Interpreting the Bible

By
J. C. K. VON HOFMANN

Translated from the German
BY CHRISTIAN PREUS

AUGSBURG PUBLISHING HOUSE
Minneapolis, Minnesota

Bible quotations are from the Revised Standard Version, the King James Version, or in free translation, whichever best illustrates the author's point in each instance.

Manufactured in the United States of America

Foreword

Nearly two hundred years ago the German scholar J. A. Ernesti published his treatise on Biblical interpretation, by which he revolutionized Biblical scholarship. Being primarily a philologist rather than a theologian he demanded that the principles by which the classical scholar was guided should also be applied to the exegesis of the Biblical books. About the same time Johann Semler insisted upon the primacy of historical investigation in the interpretation of the Scriptures. This is not the place to retrace the dramatic and tortuous history of Biblical scholarship during the past two centuries. Suffice it to say that neither Protestant nor Catholic theology has felt able completely to ignore or reject the new approaches to the study of the Bible, and also that they realize with increasing clarity that either principle, when applied consistently and unchecked, tends to disintegrate theology. The fact cannot be denied that the making of the Biblical books resembles in almost every respect that of any other book, and that the historical events recorded in the Bible did not take place in a vacuum but rather within the framework of the ancient Near East and the Hellenistic age.

Yet Protestantism stands or falls with the authority of the Bible. Unless it can be shown that there is something absolutely unique in the making of the Bible and the historical events of which it speaks, the Christian religion is engulfed in the maelstrom of relativism. Those would be right, then, who see in the Bible but the document of a millennium of religious thought among the Hebrew people giving expression to a mentality far removed from that of our time. Furthermore, even if the interpreter should succeed in rendering the Bible's content interesting and startling to the modern reader, its human authors could not claim any superiority over the brilliant intelligence and the vast learning of their modern interpreters. It would be left to everybody's discretion to decide how much, if anything, he should accept from the Bible, in order to be entitled to call himself a Christian. That is indeed the attitude adopted by a great deal of modern Biblical scholarship in Protestantism. It is the student of the Scriptures, rather than the Bible, that tells us what to believe.

There have been many attempts in the course of the years to remedy this situation. Lutheran and Calvinistic confessionalism has pleaded for a return to the views of the seventeenth century, pretending that the problems raised by critical scholarship existed in appearance only and could be ignored. Fundamentalism is a pragmatic version of that view, by which the wealth of the Biblical revelation has been reduced to idolatrous worship of the text of the King James Version and faith has become belief in a few events in the life of Jesus. At the other extreme we find the Existentialism of Bultmann and Gogarten, where first the Biblical records are thrown out completely but where at least part of the New testament proclamation is brought back again in the demythologized form of an existential experience.

J. C. K. von Hofmann's significance lies in the fact that he took the critical movement seriously and was anxious to learn from it, but without yielding an inch in the matter of Biblical authority. He succeeds, where many others have faltered, by freeing the Bible from the isolation in which previous scholarship had left it. In this respect it does not

make much difference whether according to the theory of
Verbal or Plenary Inspiration the Biblical writers are looked
upon as working apart from the life of the Church or whether
in the secularized treatment of radical criticism the claims
of the Bible to provide the saving truth are ignored. Hofmann's starting point is not an isolated Bible which an
isolated scholar interprets by means of a set of authoritative
rules, but rather he sees the exegete as a member of the
church that believes in the Bible as the book through which
God reveals His redemptive will, and who on his part is to
interpret this Bible for the benefit of his church. In the light
of that experience rather than by means of an *apriori* deduc-
tion Hofmann understands the making of the Bible as a
feature of holy history, i.e., of that aspect of history in which
the divine election calls forth man's believing response. God
is not interested in filling man's mind with infallible propositions as is the case in the Hermetic literature, for example,
but rather to illumine for him His work of redemption. Thus
Bible and redemptive history are correlated. By relating the
words of the Bible to the saving events to which they point,
Hofmann avoided that deadening intellectualism by which
the Bible had been transformed into a textbook of theological propositions. In the context of Holy History the Biblical
revelations refer to God's grace and justice and they appeal
to the reader as words of comfort, hope and admonition. By
means of this realism, Biblical exegesis has been enabled to
recover the sense of relevancy which is so essential for the
Christian message. By concentrating upon the purpose of
God, and arranging the events of the Bible in a teleological
order, Hofmann overcomes the historical relativism of so
many scholars who are unable to see in history more than
an unending and aimless succession of events. Pointing out
that this is a history which moves towards the reader and
carries him with it to God's ultimate goal, Hofmann has not
only rediscovered the significance of eschatology fifty years
ahead of Schweitzer, but also laid bare the source of the

urgency which God's revelation has for us. The interpreter, and consequently the reader, too, participates himself in Holy History and thus becomes responsible for its progress.

By this concept of Holy History *(Heilsgeschichte)*, Hofmann is also enabled to differentiate in the Biblical record between those elements which are subject to critical investigation on the one hand, and the unalterable manifestation of God's saving purpose on the other. He categorically rejects the modern differentiation between historically conditioned, and thus obsolete, features and eternal truths. The history of Biblical scholarship has shown too clearly that the socalled "eternal truths" always turn out to be the critic's own basic axioms. But Hofmann would not accept the opposite view either, according to which every detail of geographical, geological, or astronomical information in the Bible is infallible. Scripture is God's Word and revelation everywhere. But since God pursues a goal in all He does, every detail in the Bible is to be treated as part of the total picture. This applies not only to the mutual relationship of the two Testaments, but also to every particular feature in the records. Thus the meaning of the Bible will be understood by those only who interpret those "secular" informations as the means by which the writer expressed his revealed insight into the divine purpose in terms of the natural knowledge available to him. With this perspective, Hofmann succeeds in making the whole Bible relevant for the faith of the reader without subjecting him to the world view and the limited natural knowledge of past history.

In the field of Biblical philology, textual criticism, and exegetical technique great progress has been made during the century that separates us from the time when Hofmann wrote his book. But quite apart from the fact that the changes do not affect Hofmann's basic principles, one is amazed by the soundness of his learning. Some of the remarks he makes on Hebrew mentality as distinct from the Greek can be fully appreciated only in the light of most recent scholarship.

But his lasting significance lies in another field. He had not only defined the starting point of Protestant exegesis, but also discovered with ingenious certainty what the basic attitude and the guiding perspective are that are consonant with the Christian faith without in any way hampering the legitimate scholarly treatment of the Biblical books.

Otto A. Piper

Translator's Preface

This volume offers the text of a course of lectures given by J. C. K. von Hofmann at the University of Erlangen in 1860. They were edited posthumously by one of his pupils, W. Volck, under the title "Biblische Hermeneutik" and published by C. H. Beck in Noerdlingen in 1880.

Whereas in Germany, Hofmann is counted among the great theologians of the past century, his name is almost unknown in the English-speaking world, and few of his books are found even in the libraries of the leading theological schools. It is not for antiquarian reasons that this work of his has been rendered into English. Rather it is hoped that through his influence one of the basic weaknesses of our exegetical work may be overcome. Notwithstanding the flood of exegetical literature that has seen the light in the last decades little attention has been paid to the basic rules of exegesis, and particularly to its theological presuppositions. In some circles the subjective element in exegesis has been stressed onesidedly, which practically meant that the interpreter of the Bible would find his own faith in the book he studied.° In other groups, all emphasis was laid upon a

---

°It is surprising to discover that in circles which claim to be guided by a belief in Verbal or Plenary Inspiration, the author often makes an arbitrary selection of the topics he likes while others, though clearly presented in the text, are simply ignored.

"scientific" method of exegesis, which for all practical purposes meant a positivistic approach to the Scriptures. As a result the exegete could accept only as much of a Biblical book as was compatible with his world-view. For practical purposes this led to an inconsistent dichotomy, whereby the preacher's exposition of the text was more or less independent of the "assured results of scientific exegesis."

Permitting Hofmann to speak English will make available to our generation some of the insights of a keen thinker who was able organically to combine a scientific treatment of the Biblical text with a firm belief in the revealed content of the Bible. By doing so he was able to find solutions for numerous problems which are still vexing us today as, for instance, the Bible and the Word of God, the authority of the Canon, truth and history, faith and reason, church and Scripture.

In view of the fact that the conservative theological tradition in Scandinavia stands in direct succession to the Erlangen theology through Theo. von Zahn, Gisle Johnson, F. W. K. Bugge right down to such contemporaries as Sigurd Odland, Olaf Moe, and Ole Hallesby, it may seem strange that the Scandinavian immigrants of the last century did not bring these views along with them. The reason is simply that the first waves of immigrants came over before the Erlangen theology had taken root in the old country. And when they arrived here the worst thing that confronted them was their old foe, rationalism. In order to preserve their faith they seized upon the weapon nearest at hand, which happened to be the same kind of fundamentalism which Hofmann had gone to such pains to unseat in Germany. A similar development took place among German immigrants who adopted the rationalistic caricature of Lutheranism taught by Hengstenberg. As a result, the best of the Erlangen tradition has been conspicuously absent from American Protestantism, with the exception of the United Lutheran Church.

Hofmann's significance lies in the fact that unlike his contemporaries, who attempted to solve the exegetical problems by means of abstract rational principles he stated it clearly in terms of church life and religious experience. Thereby he discovered the common starting point of the theological exegete and the ordinary reader of the Bible. Experience alone might have led him to the vagaries of existentialism, church life alone would probably have resulted in a confessionalistic dogmatism. Combining the two he discovered a method which leaves the exegete constantly in the position of a learner over against the Bible while at the same time it makes him aware of the relevancy the Scripture has both for himself and the Church.

Thus we may learn from von Hofmann that our exegetical differences are not all of the either/or kind. He was a master of synthesis, able to discern the valid elements of the most diverse schools of thought. With orthodoxy he saw that the interpreter must operate within the traditions and confessions of the Church. With the critical schools he taught that the interpreter must employ proper methods of literary and historical criticism, and he showed that such studies need not be destructive to faith. With pietism he agreed that the interpreter must himself be a man of faith; and with Schleiermacher he held that the personal religious experience of the individual is indispensable for a congenial understanding of the Scriptures. From the Reformers he learned that the testimony of the Holy Spirit in the Scripture, in the Church, and in the life of faith is basic for a genuine appreciation of Revelation. He reminds us today that while the confessions of the Church are normative for the theologian, they are also historical documents which need to be reinterpreted in the light of new insights gained from the study of Scripture.

In order to remain alive and faithful to its Master, the Church must be willing in every generation to be confronted afresh with the message of the Scriptures and to apply it to its new situation. No one in the past century has more clearly pointed out the way to carry out this task of theology than J. C. K. von Hofmann.

CHRISTIAN PREUS

Acknowledgments

It is unlikely that this translation would have seen the light of day without the help of Drs. Otto A. Piper and George W. Forell. In its initial stage the difficulties of translation seemed to be almost insurmountable because von Hofmann's sentences were more involved and his Ciceronian sentence constructions were more elaborate than even theological German is supposed to be. The two friends spent several weeks of vacation time with the undersigned in order to assist him in his work. Our long-suffering wives, who endeavored to keep meals warm long after they were ready also deserve credit. To my son Tony I am indebted for reading the entire manuscript and correcting many of the remaining Germanisms. If the whole production has nevertheless retained a certain Germanic tinge the benevolent reader should realize that it is next to impossible to disassociate oneself completely from von Hofmann's manner of thinking after being immersed in it.

CHRISTIAN PREUS

Contents

xvii

Introduction

I. GENERAL AND BIBLICAL HERMENEUTICS

Biblical hermeneutics cannot be studied by itself. It is based upon general principles of interpretation, which must be applied to a particular case, namely the interpretation of Holy Scripture. It cannot be developed exclusively out of theological premises. Its derivative character has usually been obscured, however, by the fact that most of the works dealing with this subject start with a section on "General Hermeneutics." This means that axioms of hermeneutics were adopted which actually had originated within another context. While the theologian thought he was proceeding independently as he developed his general hermeneutics, he actually started from theological data. Schleiermacher, for example, in his lectures on "Hermeneutics and Criticism with Special Reference to the New Testament" established a system of general hermeneutics whose rules were also applied to Holy Scripture merely because that was the subject in which his theological audience was interested.

In order to understand clearly the real meaning of hermeneutics, we should not depend too much upon the etymology of the word "hermeneutics." The Greek root *herme-*

1

neuein means either to "proclaim" or to "interpret." In either case this verb designates an activity by means of which information is imparted to a third person. Whereas through proclamation we learn something which we otherwise would not know, through interpretation we are made to understand something which otherwise we would not comprehend. In the term "hermeneutics" the root is used in the latter sense. Furthermore, the term indicates that a third person is to understand something through us. For this reason the older text books on hermeneutics dealt not merely with the method by which we arrive at a proper understanding of a subject, but also with the appropriate way by which this understanding was to be communicated to others. For example, Ernesti (1707-1781) discussed both understanding and communication. But these are two entirely different activities. How to present correctly one's understanding of a document belongs to rhetorics. Some extended the task of hermeneutics even further. J. J. Rambach* (1737-1818), for instance, dealt not only with the method by which the correct interpretation of a passage could be proven, but also with the appropriate manner in which the accepted understanding of a Biblical text could be made useful to others and how it would bring about the salvation of others. He concluded his Biblical Hermeneutics with a section on "The Communication, Demonstration, and Application of the Discovered Meaning."

However, we should take into consideration the fact that we can interpret for ourselves as well as for someone else. In this case we can dispense with the demonstration of the correctness of the discovered meanings or with the method of its communication. Thus neither communication nor demonstration belongs necessarily to hermeneutics.

In any case, the correctness of the interpretation depends entirely on the appropriate method and principles used for one's understanding of the text. The interpreter can do no more than show that he has used the appropriate media

---

*"Institutes of Hermeneutics," Jena 1723.

and has used them correctly. No special directions for proving the correctness of the interpretation are necessary.

Hence general hermeneutics has a two-fold task. First, it deals with the possibility of understanding, and secondly, with the method of understanding in general. Every expression of thought can become the object of understanding. Thus general hermeneutics is not limited to words, certainly not to written words. I can say that I understand an expression of thought when I can answer these questions:

1. What mental processes are manifested therein?
2. What is its content?
3. How is its form related to its content?
4. What is the historical setting of that process?

First, then, we must investigate what cause has brought about this process, what factors affecting it from the outside have given it its peculiar character, and what his nature is in whom this mental process originated. The latter feature has to be recognized both in its general aspects and in its specific modification in the given case. If I want to understand a manifestation of mental life I have to go through the same mental process which produced it in the first place. Unless I identify myself with the historical development of which this mental process is a part, that process will remain an isolated and disconnected fact which is historically unintelligible to me.

Furthermore, the subject matter of hermeneutics is determined by two facts. First, the proper expression of thought is speech; and secondly, speech cannot be the object of formal interpretation until it is written down. The very nature of thought expressed in words, and particularly thought expressed in writing, implies another prerequisite for its understanding: I must know the language by which the speaker is bound. Language holds him with its laws and barriers and at the same time supplies him with means of expression. Furthermore, the interpreter must be familiar with the universal human ability through which the inner life expresses itself. In the first case we deal with a definite language; in the second case, with language in general. Grammar and rhetoric are therefore the formal presuppositions of hermeneutics; psychology and history are its material presuppositions.

To develop all this in detail is the concern of general hermeneutics, but this is not our task. For the Biblical hermeneutics with which we deal is not the application of a general hermeneutics to a special kind of literature but the answer to the question: What do we need to understand Holy Scripture appropriately besides the technique of scientific exegesis?

Not that the interpreting is itself different in this case. But how is it to be practiced so that the peculiarity of this body of literature, the Holy Scripture of Christianity, will be given full consideration? The answer to this question is our concern here. A review of the history of interpretation of Scripture will show that people were in error when they believed that the interpreting itself should be different in this case. This error started from a mistaken understanding of the character of Holy Scripture, and from an incorrect concept of our relationship to Holy Scripture. It will be apparent that there is no reason to develop an independent hermeneutics first, but it is necessary to ask what should be added to the general laws of interpretation in order that they may be applied in accordance with the specific demands made by this subject matter.

II. THE HISTORY OF SCRIPTURAL INTERPRETATION

The books which make up the Old Testament canon have been the object of learned exegesis ever since the time when their collection was completed. The main concern at first was to treat the Pentateuch exegetically, since it was necessary for the legal order of the Jewish community as based upon the law of God. . . .

From this concern with the law grew the Talmudic study of Scripture, in which the prophetic content of the Bible was neglected. Because of the differentiation between the body of Scripture (i.e., the literal sense), and its soul (i.e., the sense to be gained by this type of interpretation), the text was considered as a sort of hiding place for riddles which had to be solved through the cleverness of the interpreter. Such a method of exegesis was bound to develop where the divine revelation of Scripture was understood as implying that everything necessary could be found there.

Other perversions appeared when Jewish thought came into contact with pagan modes of thought. We notice that Philo always attempted to interpret Scripture in such a manner as to find in it the metaphysical and ethical thoughts that he brought along from his study of Platonic philosophy. It was for this reason that he interpreted Scripture allegorically, holding that each word of Scripture has a body and a soul. . . .

Both Palestinian and Alexandrian Jews were in error when they believed that through their artificial exegesis Scripture could be freed of that which seemed unworthy of it in its literal sense. They would not have found anything unworthy of Holy Scripture if they had placed themselves into the historical context of Scripture. Instead, they always dealt with individual passages which they treated without regard to the context. Taken in isolation some verses in Scripture could seem unworthy of Scripture though in reality they were not. Indeed, it was the basic error of this exegetical method, Palestinian as well as Alexandrian Jewish, to ignore the fact that Scripture is dealing with Holy History.

When Jesus, coming as the Savior of Israel, said that it was to Him that the Scriptures bore witness, He brought those who believed in Him back into the context of the history of salvation and thus they became able to understand Scripture within the framework of Holy History. The relation of Scrip-

ture to Holy History is given full recognition in the manner
in which the Apostles used and explained the Old Testament
in their own writings. They regarded Scripture as the witness
borne by Holy History to Christ, who is the goal of that
whole historical process.

Though frequently seeming similar to the rabbinic, the
Apostolic exegesis is in fact utterly different. In individual
passages the difference will not be recognized because the
New Testament writers do not explicitly point out the connection which exists between the Old Testament passage
referred to and used in its historical context on the one hand,
and the saving facts, present or future, which are therein
expressed and witnessed to on the other. Gal. 4:24 and I Cor.
9:9 are frequently referred to as proof that the Apostle
employs the rabbinical method of exegesis. But in the former
passage Paul's exegesis is based upon the significance that
Abraham's marriage has for Holy History. This is the only
use he makes of allegorical interpretation. In the contrast
between Hagai and Sara he finds the one that exists between
the two ordinances of God, namely law and promise, in Holy
History. In other words, his method is justified by the facts
and not to be excused as an application of rabbinic practice.

Similarly, when in I Cor. 9:9 he quotes Deut. 25:4 and
continues, "Is it for oxen that God is concerned?" it does not
mean that the literal meaning of this law is unworthy of God,
but that the will of God expressed here is applicable to men
too, and goes over and above God's care for cattle.

The Apostolic exegesis is similar to the rabbinical only in a
formal way. In its nature it is utterly different because it
grows out of a different relationship to Scripture. Its correctness is based on the vital relationship in which the
Apostles find themselves both to the historical life of the
Scriptures and to their Lord and Savior. Our study of the
Old Testament has no greater task than to reach a scientifi-
cally justified method of interpretation of Scripture which
will enable us to interpret it in the same way as the Apostles
did, except that we consciously point out the context which

is implicitly presupposed but not expressly stated by them.

The value of the Apostolic exegesis will be fully appreciated when compared with the exegesis of post-apostolic times. When Christian teachers stood in a less vital relationship to Scripture than the Apostles, Jewish exegesis made its influence felt. We observe a relapse into the Jewish disparagement of the obvious meaning of Scripture as unworthy of God, and we perceive an artificial exegesis of Christian ideas. We find this procedure, for instance, in Justin Martyr, especially in his "Dialogue with Tryphon," and in the so-called "Letter of Barnabas." . . .

The mistakes of the past were repeated in another way when an ill-famed Gnosis attempted to discover alleged higher wisdom where the clear meaning of Holy Scripture left no room for it. Non-Christian and Alexandrian Christian Gnosticism had one thing in common: by means of allegory they found in Scripture what Scripture does not teach. The only difference was this: that in their exegesis of Scripture Clement and Origen remained basically within the framework of Christian life and knowledge, notwithstanding erroneous exegesis in individual cases. . . .

The blame for the development of such a perverted exegesis cannot be laid to a false hermeneutics but rather to a basically false attitude towards Holy Scripture. People did not accept the Bible as a document of history, but rather considered it as a revelation of doctrines, which presumably would teach everything that one desired to know.

Compared with such treatment of Holy Scripture, the Western exegesis of Irenaeus (b. ca. 130 A.D.) and Tertullian (b. ca. 160 A.D.) was a sounder one. In opposition to the pagan Gnosis with which they had to contend they insisted that exegesis be confined to the literal meaning of Scripture. If the cleverness of the interpreter were allowed free reign for allegorizing, Scripture would cease to serve as a weapon against the disintegration of Christendom resulting from Gnosticism.

At the same time these theologians demanded that Scripture should be interpreted in accordance with the Confession of the Church. Against the Gnostics this principle was justified, but it was applicable only when the common faith of the Church corresponded to the whole content of Scripture, an integral faith to the totality of Scripture. This would imply that true faith is a prerequisite for the correct understanding of the individual passages of Scripture correctly. However, the basic error that began to develop in the Church even then was the inability to distinguish between the essential character of the Church and its temporary manifestations. No distinction was made between the "Church according to the Spirit" and the "Church according to the flesh." The result was a false subordination of exegesis to what was commonly called Tradition. Furthermore, Ireneus and Tertullian and their followers occasionally violated their own principles. They utilized allegorical interpretations both in order to rid themselves of a literal meaning which seemed to them unworthy of Scripture, or in order to find Scriptural support for a real or alleged divine truth.

The same tendency can be noted in the school of Antioch in Chrysostom (347-407) and Theodoret (ca. 386-457). In contrast to the arbitrary allegorical exegesis practised by the school of Alexandria they demanded historical interpretation. They pushed this demand so far that Theodore of Mopsuestia, for instance, followed the rabbinical exegesis of his time in his exposition of predictive prophecies, especially those found in the Psalms. He applied Messianic prophecies and passages which were considered to be such, to Old Testament persons first, and only in a secondary way to Christ.

In this respect, the other teachers of the school of Antioch did not follow him that far, but they did adopt the principle of historical exegesis. They, too, insisted that there were three types of Scripture passages: those which were to be taken literally, those which have to be understood in a "higher sense," and those which have to be understood both ways.

Thus the allegorical interpretation of Scripture, though

applied in varying degrees, prevailed in the Eastern Church and also in the West up to the time of the Reformation. It was Augustine who set the standards. His position toward Scripture is expressed in the words, "Everything in the Word of God which cannot be applied for moral conduct or for the truth of faith, must be understood figuratively."

Generally speaking, three higher senses were distinguished from the literal sense: the allegorical, which supplies tenets of faith; the tropological, which supplies moral teachings; and the anagogical, which supplies metaphysical doctrines as well as those concerned with the world beyond and eschatology.

Thus Scriptural exegesis up to the Reformation was characterized by two things: (1) The subordination of interpretation to tradition. (2) A differentiation was made between the historical and spiritual senses.

The Reformation freed the exegesis of Scripture from two perversions: First, the interpreter was delivered from the obligation which Tradition had laid upon him. The work of the Holy Spirit was finally understood when it was stated that he is personally active in the interpreter and instructs him in the understanding of Scripture. This he does, however, only through the Scripture itself. By comparing Scripture with itself the interpreter was to understand its meaning in every passage; in other words, exegesis was to be based on the "analogy of Scripture." Thus the Holy Spirit teaches the interpreter to understand Scripture through Scripture.

Second, the Reformation restored the historical meaning of Scripture to its proper place. Melanchthon said: "Next to the grammatical, dialectical and rhetorical rules, we must look everywhere for one sure and simple meaning." Or as Luther put it, the aim of exegesis is the true and certain meaning of Scripture which is identical with the literal and historical meaning. Now at last they were serious about their attempt to rediscover from Scripture the saving truth which the Church had lost. Previously the traditional teaching had made that unnecessary.

But the freedom of exegesis from the tradition of the Church which Luther had won was soon lost. Exegesis "according to the analogy of Faith" was soon given a different meaning than "letting Scripture interpret itself." Individual passages were to be interpreted in the light of the sum total of doctrines taken from the "clear" passages of Scripture and this sum total was identified with the Confession of the Church. It is true that Quenstedt (1617-1688) said, "Scripture, or rather the Holy Spirit speaking in Scripture, is his own legitimate interpreter." Nevertheless, there came into being so-called ecclesiastical interpretations of individual passages of Scripture as well as of Scripture as a whole, from which no one was permitted to deviate. These really or allegedly clear passages of Scripture in which the sum of Christian doctrine was believed to be contained, i.e., these "classic passages" *(loci classici)* or "proof texts" *(dicta probantia)* were not to be interpreted in any other way, lest the doctrines taken from them should be endangered, since by them the rest of Scripture was to be interpreted.

Another evil result of this development was that exegesis confined itself increasingly to these proof texts. They were explained apart from their context, with the result that the meaning of the latter was inevitably determined by the previously fixed interpretation of those proof texts. Thus the understanding of the context was twisted or perverted according to circumstances. Exegesis was thus again dominated by Tradition, although the doctrines which furnished the standards of exegesis were actually taken from Scripture.

Exegesis suffered further through a doctrine of inspiration which had been deduced in a purely rational way from the principle of the exclusive authority of Scripture in matters of faith. People conceived of Scripture as the Word of God in a purely abstract sense, and from this abstract concept certain rational conclusions regarding the character of Scripture were deduced irrespective of its actual nature. Scripture was not understood as the all embracing revelation of God, nor as a document and product of Holy History, but as the revelation of saving doctrine. Now if Scripture is the Word of God in this unconditional sense, no contradiction within it is conceivable. Thus the text was forced to fit the theory. One postulated a text free of error, and textual criticism was out of the question. Similarly, the canon of Scripture was placed beyond doubt, and investigation concerning its authenticity was prohibited. Here again, men became subject to Tradition. Moreover, with this view of Scripture the idea was reintroduced that every passage of Scripture deserves the same "emphasis." Rambach, for instance, asserted that each word of Scripture should be given such extended meaning and such emphasis as the text would possibly permit.

Nevertheless, the teaching of the Reformation was maintained, at least in principle, that Scripture has one meaning which is supplied by the literal sense. Whenever a reference was made to a mystical meaning, it was explained that it did not exist in addition to the literal meaning but was implied in the subject matter expressed by the words. This was indeed correct. But at this point the fixed doctrine of inspiration was responsible for another restriction. It was believed that allegorical or typological interpretation should be permitted only where Scripture itself gave the clue.

Cocceius (1603-1669) revolted against these restrictions because they made difficult a consistent interpretation, especially of the Old Testament prophets. He, too, thought that Scripture has only one meaning, the historical or literal. He declared that "allegory does not constitute a special sense of Holy Scripture," but he was anxious to protect the freedom of the exegete to interpret Scripture consistently. If it were permissible at all to use an allegorical and typological method, especially in the exegesis of the Old Testament, it would be legitimate for the interpreter independently to extend this type of interpretation to the whole of Scripture. While these principles would not have led Cocceius away from a wholesome interpretation of Scripture, his rigorous insistence upon the divine inspiration of Scripture led him

to postulate an "emphatic diction" of the whole Scripture.*
The result was that he expected more from each word than
the text was able to supply. Starting from a correct point
of departure he was led into a hopeless arbitrariness in his
exegesis of individual passages. It was his great contribution,
nevertheless, that he insisted upon the study of the context
and upon the intrinsic unity of Scripture as a whole, in opposition to the prevailing aphoristic manner of interpretation.

The first major change came as a result of the work of
Richard Simon (1638-1712). He made it clear that in the
transmission of the original text the writings of the Bible
had experienced the same fate as other ancient writings.
Textual criticism was at once taken seriously.

But as far as the content of the Bible was concerned, even
Ernesti, whose insistence upon grammatical interpretation
made such a contribution to the study of Scripture, was
nevertheless so dominated by the conviction that contradic-
tions in Scripture are impossible that he demanded that
where such seemed to exist, the interpreter was obligated
to make them disappear.

The certainty that Holy Scripture was in a special sense
the work of the Holy Spirit was so deeply rooted that it
remained a guiding principle even when the interpreter
had lost his confidence in the faith of the Church. This
explains the fact that when the common faith of the Church
was openly abandoned, the Holy Scriptures were nevertheless considered as a peculiar work, which merely needed to
be brought into conformity with reason. Some held that it
was actually identical with "reason." This was the principle
that H. E. G. Paulus (1761-1851) followed in his interpretation of the New Testament. Others openly admitted that by
itself Scripture did not conform with reason and that by
bringing it into conformity with reason they were doing
violence to it. This was the case with Kant (1724-1804).

It was only when every appearance of respect for Holy

---

* That is, that every word has equal value.

Scripture was given up that people dared to do what Semler (1725-1791) had already demanded, namely, to interpret Scripture like any other book, or its individual writings like any other literary work. He had demanded a purely historical interpretation of Scripture. Such a method was adopted when people had no more reason to consider Holy Scripture as something peculiar. People did not hesitate to pronounce its historical elements as mythical and the doctrines expressed therein as popular and historically conditioned. As far as the historical elements of Scripture were concerned, most felt with Strauss (1808-1874) that it was enough to explain how these mythical elements might have come into being, and concerning the teachings of the Bible it seemed satisfactory to be able to show the gradual development of the popular views recorded therein. In this manner it was no longer necessary for the exegete to force himself or Scripture into some unnatural pattern. Not only was the historical understanding of the text considered sufficient, but some interpreters were pleased to emphasize the alleged irrationality of Holy Scripture. This was done by Strauss in regard to its historical content and by Fritsche in regard to its doctrine. Since no need was felt for a miraculous salvation outside of the natural development of humanity, Scripture was not permitted to witness to the reality of a miraculous history which could not be explained by the laws of ordinary life. Everything that Scripture reported in this respect was declared mythical. In the same manner there was no longer any room for prophecy in the original sense of the word. Prophecy was reduced to divination.

From these principles the history of origins of the Holy Scriptures was reconstructed. Victims of self-deception, these writers boasted that they were guided by no presuppositions whatsoever in their work, in contrast with the type of interpretation which was determined by the common faith of the church and the presupposition that Scripture is the word of God in a unique manner. These men did not realize that they too were dogmatically determined, although by the opposite presupposition. In fact "a complete lack of presuppositions" on the part of the interpreter would be unthinkable. It is impossible for the interpreter to be neither Christian nor non-Christian, neither religious nor irreligious, but merely interpreter. He approaches Scripture as a person with a definite character and nature and experience, not as a "blank sheet" upon which Scripture inscribes itself.

By the time the Christian faith was again applied to the study of Scripture, the non-Christian interpretation had supplied two things: (1) A well grounded, grammatical understanding of the words themselves to which Gesenius (1786-1842) in the Old Testament and Winer (1789-1858) in the New Testament had made outstanding contributions. (2) An understanding of the historical content of Scripture, which Semler had made necessary.

A realization of the nature of grammatical interpretation prevented the general adoption of the differentiation between the "higher" and "lower" meaning of Scripture, when this was attempted again by Olshausen (1800-1882) and Stier (1800-1862). Theologians had become immune to this type of interpretation through a sound grammatical training. Moreover, the fact that they had acquired a historical understanding of Scripture protected the theologians against the errors in Hengstenberg's (1802-1869) exegesis of the Old Testament, as found in the first edition of his "Christology." By emphasizing exclusively the unity of the truth of salvation supplied by Scripture, he gave too little attention to the historical background and the historical form of Scripture. By this procedure he was in constant danger of finding everything prophesied in every passage of the Old Testament.

These relapses into errors of a previous period had their cause in a false emphasis laid upon the fact that the Scripture is inspired and is the work of the Holy Spirit. It was Beck (1804-1874) who, in his treatise "On the Pneumatic Interpretation of Scripture," showed that it was possible to recognize fully the inspiration of Scripture and the unity of its saving truth, and at the same time acknowledge the diversity which results from its historical character.

Still another early error threatened to reappear. When the Christian faith, which had again become the clue to the understanding of Scripture, realized the significance of the Church, there was again a tendency to subordinate interpretation, in a false manner, to the Confessions of the Church, and to ignore the plain meaning of the text in favor of the Confession. Theologians would speak of an ecclesiastical interpretation of individual passages, deviation from which was considered unchurchly. Instead, the interpreter must share faith of the church and read Scripture with the eyes of this faith.

Our review of the history of Scriptural interpretation has shown one fact. Wherever exegetes departed from a method of interpretation based upon the laws of general hermeneutics, it was not because they did not know these laws but because they took a false attitude toward Scripture, and as a result they felt unable or unwilling to remain on the right path of interpretation.

This false attitude toward Scripture manifested itself in a number of ways. We noticed:

(1) An erroneous conception of inspiration, that is, of the fact that the Holy Scripture is the work of the Holy Spirit. One result was an emphasis upon individual passages which is irreconcilable with the nature of speech. More was expected from the letter of the text than it could possibly supply, since the interpreter felt obliged to search, by means of artifices not justified by the nature of speech, for hidden secrets or a manifold sense. Another result was the belief that the obvious literal meaning of those passages of Scripture which were considered unworthy of the Holy Spirit was to be excluded a priori. Finally, without consulting the text in individual cases, it was contended that any disagreement between individual portions of Scripture was out of the

question. All this was a result of a false attitude toward Scripture, based upon an erroneous concept of inspiration.

(2) Another wrong attitude toward Scripture consisted in conceiving of it in an erroneous way, which obviated the understanding of its historical character. The result was that each individual passage, rather than being weighed according to its position within the whole of Scripture, was supposed to supply the same insight without any regard to context.

(3) A false attitude towards the Church made a correct appreciation of Scripture impossible. This occurred when it was postulated beforehand that nothing could be found in Scripture which would contradict not only the truth of the Church rightly understood, but also the teaching of a particular church at a particular time, notwithstanding the fact that the latter may be in error.

(4) A false attitude to the saving truth made a correct appreciation of Holy Scripture impossible, namely when scholars had postulated beforehand that nothing could be found in Scripture which contradicted the natural development of humanity, the laws of nature, reason, etc.

This survey shows how diverse was the wrong understanding of Holy Scripture as a result of which its interpretation deviated from the method based upon the laws of general hermeneutics.

There may be agreement in the understanding of details of Holy Scripture between an exegete who refrains from doing violence to it because he is indifferent with regard to the significance which it claims to have for his eternal salvation, on the one hand, and an exegete who reads Holy Scripture with the kind of freedom that originates in the fact that he actually lives in the saving truth of which it bears witness, on the other.

Yet this agreement exists only in the particulars. At the same time there may be less agreement between the results of such truly free exegesis on the one hand, and the interpretation of an exegete who, while recognizing the claim the Scripture makes regarding eternal salvation, takes an unfree attitude toward it, on the other.

It frequently happens that the "unfree" interpreter will blame the one who used his rightful Christian freedom in regard to Scripture, because his exegesis is similar to that of an unbelieving interpreter. But this disagreement in the interpretation of particulars disappears when it is shown that the results of such exegesis serve to support that claim of Scripture. Furthermore, there is no agreement as to the importance which each individual part of Holy Scripture has for the whole. In the former case, it is a miracle which becomes the stumbling block for the alleged independent interpreter. His alleged impartiality is hardly compatible with the offense given to him by the fact that the miracle which in his opinion is impossible should actually be verified. As far as the understanding of the significance is concerned which the particulars have for the whole of Scripture, the so-called neutral interpreter, who would better be called indifferent, lacks the ability to comprehend the context of Holy History to which each individual part belongs. Lacking salvation, he is unable to comprehend its nature.

III. THE PROBLEM OF SCRIPTURAL INTERPRETATION

We have discovered that in order to interpret Scripture according to the general laws of hermeneutics, we must first of all have a correct appreciation of Holy Scripture. Then we are able to clarify the task of Biblical Hermeneutics. We have to investigate what is meant by a correct appreciation of Holy Scripture in order to discover the consequences it has for the exegesis of Holy Scripture. We do not mean that in Biblical hermeneutics rules ought to be given for the interpretation of Holy Scripture, but rather that the one who is capable of interpreting Scripture in a correct way has to give an account of the conditions under which a correct interpretation is possible. It is not proper, therefore, to begin with the particulars of Holy Scripture as is being done and necessarily must be done by those who start with general hermeneutics and simply apply it to the interpretation of Scripture in each individual case.

The procedure of Biblical hermeneutics must be the reverse of that of general hermeneutics. In general hermeneutics we investigate what it is that gives to the expressions of a mental process, whether sign, speech or writing, both their necessary identical character and also their diverse possible connotations. On this basis we ascertain what is required for the understanding of these expressions. In general hermeneutics we proceed from the simplest elements to the more complex ones, from the details to the larger units, from word to sentence, from sentence to paragraph.

In Biblical hermeneutics, however, we have to proceed in the opposite direction. Its task is to show how the interpretation of Holy Scripture, done according to the ordinary rules of hermeneutics, is at the same time determined by the distinctive character of its object. The interpreter is in the first place confronted by Holy Scripture as a whole, which in this capacity is the Holy Scripture of Christendom. It is in its totality and intrinsic unity that it forms the object of Biblical hermeneutics. The foremost question is how the activity of the interpreter of Holy Scripture is determined by the specific way in which he is confronted by the Bible in its totality.

Furthermore, there is the difference between Old Testament and New Testament that has to be considered, and finally, the differences which characterize the content of Scripture in both parts. We emphasize the content. For it is not Holy Scripture as a special kind of literature which makes Biblical hermeneutics necessary. In that case its law of interpretation would be but a portion of general hermeneutics. Rather its peculiarity is derived from the nature of its content which has caused it to be the Holy Scripture of Christendom. Its intrinsic diversity is not to be found in the realm of rhetorics, but rather in the nature of its content, namely, that it is the document of prehistory and of the history of origins; and in the second place, that it describes the past, the present, and the future of that history. The former differentiation divides Scripture into two successive parts; the latter pervades both parts.

(This method of Biblical hermeneutics is similar to that which the doctrine of Inspiration should follow. Here, too, it would have been more fruitful if the procedure had been from the whole to the individual problems, instead of beginning immediately with minutiae.)

Part One

THE UNITY

OF

SCRIPTURE

CHAPTER ONE

The Bible as the Actual Possession of Christendom

The Holy Scripture comes to the interpreter in a two-fold way, namely, (1) as the present possession of Christendom, cherished as its sacred writing; (2) and as a product of an historical past. In the former respect it confronts him as a homogeneous whole, and in the latter respect as the sum total of its parts. We shall consider the Bible from both points of view.

If the Biblical writings were merely portions of the literature of mankind we would not need Biblical hermeneutics. But this would be the case only if Christendom were the product of human culture. Biblical hermeneutics is concerned with the specific function of the Biblical writings, namely, their being the sacred writings of Christendom. This significance they must have for the interpreter whose activity we want to describe. He approaches them with a presupposition which is rooted in the faith which he shares with all Christian people, and he expects that this presupposition will be verified through his methodical study of the Bible. What is this presupposition, and what is its justification?

The interpreter enters upon his investigation of Scripture as a Christian and as a theologian. His understanding of Scripture does not start with a scientific theory but with a belief concerning its distinctive character in general. This belief is not based upon the testimony of Scripture itself, i.e., upon individual passages of Scripture, for that would not be belief, even if Scripture described its own nature in so many words. But there is no such testimony of Scripture concerning itself. Passages like II Peter 1:21 or I Peter 1:11 do not supply it. We do read that the prophets whose utterances are recorded in Scripture spoke not of themselves but were moved by divine power, and that the spirit who was active in them was the Spirit of Christ. But the same is true of all those who have prophesied without having their prophecies incorporated in Scripture. What then is the distinctive characteristic of Scriptural prophecy?

In II Tim. 3:16 we read that the Holy Scriptures of the Old Testament have their origin in the Spirit of God. But this is not true exclusively of the Old Testament. We do not read, "All scripture is inspired by God," as if "God-inspired" referred only to the Old Testament, but we read "All God-inspired Scripture is useful for teaching," etc. Were there no other writings which were "God-inspired"? It is plainly evident that in the New Testament the writings of the Old Testament are clearly differentiated from all other literature concerning both their origin and their content. This is reflected in passages like John 5:39 ("You search the Scriptures," etc.) and also in the manner in which Jesus and the New Testament authors used the Old Testament and quoted it as the Word of God or of the Holy Spirit—as Eph. 4:8, Heb. 8:8, 10:15. They did not refer to some individual God-given oracles or books but to "the Scripture." They treated Scripture as a whole to such an extent that every individual verse is considered a word *of* Scripture, not merely a word found *in* Scripture.

But what is the position of the New Testament writings whose witness in this respect has to be evaluated according to whether or not the same applies to them? Some quote promises of Jesus like John 16:13, or such passages as I Cor. 2:13 to substantiate the claims of the New Testament. However, neither passage applies to the Apostles exclusively, but to every one who has received the Spirit of Christ. There is nothing in these verses to show that the New Testament writings are essentially different from all other Christian literature. Yet it is our basic concern to discover whether there is a difference. It cannot be proven from II Peter 3:15, although here the Epistles of Paul are put on the same plane as the Old Testament books. For quite apart from the fact that the Apostolic authorship of this letter is questioned, does the fact that here the Epistles of Paul are put on a par with the Old Testament writings apply to all other documents which make up the New Testament canon? The fact of the matter is that there is no external witness which could verify that the whole Scripture as we have it today, Old Testament and New Testament alike, is Holy Scripture in contradistinction to all other Christian literature.

But even granted that there were such a witness, it could not produce a belief worthy of the name, for it is not of the nature of Christian faith to consider something true merely on the basis of some external witness. It is at this point that the testimony of the Holy Spirit has been adduced. But even this testimony goes no further than to assure us of the divine origin of the saving truth of salvation which is documented in Scripture. It does not assure us that here in Scripture this truth is the Word of God in a different way than when it is proclaimed anywhere else orally or in writing. It does not prove to us that these writings as a whole are the work of the Holy Spirit in an exclusive sense.

Yet if this assurance is to be an assurance of faith, that is an assurance commensurate with the things in which we believe, the witness of the Holy Spirit must render me certain of it in the same manner in which he makes me sure of Christ and His salvation. However, this can be done only in an indirect way. For what is directly given to me as a Christian is the assurance of the special relationship in which I stand to God by the fact that I am a Christian. Of that relationship I am certain in a direct manner, namely, through the personal experience which I have of it and not by means of something else apart from it. For that reason this assurance cannot be given by way of logical demonstration; one can have it only by way of personal experience. The statement of this relationship to God must be the starting point of all theology.

As a theologian I have to formulate that fact in a scientific way, i.e., in such a general manner that no one who is truly a Christian is thereby excluded, and also in such an exhaustive way that everything by which Christians differ from non-Christians is included therein. We should not go so far as to ask, what is it that in the broadest sense might be included under the concept of Christianity? Also we should not include those features in which the direct assurance of faith is analytically set forth. The concepts thus arrived at imply the possibility of doctrinal diversity.

The fact of which I am so directly certain that I find in it my salvation, is the personal relationship to God which has been mediated to me in a personal way through Christ, who is not only a being of the past but also the present one. Thus my relationship to God is also one to Christ, and vice versa. It implies both the forgiveness of sins which God grants me in Christ and my love of God which is rooted in Christ.

Our certainty of the facts of salvation does not come as a result of the natural development of our life as creatures, but rather as something that becomes real in ourselves in opposition to it. We are also certain that the Mediator of these facts is not a being that proceeded out of the natural development of the human race, but rather as one sent into it by God.

Furthermore, we are assured of this fact as something effected in us through the ministry of the Christian community, and actualized in us as a result of our membership in it. However, we appraise the genuineness of the historical and local realization of the Christian community according as it is a community founded upon that saving fact. The only place we will find a community that is in agreement with this body of facts is where Holy Scripture is normative and only to the extent that that is the case. That we are truly Christians only inasmuch as we are Protestants is an assurance that is inseparably joined with our assurance of faith. And thereby in turn it is part of our assurance of faith that Holy Scripture, taken as a whole, has been appointed to be the rule for the Christian Church. The birth of the Christian Church is to be understood accordingly. In the measure that it accepts the whole Bible and considers the Bible as the purpose of its existence, the Church is God's work through His Spirit.

Just as the Protestant Christian is the only one to have a firm assurance of salvation, so he alone has an unhampered certainty concerning the nature of Holy Scripture. His certainty of salvation is the basis for the analytical exposition of the content of his faith, i.e., for systematic theology, while the certainty about Holy Scripture is the basis for the exegesis and study of the Bible. Hermeneutics supplies the rule for this activity. However, this rule is rooted in faith and presupposes such faith in those who are to apply it. The prerequisite of Biblical study is not a theoretical doctrine of inspiration but the belief in Holy Scripture as that which Christians know it to be through experience.

This statement is true with reference to Scripture as a whole. The question whether it applies to everything that today is considered as belonging to the canon remains open, and is subject to Biblical scholarship. For that reason, the results of such investigations may produce a scientific certainty, but not a certainty of faith. The intrinsic certainty about the nature of Scripture which is rooted in the Christian faith precedes all scholarly investigation of Scripture. It differs therefore essentially from the results of exegesis by which a doctrine of inspiration is provided.

In what way is the interpretation of Holy Scripture determined by the fact that the Bible in its totality is the common possession of Christendom? What does the belief in this fact signify for its exegesis? We would say three things:

(1) The Holy Bible bears authoritative testimony to the historical development which has taken place in the Church. Like the Church and that development, the Scripture is not the result of the historical growth of mankind but the work of God. Within human history, its specific function is to serve the realization of God's ultimate purpose both for history and in conflict with it. All those historical events and results which are the realization of God's ultimate purpose, that is, all Holy History and its effects, we call "miracle,"* because they stand in opposition to the natural development of man. We differentiate between past history, which forms the basis for the present existence of the Church, on the one hand, and the actual life of the Church for which Holy Scripture is the standard, on the other; that is, between Holy History and "saving presence."

Scripture shares in this "miracle" of Holy History. Not only is it given to be the standard of the actual life of the Church, but it also belongs to the miraculous history of the Church. Scripture is "miracle" both in its origin and in its content because it is the document of Holy History.

(2) The personal mediator of our relationship to God was an Israelite, and his people came out of Israel. It is the Israelites therefore who are called to carry out Holy History. In this light the Israelitic character of Holy Scripture, which is both the product and document of Holy History, is to be explained.

(3) The historical process of which Holy Scripture is the document is a unified whole. As a result the truth of salvation, which is concerned with this process, is also a unified

---

* von Hofmann invests the term "wunderbar" with a technical sense for which our adjective "miraculous" seems inadequate. We therefore try to indicate some of this sense with the abstract term "miracle."

whole. The variety of the content of Scripture must be judged accordingly.

In the light of these three characteristics of Holy Scripture in its totality and as the actual possession of Christendom, what is the task of the interpreter?

A. THE MIRACLE OF SCRIPTURE

1. The Miracle of Its Origin

Holy Scripture is a product of the history which forms the basis for the actual life of the Church. Its origin shares in the miracle of this history, as it is the work of God through His Spirit. Its specific function, unlike all similar literature, consists in its being given for the purpose of being normative for the Christian Church. The interpreter does not begin with a critical treatment of its component parts, or with questioning the value which Christianity ascribes to them on account of the fact that they are parts of its Holy Scripture. Rather he approaches them with an assurance rooted in his Christian faith that Scripture will verify his belief in its unity. This assurance is the spiritual disposition which precedes and accompanies his scientific study. The scientific approach is demanded by the nature of the object he is to study, if our characterization of the Christian life is correct.

Since the distinctive miracle of Holy Scripture lies in the fact that as God's work performed through His Spirit it has those characteristics which are needed to make it normative for the Church, the interpreter's attention must be directed above all to them. He should not read it as a part of the world's great literature, or as a product of the historical life of the Church, but rather he searches Scripture for those features which make it fit to be normative for the life of the Church. Only in so doing does he read Scripture as a theologian, not merely as a Christian for his personal edification. To the extent that he succeeds in this task he becomes aware of the canonicity of its parts.

As trust in the unity of Scripture forms the disposition of his mind, so the search for its specific normativity determines its direction. Apart from that disposition, doubt will prevent him from correctly understanding what he reads. Doubt clouds, while confidence sharpens our eyes for the incomparable value of Scripture.

2. The Miracle of Its Content

Christianity is the relationship between God and man which has been mediated through Jesus Christ. It did not originate from the nature of this world as given through creation and perverted by sin. Rather it is in opposition to that nature which is ours by birth, and yet to those who through personal experience participate in that relationship it is the most real reality and the most certain certainty. The Christian is more sure of Christ, in his past work and active presence, as the one who personally mediates his relationship to God, than of anything that is perceptible and given to his senses. In accordance with that fact, he evaluates the witness which Scripture bears to the history which forms the basis of that awareness and of which he is the result.

Holy Scripture must share the nature of Christ Himself. Like Him, the Bible is not the product of the world in its natural condition, or a result of the historical development of human life, but rather it has been made part of them in order to change them into their opposite. It must be miraculous like Christ, and that notwithstanding the difference that there is between Him and the Bible. That difference is rooted in the fact that Christianity in its actual realization is the result of that past event in which He entered into the world and into mankind, whereas He, as the salvation of the world, is not only present through the effects of the incarnation but is Himself perpetually at work in it.

The presence of Christ, the word by which He bears witness of Himself, the change in man which He brings about through the word, are miraculous. Yet their miraculous character lies in their abiding presence, and therefore escapes sense perception because the miracle takes place in the regular succession of processes which can be perceived by our senses. In that respect it is distinct from the miraculous nature of that history from which this abiding presence has resulted.

This latter history is a chain of events which by entering individually into this world made manifest their contradiction to the nature of this world. They are therefore called "signs," because through their contradiction to the laws of nature they make themselves known as facts belonging to an essentially different history. This is the specific nature of the miracles of Holy History, in distinction from the miracle of the saving presence and its ever repeated manifestations.

Since Scripture is the document of Holy History, its content too must be miracle. Since basically Christ is the content of this history, He is the absolute miracle. All miracles in the Bible, both those which point towards Him and those which He performs Himself, must be understood and measured with reference to Him. To the interpreter who approaches Scriptures as a believing Christian no miracle recorded in Scripture will appear as an isolated fact, but rather he sees it as a component part of that history which resolves around Christ, tends toward Him, starts from Him, and therefore shares the nature of Him who is the absolute miracle.

The problem then is no longer whether this or that event which Scripture reports is possible, but rather: in what relation does it stand to Christ? It is judged from that point of view alone, not according to the laws of nature. We do not have to deny these events when they contradict these laws or to reinterpret actual miracles and prophecies in conformity with these laws, or to look for some compromise by means of which they would be compatible with them.

Rather, we accept the event as it is recorded without postulating for the Scriptures an origin which would invalidate the historical trustworthiness of their records. This would be the case for instance if we ascribed to them such a late date that the actual events might have been transformed into legendary fiction or if we interpreted the prophecies as fabrications made after the event, or as mere soothsaying.

But since we understand and evaluate this history (whose product and testimony is Holy Scripture) in the light of Jesus, the individual miracle has to be interpreted as part of an historical process which has Christ as its center. A Biblical miracle remains unintelligible and lacks true value for theological understanding when treated by itself and apart from its special place and significance for Holy History.

It has been said that this symbolic type of narrative is characteristic of myth. Yet a history which has a center toward which it tends and from which it derives its completion must be of symbolic nature because it points either to the future or to the past. Its character manifests itself in its epoch-making events.

The reason that this occurs so rarely in other types of history is that their development is not a purely intrinsic one. The paths of world history cross each other and do not permit such a purely intrinsic development. Holy History, which is the realization of the ultimate purpose of God, has such an exclusive pattern. Hence it is particularly symbolic in all its epochs, pointing to Christ, either backward or forward.

According to the Bible, the very beginning of Holy History is miraculous, because the world in which we live had a beginning because God willed its existence. The beginning of the universe is inconceivable to a mind that thinks in terms of the laws of nature. But everything that has a goal must also have a beginning, and the goal in this case is that all things shall be gathered into a unity under Christ.

The description of the beginning of mankind is also miraculous. According to Genesis man is not the product of the natural evolution of this world, but rather, mankind has had an independent beginning towards which the rest of the world was pointed and in which it will be concluded. An evolutionary theory based upon the laws of nature will not and cannot reach such a conclusion. But if man were merely a part of the universe his relationship to God would be a part of the relationship of the universe to God. Actually however, the history of the world is basically the history of mankind becoming united in Christ, and all things are subordinated to this goal of mankind.

What Scripture reports about the creation of woman is also a miracle. But if mankind was to have more than a merely biological life, and was to exist for a relationship to God as completed in Christ, this unity which mankind was destined to reach under Christ had to be initiated by the fact that man was at first one; not dependent upon his kind but upon his creator and destined to live in a personal relationship to Him.

Concerning the origin of man's sin we are told that the serpent had spoken to the woman. In view of the fact that sin was to be forgiven in Christ, it must have originated outside of mankind rather than in man himself.

The fact that through Noah mankind was saved through the flood to a new miraculous beginning is attributed to a divine revelation which urged him to do what was necessary for that purpose. Thus it is made to prefigure the salvation of mankind through the Savior who joins it and saves His people through judgment.

The origin of the differences in language is a miraculous process. Were it the result of a self-willed emigration rather than its cause, the dispersion of mankind into nations would be the result of their own decision. This could not be the case since its reunion is the work of Christ. God decreed that men should go their own way so that there would be no other unity for them than Christ.

Abraham's wanderings were not the result of his own decision nor of circumstances beyond his control. The beginning of a chosen people had to be as miraculous as the goal of its history. This history is characterized by the

miraculous intercession on the part of God and the corresponding obedience of faith on the part of man. Miraculously
Abraham had to become the ancestor of the people from
which Jesus was to descend in a miraculous way.

The same law appears again when his descendents are
established as an independent nation in their own country.
This did not happen gradually or through their own decision or power.

The call of Moses, the evidences of his vocation, and the
judgment through which the resistance of the Egyptian king
was broken, were miracles. When we read that the last of the
miraculous plagues in Egypt which brought about Israel's
salvation consisted in the death of all the first born children
of the Egyptians, we must not think immediately that not
only the first born may have died, and perhaps not all the
first born. To think this way would rob this event of its
main characteristics, namely, that in a way this was a sentence of death passed over the entire people. The Egyptians
experienced a judgment of God which affected not merely
a number of individuals here and there, but rather, every
first born male, which represented the head and leadership
of the people.

Miraculous was the fact that Israel found its way through
the Red Sea, and was fed in the desert. If we attempt to
explain the former event by the tides, and reduce the manna
to a small supplement made to their other provisions, we
stand in clear contradiction to both narratives. For example,
in Numbers 11:6 the Israelites complain that they see nothing but manna.

The revelation of the law had to be miraculous if the
people to whom it pertained was to prefigure the Church of
Christ which descended from it. Likewise, the temple of this
community could not be the result of human wisdom if it
was to symbolize the relationship of God to His people which
was to be completed in Christ. In the tabernacle this relationship was prophesied, and thus in a sense already present,
and in another sense yet to be realized.

Israel's entrance into Canaan had to be as miraculous as its flight from Egypt. Both events together correspond figuratively to the salvation of the Church of Christ which will occur simultaneously with the judgment of the world.

Jehovah proved to be the God of the soil on which Israel was to dwell when the walls of Jericho fell, and the God of the heavens that vaulted over Canaan when meteors killed the fleeing army of the enemy and when the day became longer so that Israel might reap fully the fruits of its victory. Therefore we must not try to reinterpret the latter event though we cannot understand how it happened and whether it had anything to do with the falling of meteors. We let it go at that, that no day either before or after was like that day.

We deal the same way with the miraculous experience of Balaam. His prophecies were of the greatest importance both for Israel and her enemies. It was the same Jehovah the God of Israel who spoke through this non-Israelite. Balaam wanted to speak against Israel in the service of Balak but was not allowed to do so. The animal which carried him had to remind him of this fact. The miracle is not diminished by the fact that the natural cry of pain of the animal became, in his ears, human speech. It was surprising that at his farewell from Balak Balaam should foretell the historical developments of the world into the far distant future. But when people try to rationalize the story by claiming that the original prophecy has been enlarged upon by later generations, the very existence of Balaam loses its true significance in the context of prophecy.

His importance lies in the fact that when Israel first entered into the rank of nations, a prophet who was not an Israelite foresaw the future of nations and world powers from this point on. This notice of the future sufficed for Israel for centuries ahead until the day of Daniel, who continued from the point where Balaam left off, and thus supplied comfort to them in the midst of threatening historical developments.

The king whose rule was to predict figuratively the reign of Christ was to be appointed by revelation, and through revelation it had to be made sure that the rule over God's people would remain in his family until that people's destiny had been fulfilled. Through awareness of this fact Israel was prevented from engaging in a kind of political life where it might lose sight of its eternal destiny. It realized that the stone had been laid on Zion which was the foundation of its future, and that it had to remain there through all the vicissitudes of its history. When the kingdom of David disintegrated, it was the task of the prophets to keep Israel aware of its destiny. This task was accomplished through the same miraculous spirit of revelation through which David had received his promises and had been made king.

But when Israel deserted its peculiar national task little attention was paid to such prophecies. Elijah and Elisha rose up against this danger. When Elijah punished with a drought the country which was given to the service of Baal, when by his prayer the sacrifice which he offered to the God of Israel was set on fire by lightning, or when Elisha in a miraculous way knew of the movements of the enemy's armies and disclosed them to the king, it was all for the same purpose: namely, to keep the people in that awareness and to bring the people back to the service of God. The sheer miraculousness of their acts corresponded to the desperate situation of their kingdom.

Finally when Daniel received revelations which depicted the future as a succession of powers until the end of the present world, and even mentioned some of them by name, we have to keep in mind that his people were in need of these prophecies. They were in danger of falling into despair because the historical situation remained unchanged and nothing came to pass that had been prophesied concerning Israel's final redemption and glorification. And the only names disclosed to him were those of the Mede-Persians and of the Greeks who immediately succeeded the Chaldeans.

The reason for this was that his people had to be familiarized by previous revelation with the course of events which would result for them in an unprecedented oppression. For this reason these events were foretold to him with unparalleled exactness so that when this persecution began the people would be able to figure step by step that this persecution had been predicted and that this persecution as well as its final end had been predicted.

The history of the New Testament begins with miraculous events and announcements. If the conception of Jesus had been the result of human procreation, He would have been the product of humanity and like them in need of salvation from sin and death. The miraculous beginning of His life, which differentiated Him in the same manner from all others as the Savior is differentiated from those He saves, corresponds to the miracle of our restoration into the life of fellowship with Him. In both instances no more is demanded than the obedience of faith to the Word of God. The announcements which preceded and followed this event corresponded to its greatness.

The fact that this was the beginning of the fulfillment of the prophetic promises had to be proclaimed in a manner different from the prophetic promises themselves. Like the basic promise, it had to be manifested in such a way that those who would receive the announcement could have no doubt that they were dealing with something that had not grown from human thought. Similarly, when John the Baptist was to receive certainty that Jesus was He whom he had proclaimed, he received a divine witness through an outward sign.

John performed no miracles, but Jesus did. He had to substantiate his own witness to his Saviorhood through actions which would reveal Him as the Savior from all evil and also from death. What He taught was illustrated by His wonderful deeds. In Cana His disciples experienced what it meant to pass from life under the law into the joy of the

Gospel. What He meant by speaking of the eating of His flesh and the drinking of His blood could be comprehended in the light of His miraculous feeding of the thousands and His miraculous crossing of the stormy sea. By making some of His disciples to become witnesses of His miraculous transfiguration, He gave them a foretaste of the glory of His transfigured life to which His body was to arise after death. That the members of the New Testament community were free from obligation to the ordinances of the Old Testament was an insight sufficiently important to be made sure to Peter by means of a miracle, i.e., by finding the money for the temple tax in a fish which he caught upon the command of Jesus. Similarly, the fact that in the hour of Jesus' death the veil of the temple was rent, corresponded to the significance of this moment at which the wall between God and His Church fell, and also to the significance of the sanctuary which heretofore had been the house of God upon earth.

Just as Jesus' human life had begun with a real conception and birth, so it was necessary that He should really die, but also that He should rise from death to a new bodily life. Thereby He was to initiate the restoration of mankind to a perfect existence, physical as well as spiritual, and by the innate power of His life in the body to lead it towards that perfection. For man is not a mere spirit, but is essentially a being that lives in a body.

When after His resurrection, Jesus appeared and disappeared in a miraculous manner before the eyes of His disciples, His appearances taught them how He would be with them in the future, and His disappearing that He would no longer be visible to them. When nevertheless He converted Saul through an appearance which could be perceived through the senses and thus showed him that He, the Crucified, was alive, that manifestation corresponded to the purpose for which it occurred. It meant that the conversion of the Gentiles was to be a special work independent from the conversion of Israel, and that he who had been called and converted apart from the Apostles through the glorified Savior was to gather gentile Christianity into an independent existence alongside the Jewish Christian Church.

Those who attempt to explain Paul's vision by assuming that Paul was already in an inner conflict as to the appropriateness of his persecuting the Christians, and by thus reducing his conversion to a psychological process, which was incidentally accompanied by a vision, neglect the most essential aspect of the event, namely that it pointed to the mission for which Paul was destined.

After the Ascension of Jesus, the promise that the Spirit of God would begin a new phase of activity in Christ's disciples as the spirit of the glorified Son of Man was fulfilled through a perceptible event on the day of Pentecost. It indicated that they represented the people of God, who within their earthly existence prefigured their own future glory. The fact that at this moment the differences of language did not prevent the Church from speaking to the witnesses of this event in their various languages, revealed that in the future the Word of God would no longer be confined to Israel, but would be proclaimed in every tongue.

Later on, when the priestly party of the Sadduccees had the Apostles arrested, they were miraculously freed. Their work was not to be interrupted until the Jewish Christian Church had been firmly founded. Nevertheless Stephen did not escape death. For when even the Pharisees became his enemies, this enmity was given free reign so that the Church in dispersion would bring the message about Jesus to the non-Jewish world of the Samaritans and Gentiles. James had to die, while Peter was miraculously freed. This meant that the Apostles were not destined to stay with the congregations until the return of the Lord, but also that it was not left to the arbitrary whim of man to take them away as long as their work was not yet finished.

In Philippi Paul was freed miraculously from his chains because this was the first case of hostile action which pagan rulers took against the messengers of Christ in the Gentile world. Later however, when his work in the East had been accomplished, he remained in jail for five years. His work would now proceed without his help; the Word of God is not fettered (II Tim. 2:9).

Whatever happened to the Apostles or through their instrumentality, whatever occurred through their proclamation of the Gospel, whatever miracles were performed in and through the Church, took place according to Heb. 2:4: "while God also bore witness by signs and wonders and various miracles and by gifts of the Holy Spirit . . . ." Among the gifts of the Spirit mentioned in I Cor. 12 however, there is to be found "the utterance of wisdom and of knowledge" no less than "the speaking with tongues and healings." The further the gospel expanded beyond the original establishment of the Church in Israel, and in the Gentile world, the more the latter gifts recede behind the former.

Thus all the miraculous aspects of the history recorded in Scripture must be understood in relation to its center point, and to be evaluated according to the relation in which they stand to it. This applies particularly to theophanies and to the appearances of angels. It is objected that these convey a mythological character to Biblical History.* We start with the fact that God was revealed in Christ, as we read in John 14:9 where to Philip's request, "show us the Father," Jesus answers, "He who has seen me has seen the Father." This teaches us that God's active presence becomes perceptible at precisely the moment when man needs a tangible manifestation. Man was never intended to attain a knowledge of God exclusively through a process of mental development; because the Word is the means through which God creates faith; and partaking of bread and wine is the means through which the glorified Christ is at work in His Church. Concerning theophanies it should be remembered that appearances of God and of angels are one and the same thing.

_____

* Translator's note: cf. for instance D. F. Strauss and Rudolf Bultmann.

The creature is able to see and to hear his creator. He does not have to seek him in his own spirit,** for since he is created for a personal relationship to God he experiences through his senses that there is a God and that this God deals with him in a personal way.

Whereas in Genesis 3:8 we read, "and they heard the sound of the Lord God walking in the garden," it is said in verse 24 that, "at the east of the garden of Eden he placed the Cherubim." In other words, in the latter instance, the manifestation of the presence of God appears as the visible manifestation of His serving spirits. Conversely in Genesis 16:7, "the angel of the Lord" appeared to Hagar and spoke to her, yet in verse 13 she says that "the Lord" had spoken to her. In Exodus 3:2 it says, "the angel of the Lord appeared to him," but in verse 4 we read, "the Lord saw." Again in Exodus 13:21 it says, "the Lord went before them," but in 14:19, "the angel of the Lord" did so. Notwithstanding the fact that in Exodus 19:19 it is said that Moses spoke on Sinai and God answered him, Stephen was perfectly justified in saying that it was an "angel" who spoke to Moses on Sinai (Acts 7:38). In the story of Gideon's call we hear that Gideon saw an angel of the Lord speak to him, while later we read that "the Lord" had spoken to Gideon (Judges 6:22).

We are justified in maintaining that whenever Biblical History reports appearances of God it means that God has made His active presence physically perceptible in such a way that the angelic world mediates this manifestation of God.

Furthermore we must note that the manner in which God becomes perceptible differs according to the purpose for which the appearance occurs. According to Genesis 3:24, for instance, men saw the lightning of a menacing sword, a terrifying manifestation of fire at the place where they were

---

** Translator's note: i.e., as in Idealism where God is an idea in the human mind.

no longer supposed to enter. In Genesis 15:17 however, Abraham sees "a smoking fire pot and a flaming torch" because the sacrificial pieces on the right and on the left were to be consumed. By this fact he was to be assured through a physical sign that God had made a covenant with him, just as one man does with another.

Again in Exodus 3:2, Moses, when he is called, notices a burning bush which is not consumed, and hears from it a voice just like that of a man. The bush was a symbol of the presence of God in Israel. This God is a consuming fire and makes His dwelling among a sinful people without consuming it. The calling of Moses thus serves to actualize this arrangement.

Exodus 13:21 speaks of a suspended cloud in the form of a column which was lit up at night as a wonderful caravan fire to give direction to the people on their way. Mt. Sinai was hidden by storm clouds, out of whose darkness the people heard a human voice and above which they saw a consuming fire. For since the law was to be received, they were to be impressed by the fact that God must be feared. The law however was given by angels (Gal. 3:19, Heb. 2:2, Acts 7:53). As a matter of fact, the whole event of God's visible presence on Sinai is attributed in Deut. 33:2 to the activity of the heavenly hosts. It was a self-revelation of God through the service of His angels (cf. Ps. 68:18). This appearance was terrifying, but the Elders who being initiated into the relationship between God and Israel were led into the darkness of the mount by Moses, saw in its midst the God of Israel (Ex. 24:10). Below him it was like sapphire and the clarity of heaven, for they were supposed to receive a glimpse of the blessed glory of their God's peace. Whenever Moses entered into the holy tabernacle to receive a revelation, the pillar of cloud descended at the door of the tabernacle and from it he received the Word of God (Ex. 33:10). The people had to see with their own eyes that the orders given by Moses were not on his own authority. But what he perceived in Ex. 34:5 f. where he did not face Jehovah

but saw Him from the rear has not been expressed in words
(cf. 33:23). We only hear about the impression which it
made upon him.

When Elijah saw God at Mt. Horeb (I Kings 19:11), it
was in order that he might experience the same thing in the
same place as Moses. But when God revealed Himself to His
prophet, neither in the storm nor in the earthquake nor in
the fire, but in the still small voice, it was in order that he
might receive precisely that idea of God which his calling
as a prophet required, because his mission implied that he
be a man of terror for his people.

Elisha's servant experienced the protecting presence of
God by seeing everywhere around him fiery wagons and
horses. Thereby he was to gain courage to follow his master
in the midst of enemies (II Kings 6:15). But the shepherds
on the fields of Bethlehem who were to receive the good
news that the Savior of the world had been born, saw creatures of light and heard songs of praise. Thus the manner in
which the active presence of God manifests itself always
corresponds to the situation in which this appearance occurs.

But God may approach man also in human form. In Genesis 18:2 for instance, we read that Abraham saw three men
stand before him, whom he invited to stay. However, in the
course of the same narrative we read in verse 13 that "the
Lord" spoke to Abraham, just as the entire story opens with
the statement that "the Lord" appeared to him. Likewise in
chapter 19:1 the "two angels" came to Lot, as they had
come to Abraham, and he takes them for travellers. He recognized them as messengers of God only when they revealed
to him the purpose of their coming. The fact that they ate
is of the same nature as their walking and standing or using
the human language or being dressed in human dress, as we
read, for instance, in Daniel and in Revelation. All this does
not indicate that they have physical bodies, nor that they
are in need of physical nourishment, but rather it symbolizes
their superiority over the earthly and physical nature of man.

Because similar narratives are found in pagan legends it

is alleged that these divine manifestations are mythical too. But here we find them in the context of Holy History. When Jacob fled from Esau, who had become his enemy, he had to fear not only for his life but also for the promises connected with his person. Therefore he remained at night on the other side of the river after letting his people cross. In this night of terror he is attacked by a "man" who wrestles with him. This wrestling was not to last beyond the dark of the night, by which his dread was increased. He had to learn what is expressed in Genesis 32:28, " . . . you have striven with God and with men, and have prevailed." His prayerful wrestling with God assumed this form to make him sure that God would grant his prayer and to rid him of his dread. Thinking that he was wrestling with a human enemy and fearing that he might lose in this situation, he became aware of the fact that he had seen God ("I have seen God face to face," verse 30). Our assertion that the appearances of God and of angels are identical is substantiated further by the fact that in Genesis we read that Jacob wrestled with God, while in Hosea (12:4) we read that "He strove with the angel and prevailed."

Similarly, when Joshua (5:13) sees before him a being completely human in form, and brandishing a sword, this was to remind him that he and his people were under God's guidance. Gideon too, who was to free his people from grave persecution, sees what at first seemed to be merely a human being. He speaks to the one described as the "angel of the Lord" (Judges 6:12), as though he were a man, and only later on does he realize that this person is bringing the Word of God to him, and then he calls him "the Lord" (v. 22).

So we notice that the manifestation in which a divine revelation is given to man assumes human shape unless there is reason for it to be different. This is the case also in the New Testament, as for instance with Zacharia, or Mary. In Luke 1:28 an angel came to her; in verse 38 it says that he went away. Yet of the shepherds at Bethlehem we read that they saw creatures of light which "went away from them," and "into heaven." When Jesus saw His first disciples around Him, He said in John 1:51, "You will see heaven opened, and the angels of God ascending and descending upon the Son of Man."

But these spirits of God were not to be physically perceptible to men as long as Jesus was with them, because His miracles assured them the service of these spirits. The centurion at Capernaum correctly assumed that Jesus ruled over the invisible powers, just as He ruled over His servants (Luke 7:8). The disciples saw this service of the spirits who were at Jesus' disposal only in the miracles which He performed. However, the fact of His resurrection was attested to them by the appearance of angels. The women saw but one angel (Mark 16:5), but Mary of Magdala saw two. In her case the miraculous appearance was not merely to tell her of the miracle that had happened, but also the place where the Lord's head and feet had lain was to be shown to her in a miraculous manner (John 20:12). After the disciples had seen Jesus ascend we read in Acts 1:10, "two men stood by them in white robes," and when Peter was to be freed miraculously from prison, the angel of the Lord stood by him and having led him out he suddenly disappeared (Acts 12:7).

The fact that these manifestations can be perceived with the senses does not mean that an angel is a corporeal being and always perceptible. It is like the sound from above which answered Jesus' prayer during His last address to His people when Jesus made the request, "Father, glorify thy name" (John 12:28). The multitude said, "it thundered." Others said, "an angel spoke to him." But the Disciples heard the words: "I have glorified it, and I will glorify it again." Daniel likewise saw a majestic form, but those who were with him did not perceive it (10:7). A light from heaven shined suddenly upon Saul and his companions, according to Acts 9:3, so that they fell terror-stricken to the ground. They heard somebody speak to them but they saw no one and did not understand what was said. In other words, an effect was produced in their senses which made them see and hear as much as was necessary for the intended purpose. The appearance was experienced only by those for whom it was destined, and they perceived only as much as was demanded for that purpose. Otherwise the nature of the event depended entirely on the purpose intended.

Those manifestations which by nature are outside the realm of physical perception appeared real to those who were awake, but as dreams to those who were asleep. In Gen. 28:12 Jacob saw in a dream angels of God ascending and descending when he went abroad, while in 32:2 he was awake when he saw an apparition which made him exclaim "this is God's army!" Joseph heard an angel of the Lord in a dream (Matt. 1:20) while Mary had the same experience while awake.

In the gospel according to Matthew all visions occur in dreams, while Luke reports them as appearing while people are awake. Some have therefore maintained that both types of reports are suspect of being unhistorical. But in Matthew only those cases are reported where the remembrance of a dream is sufficient to bring about action when the person has awakened, whereas in Luke we find proclamations which are intended to give complete certainty. A vision in a state of rapture can be compared to a dream. In both instances the outer senses are closed off and the seeing and hearing are forms of inner experience. While such raptures are not confined to the realm of Holy History, here they are in the service of God's redemptive work. That which is seen and heard in this condition serves the same purpose as those appearances which are perceived by the conscious senses.

When he receives his prophetic call, Isaiah sees the God of Israel sitting on a throne and the spirits about Him, and He hears his word, "Whom shall I send?" he replies, "Send me" (Is. 6:8). Similarly Ezekiel, in a rapture, sees Jehovah coming towards him carried by the cherubim as though by a living carriage, to call him (Ezek. 1). In Revelation 4 John, having been transported to heaven in a rapture, sees God sitting there on a throne. The differences between these three visions correspond to the different purposes of their respective raptures. The cherubim of Ezekiel carry him who is enthroned, while those of John stand about him. In the former instance they serve as a living carriage, while in the latter they are a living ornament of the throne. Those of Ezekiel have four wings because they fly and carry him who is enthroned above them, whereas those in Isaiah 6 have six wings because they stand around him who is enthroned. It would be erroneous to conclude from the different number of their wings that there was a difference of opinion concerning the number of wings of a cherub. Rather their number is in accordance with the mental picture that the seer has of the presence of God.

The belief that the Apocalypse was written by the Apostle John was opposed by some on the ground that John would never have described the Jesus with whom he had lived in the manner it is done in chapter one. But in chapter 5:6 he sees Him in the figure of a lamb with a mortal wound, healed, in contrast to the dragon, and in 9:11 ff. he views Him like a king with a diadem, sitting on a battle horse. The form in which he sees Him depends in every case upon the specific revelation which he is receiving.

The miraculous character of the appearances of God and of angels differs in no respect from that of the healings performed by Jesus. Like all the miracles of Holy History they are to be evaluated according to the purpose which they serve. It is necessary to recognize the place which each of these miraculous events occupies in the context of Holy History, which in turn is to be interpreted in the light of Christ. The more clearly this relationship is recognized, the more firmly the historicity of the event is also assured, and to ascertain its historicity is demanded by the nature of our faith in Christ. Faith presupposes the existence of a holy history in which God deals with mankind rather than a natural order rooted in God. For in the latter case everything would happen out of natural necessity. In view of the certainty which faith carries with it, the naturalistic or deistic interpretation must be considered as resting on preconceived assumptions.

Obviously therefore it is absurd to conclude from the Old Testament appearances of God that they presuppose belief in a God who has a body or definite shape, as has been inferred from the manlike figure which Ezekiel (1:26) saw above the chariot of the cherubim, or the appearance of fire which Moses beheld on Mt. Horeb, or which the congregation of Israel noticed on Mt. Sinai.

Similarly we now have the explanation of those passages of Scripture in which either the terminology by which the activity of God is described, or the things predicted of God appear too human and manlike. What we have in mind are passages in which it is said, for instance, that before the judgment of the great flood God "repented that he had created man," or that he was "angry" with those who were against Him, or that He felt "pity" for the suffering of Israel in Egypt, or that His heart is moved by those who call upon Him, or that He may forgive sin or refuse to do so, or that in the fulness of time He sent His Son.

Such features cannot be reduced to expressions of the eternal unchangeableness of God. For as a result of such reasoning the diversity of God's inner life and His dealings with this world no less than the diversity or the successive character of that which takes place in Him, would disappear in His eternal self-identity. By such a method we would empty Scripture of its specific character. It would be more reasonable to content oneself with giving to Scripture the questionable praise that it has a childlike understanding of God. But by knowing Christ and the salvation of the world that has been brought about in Him and through Him, we also know that a history that is going on between God and mankind from the beginning of time to its end. There is a history of a reciprocal interchange of life and of mutual relation between God and mankind, and thus an historical nature of God which is no less evident than His eternal self-identity. It is on this basis, in turn, that we evaluate the records of God's historical dealing with mankind. While we are aware of the part that the expressions by which God's historical activities are described are taken from analogous processes in human life, we are not thereby prevented from recognizing the historicity of these manifestations of God's life.

Faith thus enables the theologian correctly to understand Scripture in two regards. The fact that he owes his salvation to Christ has not only been proclaimed to him but it has also become a matter of personal assurance to him. Accordingly he will comprehend both the miraculous character of the things recorded in the Bible, and the human way in which the things predicated of God are expressed therein.

The assurance of its miraculous origin will determine both the mental attitude with which the Christian interpreter approaches Scripture, and the goal he has in view when he reads it as literature. The assurance of its miraculous content will determine his appreciation. Since the Bible as Christendom possesses it is a homogeneous unity, we are by faith led to the recognition of a second essential aspect of it, that is, its Israelitic character.

B. THE ISRAELITIC CHARACTER OF SCRIPTURE

1. Its Israelitic Origin

The mediator of that distinctive relationship between God and man which we call Christianity came out of Israel; as His Church did too. Thus Israel, in contrast with all the other nations of mankind, is the chosen people of Holy History.

Recently this religious distinctiveness has been extended to all Semitic peoples so that Israel's peculiarity would be only one derived from a specific development of these general Semitic characteristics. This tendency has been accentuated ever since recent investigations of legends of Assyria and Babylonia have shown certain similarities with the history recorded in Holy Scripture. However, while this similarity can be attributed to a common tradition it has religious value only where it is related to the Holy History whose goal is Christ. This relationship has been preserved only in Israel because in Israel alone Holy History takes place.

The history of Israel's origins teaches how it happened that this nation was singled out for this mission. Abraham had to leave his country and his ancestral home and live a solitary life in Canaan among foreign non-semitic nations, as did his progeny. His descendents had to move to Egypt and to grow into a nation in the midst of an equally foreign and non-semitic people. They were held together only through their manner of life, their memory of their forefathers, and their hope for the fulfillment of the promises given to them. When this people left Egypt it stayed forty years in the desert of the Sinaitic peninsula. During this time it was separated from all outside influences and grew into the distinctive law of its common life which they had not evolved themselves, but which had been given to them. Thus they became the "peculiar people" which Balaam called "blessed."

In order to interpret the history of Israel's origin by which it differs from all other nations as being merely the development of a branch of the Semitic race, it would be necessary to consider Abraham, Isaac, Jacob, and Joseph as different tribes of a migrating Semitic people, to have them live in Egypt in a Semitic environment, to change their forty years sojourn in the desert into a simple migration from Egypt to Canaan, and to transform the legislation on Mt. Sinai into a century long process of an intrinsic national development.

We acknowledge the miraculous character of this history and the exclusive significance which the people of that history had for Holy History. Since Holy Scripture is a product of this history its Israelitic character must be evaluated accordingly. It is permeated by it everywhere because it is everywhere of an Israelitic origin. This is proven by the language of Scripture, including the New Testament. The Jewish idiom of Luke, for instance, is obvious. It has been objected that in Colossians 4:14 Luke is differentiated from the Jewish companions of the captive Apostle and thus shown to be a Gentile. This view, however, is the result of an erroneous interpretation of this passage. It refers only to those Jewish teachers of the Christian message who had not accompanied Paul to Rome and did not belong to his circle but were there independently of him. Of them the Apostle says that only a few had helped to spread the kingdom of God in a profitable way. The fact that Luke is not mentioned among those does not mean that he was not a Jew, for he could not be mentioned in this context since it was taken for granted that a companion of the Apostle would participate in the spreading of the Gospel for which those few are praised.

The Israelitic origin of Scripture imparts its character to Biblical language. It is true of course that we do not understand the content correctly until we translate it into our own language. But since our language is the product of a national life, lived originally outside the realm of Holy History, its character would make it unfit to be the expression of the content of Holy History had not the Biblical language reshaped ours. Just as the Greek language had to be reshaped in order to express the content of Holy History, so did ours. By disposing of that which our language has thus become, one de-christianizes it; and thus Christian thoughts, when expressed in such a manner, become un-Christian. This transposition of the content of Scripture from the Semitic into the so-called Japhethetic does not merely mean the loss of the peculiar Israelitic expression, but also of the mentality which Holy History has brought about.

Holy History provides concepts which language in its

natural state cannot express unless elements of Holy History
are injected which give the language its peculiar connotations. This is what happened to the Hebrew language and
later to the Aramaic and Greek.

When, in Genesis 24:7 for instance, Jehovah is called "the
God of heaven"; or in Psalm 2:4 He is called "He who sits
in the heavens," or in Psalm 33:13 it is said of Him that He
"looks down from heaven," heaven in all these instances
does not designate that visible part of the universe which
can be seen from the earth. For in I Kings 8:27 it says
"heaven and the highest heaven cannot contain thee," and
in Isaiah 66:1, "Heaven is my throne." So little is heaven
conceived of as a place that limits God, that we read in
Psalm 139:8, "if I ascend up to heaven, thou art there; if I
make my bed in Sheol, thou art there." In other words, the
transcendence of God is named after the visible beyond.
Accordingly we read in the New Testament "Father who art
in heaven," and concerning Christ Heb. 9:24 says "He entered into heaven itself, now to appear in the presence of
God." On the other hand Heb. 4:14 says that He "has passed
through the heavens"; and Eph. 4:10: "Who ascended far
above all the heavens . . . ." This is to say that He who has
been lifted up to God has to be conceived of as beyond
everything that may be thought of in special terms. Furthermore when the *goyim* are differentiated from the *ha'am* the
former term designates the nations of mankind as left to
themselves, in contrast with the people whose national life
is ordered by the revealed law and which forms the realm
of Holy History.

When we translate the Old Testament *goyim* by "Gentiles"
it is usually assumed that the nations of Islam and of Christendom are not part of the *goyim*. And yet the Apostle in
Rom. 11:13 says "I am speaking to you Gentiles" . . . and
in Eph. 2:11, "you Gentiles in the flesh . . . ." Within the
Church of Christ the New Testament differentiates between
an Israel of God on the one hand and a converted world of
Gentiles on the other. However we read in Heb. 2:17 "to

make expiation for the sins of the people" where *laos* does not designate the Jewish people or the Jewish Christians, but the whole people of God which in the New Testament consists of Jews and non-Jews indiscriminately and which is a continuation of the former national existence of God's people. The Israel which continues to exist beside the Church is the "Israel according to the flesh." However, the usage of the word *ethne* ("nations") remains the same as it was in the Old Testament. It serves to denote the contrast created by Holy History between the unbelievers and the chosen people of Holy History.

To add a further example: The contrast between "spirit" and "flesh" is originally a material one, as for example in Isaiah 31:3 where the expressions God and spirit *(ruach)* are used parallel and in contrast to man and flesh *(basar)*. But when it is realized that together with our physical nature sinfulness is also inherited, the contrast becomes an ethical one. In Gal. 5:17, for instance, "flesh" denotes all mankind as a biological entity in contrast to the Spirit through which God works upon the ego as it is conditioned by its origin. When we read in John 7:39 "the Holy Spirit was not yet given," it seems to imply a denial of the fact that God's Holy Spirit had been present and active in the Old Testament. But we must remember that when John wrote this, the Spirit of God dwelt actively within the congregation of God as the Spirit of Jesus Christ and as such was Holy Spirit in that capacity.

John refers to the Spirit of God as he was actually at work when the Holy Spirit had been poured out on the Church of Christ. But in order to understand the evangelist's statement properly, one must know what "spirit" means in the language of Scripture. In secular Greek, pneuma has merely a physiological connotation, but the Spirit of which the Old Testament is speaking is in the first place "the Spirit of God." The term refers to God as "the living one" whose Spirit is described as "life-giving." This Spirit as the Spirit of the Son of Man, Jesus Christ, began His active presence here on earth after Jesus' ascension. It was in this sense that the Holy Spirit "was not yet" when Jesus was still in the flesh, and prior to glorification.

The Biblical "righteousness" *(zedekah, dikaiosyne)* does not merely denote what the ancient writers call "justice which gives everyone his due." For wherever the term is applied in Scripture to God it sounds as if it meant "grace." This is so because God is "righteous," that is, true to His plan and promise. His "righteousness" consists in the fact that He follows the plan He has laid out, therefore His deeds in Holy History are called "acts of righteousness" because in them He executes His revealed plan.

This makes it understandable why it can be said of the same God that He is "righteous," and that He "justifies the ungodly" (Rom. 4:5). He declares the sinner just on the condition which he has established himself, namely, on the basis of his own saving activity in the life and death of Jesus Christ. . . . Therefore the interpreter has to take care not to interpret Biblical terms in the sense which they have in non-Biblical language.

As we said above, our language has been recoined for the expression of the things with which Scripture deals. It might therefore appear as if it were sufficient to translate the Hebrew and Greek terms with the traditional or the specially coined words of our language. However, we can never assume in advance that the most adequate word in our language has actually been used. It is possible that the distinctive meaning of the Hebrew or Hebrew-Greek expression in question was not fully understood when the corresponding word in our language was selected or coined by the lexicographer. Futhermore, the words of our own language, by virtue of their origin in everyday life rather than in Holy History have connotations which do not agree with that which they are to express. One has to limit these connotations in one's mind in order to grasp the full content of the original expression without inappropriate and disturbing associations.

The interpreter should therefore always keep in mind the distinctive meaning of the Hebrew or Hebrew-Greek term, and transcribe it to those for whom he interprets. This procedure is required, for instance, in order to interpret correctly the much quoted words in Heb. 2:4, "the just shall live by his faith." First, let us consider the term "just." If we decided to translate this term without keeping in mind the peculiarity of the corresponding Hebrew term, it could easily be understood in the secular sense where it means merely "to give each his due." But the Hebrew term, as we have said above, is used of him who follows his plan. Thus the word is used by the prophet in contrast to the Chaldean, of whom it was said earlier that his soul was not "upright." In his relation to God and his neighbor, a man is "just" when he lives in accordance with the goal which God has appointed to him. This is particularly true of his relationship to God. For it is God who has made the rule according to which he has to act.

Furthermore, of such a one it is said that he has Life "by his faith." We say "Life" because the corresponding Hebrew word is used emphatically. Faith is not merely a belief that something is true, and not merely faithfulness in the sense of constancy. According to the basic meaning of the Hebrew verb, it means to be established in one place (Job 39:24). Here, in relation to God, faith means "to trust in him, to hold firmly to him." God is the "place" upon which man has been placed and established. Thus it becomes clear here how closely related the concept of faith is to the concepts of trust and perseverance in God.

The terms by means of which the New Testament expresses the saving facts are also rooted in the Old Testament. This can be shown for instance in the way the Greek word *hagios* ("holy") is used. *Hagios* in the New Testament is the translation of the Hebrew *kadosh*. Thus it does not merely describe a condition of the will, but a quality of being. *Kadosh* describes first and foremost God as He is contained within Himself. Consequently, in the Old Testament "to sanctify" designates separation from everything outside of God and reception into communion with God. This must be kept in mind in order to understand why the Christians are called "saints." They are those who have been sanctified, i.e., who have been taken out of the sinful world and placed in the community of God. And what has been done to them precedes their new behavior, which has to be shaped in accordance with their sanctification.

Similarly, when Jesus is called in the New Testament "priest," or "high priest," or when it is said of His death that He "sacrificed Himself" to God, secular Greek usage does not help us to understand how the term "priest" or "sacrifice" are meant here. Rather we have to turn to the Old Testament and to consider the priesthood and the sacrifices rooted in Holy History. Jesus and His death in the New Testament are described in the same terms as the Old Testament applies to the priesthood and to sacrifice.

It is indeed true that Christianity came into the world as something new, but its newness does not stand in conflict with what has just been said. Notwithstanding its newness, its relationship to the Old Testament is a great deal more than a mere continuation. What is prophetically and figuratively present in the Old Testament has been brought to its completion and fulfillment in the New Testament. We have only to keep in mind those historical events by which the Old Testament concepts have been changed and developed.

So much about the Israelitic character of Scripture as far as its origin is concerned. Now we must deal with:

2. The Israelitic Character of Its Content

In Gen. 10, three national groups are traced back to the sons of Noah. Thereafter Bible History limits itself to one of these groups, and eventually to one single branch, until it rests upon Abraham and his special call. Noah's prophetic blessing had already promised Shem that God would make his dwelling in his tent (Gen. 9:27), in other words that

here the original communion between God and man would
be restored. Now the recipients of this blessing are the descendents of Abraham. From them however, some branches
are cut off until the promise finally rests on the descendents
of Jacob. Through participation in this blessing, all the
generations on earth will eventually be saved. The whole
subsequent history is concerned with the realization of this
promise. Its ultimate fulfillment as shown in the New Testament still lies in the future.

If this is considered "national particularism," it is one that
is continued in the New Testament, in Rom. 11 as well as
in the Book of Revelation. The fact that Jesus and His
Church descended from Abraham, Isaac and Jacob is further
confirmation of the election of Israel, belief in which must
not be attributed to the imaginations of self complacency
and national vanity. When subsequently the Old Testament
deals only with Israel and considers the history of the rest
of mankind only insofar as it affects Israel, such concentra-
tion is due to the distinctiveness of Israel's calling. Israel is
the realm of history which has its goal in Jesus. Thus its history has to stay within the limits set thereby. The law of its
national life differs from all other orders of national life by
the fact that the thoughts of God for Holy History have
found therein an expression which is in accordance with its
goal. Israel's priesthood truly mediates holiness to this community of God. Likewise, when this community gives itself
the political form of a kingdom, the reign of its king is indeed
the reign of Jehovah upon earth. Similarly, Israel's prophets
are not like the spokesmen of other nations (Paul speaks,
for instance, of the prophets of the Cretes in Tim. 1:12), but
exclusively the spokesmen of God, who coming prior to the
Son of God nevertheless served the same purpose.

Accordingly, Israel's hope aims at the fulfillment of the
promise given to them. Its fulfillment will imply that Israel's
God will eventually be recognized as the only God. The subsequent establishment of the Kingdom of God is the antitype
and completion of David's kingdom. The expectation of him

who will expand his kingdom as God's Kingdom over the whole world is attached to the family of David, and after Zion had become the center of the national and religious life of Israel, this hope was connected with that locality, just as for Abraham it was connected with Canaan. Likewise, insofar as the Gentile world takes a hostile attitude toward Israel, Jehovah's eventual glorification becomes a victory of Israel over a hostile world.

The Israelitic character of the content of Holy Scripture must not be obscured by interpreting Israel, Canaan and Zion as the Christian Church, whose establishment, nature and future would here be prophesied. When for instance the author of the 100th Psalm says in verse 3, "we are his people and the sheep of his pasture," it is an Israelite who speaks of his people as a community of the true God, yet implying that it is that community as a result of God's call. It is with such a view of the community in mind that over against the hostile world the author of the 47th Psalm is comforted by the hope that "he subdued peoples under us, and nations under our feet." This hope is connected with Zion, of which Psalm 68:16 says, "The mount which God desired for his abode," and verse 29, "Because of thy temple at Jerusalem kings bear gifts to thee." As the ruler of this people, appointed by God, the king of Israel can say as in Psalm 2:8 that God has promised him, "Ask of me, and I will make the nations your heritage, and the ends of the earth your possession." Likewise to him in whom he sees the fulfillment of his kingdom and his Lord, David can say in Psalm 110:2 that "The Lord sends forth from Zion your mighty scepter." In Psalm 72:8 Solomon prays that the king of the future should rule from ocean to ocean and from the river to the ends of the earth.

When the Kingdom of David collapsed and his people were scattered, the prophets predicted the return of Israel to its country and the restitution of the house of David (see Micah 7:14; Is. 11:16; Ezek. 37:25; Amos 9:11). Zion remains God's place on earth, that is, the place with which the fulfillment of the promises is connected, to which all nations of the earth will come to receive their law and from which justice goes forth over all lands (Micah 4:2; Is. 2:3 f.).

Before that, however (Zech. 12 and 14), Jehovah's judgment over the armies of the Gentiles which are threatening Jerusalem will take place, and as a result Jehovah will be the only God on earth and the Gentiles will come annually to Jerusalem to celebrate with Israel the feast of the tabernacle.

In Dan. 7:27 "the people of the saints of the Most High . . . " is the one which will receive dominion over all the world, and when God addresses David the same nation is called "your people" in 9:24 and 12:1.

The Israelitic character of all these statements must not be obscured.

There is even less reason why those statutes of the Sinaitic law which concerns food, agriculture, and equipment of the sanctuary should be reinterpreted in order to make them worthy of Scripture. Similarly in Ezekiel 40-48 which visualizes and describes the form and order of the national life of Israel after its restoration, one should not attempt to reinterpret every detail; rather the whole must be interpreted in the light of chapter 37, which shows that the future state of things will be according to the law of Moses and yet entirely different. Those chapters refer definitely to the historical Israel as restored to its country.

Safeguarding the Israelitic character of the Old Testament does not prevent us from evaluating the Old Testament in the light of the New. But all that has to be said along this line will be mentioned when we deal with the influence which the difference between the Old Testament and New Testament has upon interpretation. Right now it suffices to point out that even the New Testament is Israelitic in its character. When, for instance, it says of Christ in Luke 1:32, "The Lord God will give to him the throne of his father David," this means that the same Old Testament promise that we find in the prophets has been reiterated here. Matthew and Luke emphasize the fact that Mary was the wife of Joseph, the son of David. The birth of Jesus fulfilled the promise made to David that the kingship over the people of God should remain in his family (II Sam. 7).

In Luke 1:54 Mary praises God because He has accepted His servant Israel and will show to Abraham and his descendents His mercy forever. In Matt. 1:21 the name of Jesus is interpreted as meaning that He will be the Savior of His people. This is the same hope that in Psalm 130:8 was expected of Jehovah. Similarly in Luke 1:68-71 Zecharia praises God because he has secured salvation for his people, "and has raised up a horn of salvation for us in the house of his servant David . . . that we should be saved from our enemies and from the hand of all who hate us." We rediscover here again the Old Testament contradiction between Israel, the people of God, and the Gentiles who are the enemies of Israel.

In Luke 2:32 Simeon recognizes in the child Jesus the light of revelation for all the Gentiles and the glory of Israel. It is true that in Matt. 3:9 we see John the Baptist reprimanding those who rely on their racial descent from Abraham, and yet Jesus in Matt. 15:24 says that He was sent to the lost sheep of the house of Israel, and in John 4:22 He says that "salvation is of the Jews." Jesus also refers to the conversion of Israel when He says in Matt. 10:23 that His disciples will not complete the evangelization of the cities of Judah until the Son of Man will come again. To be sure, in Matt. 21:43 Jesus says to His fellow Jews that the kingdom will be taken from them, but at the same time He foretells an age when His people will praise Him and greet Him as their Savior (Matt. 23:39).

Paul, the Apostle to the Gentiles, does not fail to instruct the Gentile Christian congregation in Rome that "God has not rejected his people whom he foreknew" (Rom. 11:2). Not only in Romans 15:8 do we read that Christ was "a servant to the circumcised to show God's truthfulness"—while the Gentiles can praise God merely for His mercy's sake—but also in Romans 11:25 ff. we read that "a hardening has come upon part of Israel," and that after "the full number of the Gentiles" has entered the kingdom of God, "all Israel will be saved," so that the history of Israel will reach its culmination in the forgiveness of its sins (Deut. 32:43). Furthermore, in II Cor. 3:16 we read that the veil which covers Israel's heart will be taken away, not on condition that they are converted, but at the moment when they are converted.

The Jews have a great advantage in every respect, says the Apostle Paul in Rom. 3:1, primarily because they are members of the people to whom God's revelation was committed and which for that reason forms the congregation of God on earth. The members of the Gentile world which are converted to the New Testament salvation, are like branches of a wild olive tree that are grafted into the cultivated tree whose roots are sacred (Rom. 11:17). Thus they become parts of the history of Israel which goes back to Abraham (Rom. 4:16). The congregation of Jesus Christ which had its beginning in Israel now has become coextensive with mankind. But if a particular nation should be needed again to bring the history of salvation to its ultimate completion, it will be Israel.

It would be a mistake to interpret Rom. 11 or Rev. 7 and 11 in such a manner that the providential role of Israel and of the Holy Land are thereby obliterated. The vision described in Rev. 12:7-11 is of special significance because it shows that when Israel as a nation is acquitted from Satan's accusation, the history of salvation has reached the point which is the prerequisite of its consummation. In the same way as Israel, through giving birth to the Savior (Rev. 12:5), had become the place where the salvation of the New Testament had its beginning, so also will it become the place where this salvation reaches its final goal. The conflict between God and

Satan, between Christ and anti-Christ, will enter into its final phase in Israel; and it is in Israel that Christ's New Revelation will occur first which will be the decisive factor in that struggle.

The prophecies concerning the end of the present age do not detract from the dignity and significance of the Church of Christ which at present is the congregation of God on earth, when they show that for the benefit of the whole of mankind and all the nations the particular place of Israel in Holy History will be renewed, and that the land where Jesus appeared will be again the locale of Holy History.

For this promise applies only to that Israel which is converted to Christ, and it will be the same Church to which we also belong though in a particular way, for the sake of Holy History, it will have its location in Palestine. The salvation granted to Israel will in no way differ from that given to us. Its precious treasure is none other than the blood of the lamb, as stated in Rev. 12:11. Therefore, the vision does not speak of a special salvation which would detract or be different from that imparted to the rest of the believers, but it refers to the special role in Holy History, past and future, for which Israel is called.

Thus the Israelitic character of Holy Scripture is seen to extend also to the New Testament. If we interpret all the material which we have gathered from the Old Testament and New Testament in view of Israel's calling in Holy History, certain misunderstandings will be avoided, for instance that where Scripture deals with the national history of Israel, it is therefore particularistic, that is, manifesting and expressing merely national pride. We do not have to spiritualize the nationalistic elements in Old Testament law, history and prophecy. When we understand them from the point of view of Israel's calling in Holy History, they are rid of everything which is inappropriate to the Christian idea of salvation or incompatible with the spiritual nature of Scripture. When the descendents of Abraham for instance are promised Canaan it doesn't mean merely that they are to have a territory of their own like any other nation, but rather it means that since mankind is composed of nations, Holy History too needs a nation and a land in which a history can take place whose goal is the salvation of all nations.

This history—what is it other than the revelation of heaven on earth, the accomplishment of God's eternal counsel of salvation in time? Thus it is correct when we read in Heb. 11:16 that the desire of the patriarchs of Canaan was indeed a yearning for a better, a heavenly fatherland. What they desired was not a piece of ground which they could call their own, but rather God's return to man, which Noah in his blessing once had promised to Shem.

It is in this sense that we have to understand the Old Testament promises mentioned above. For instance when the risen Christ had directed the disciples' hopes to the moment when they should be baptized with the Holy Spirit they would ask Him, "Lord, will you at this time restore the kingdom to Israel?" (Acts 1:6.) Yet the nation they were thinking about was in accordance with Daniel 7, the people of the Holy God, the establishment of God's kingdom on earth, in which all the world would be ruled according to the decrees of God as revealed in Holy History. But this congregation, or kingdom of God, which at that time consisted of believers who were Israelites, later received into its membership Gentile Christians. Thus "the people" in Heb. 2:17 is no longer the Jewish people but the congregation of God consisting of Jews and Gentiles, the Christianity of the New Testament. The only nation which plays a providential role in Holy History is Israel, as will be seen in the future. There is no people of the New Covenant by which Israel is replaced.

In addition to the fact that Holy Scripture is miraculous and Israelitic in character, we must consider it as containing the truth of salvation and as the document which in a normative way presents it to the church from the beginning to the end of its history.

C. SCRIPTURE AS WITNESS OF THE SAVING TRUTH

We need to ask two questions at this point:

(a) How are the statements in Scripture which are based upon natural knowledge and experience related to the witness of the saving truth?

(b) What is the relationship between the unity of the saving truth witnessed to in Scripture, and the variety of its documentation?

1. Natural Knowledge and the Witness of Scripture

As Christians, we begin our study of Scripture with the certainty that it is the authoritative witness to saving truth. However, this certainty does not apply to those facts which by themselves are objects of natural knowledge. They do not carry with them the kind of certainty which is implied in our belief in Holy Scripture. For the assurance that the Scripture is the authoritative witness of the saving truth is rooted in our saving faith. At the same time, however, everything in Scripture is in some way related to the witness of the saving truth. Our problem must therefore be treated in these two respects. That which belongs to the created order of things is the object of our natural knowledge and experience, whereas the certainty of faith applies only to those things which are objects of faith. Holy Scripture is Holy Scripture for us only as the authoritative witness of the things which are apprehended by faith. Therefore, the certainty we bring to our study of Scripture does not apply equally to that which is to be apprehended by faith and that which is not.

In other words, Holy Scripture is not an infallible textbook of cosmology, anthropology, psychology, etc.; and the history recorded in the Bible is not to be understood as an errorless segment of a world history. This must be taken into consideration by the interpreter from the very first page of Scripture. Every interpretation of Genesis 1 which would make scientific investigation of creation unnecessary or dependent on the Biblical record is erroneous. The task of the natural scientist differs essentially from that of the interpreter of Scripture. The creation story must be understood from its goal, which is man. Its purpose is to show that the world was created for man and has reached its climax in man.

The thought expressed in the creation story according to our interpretation stands in close relationship to the saving truth to which the Scripture bears witness, namely to the purpose of God, as ultimately realized in Christ. It is from this point of view that the interpreter will correctly understand the elements of the creation story. He will thus avoid giving a significance of their own to those passages which have a subordinate meaning only, and which must be understood in the context of the whole.

It is a misunderstanding to reinterpret Genesis according to the most recent investigations of natural science, or to reinterpret natural science according to Genesis. Perhaps the worst thing we can do in this respect is to force Scripture into a strait jacket in order to bring it into conformity with natural science.

When the correct interpretation of the creation story is adopted which is in keeping with the general character of Scripture one will not attempt to learn from it how much time it took to create the world, for instance whether the creation lasted 6 times 24 hours; or contend that the stars were created all at the same time, and that terrestrial vegetation preceded the creation of the stars, etc., etc. The creation story is not concerned with this type of question.

How many things which touch upon natural science are found in the book of Job! But none of the things which belong to natural science, particularly such as are mentioned by Jehovah in His talks to Job, are guaranteed genuine just because they are found in Scripture. These talks are not lectures on natural science, but rather they are designed to put Job, that is *man*, in his proper place before God.

Likewise, when Joshua calls upon the sun to stand still,

this has nothing to do with the Copernican system. But the phrase is used in the same manner that we say the sun rises and sets.

It is also a serious error when expressions concerning the "life" of man, such as *ruach, nephesh, pneuma, psyche,* etc., are interpreted as if they were found in a text book of psychology. They serve to express, by means of a common language, what has to be said concerning man's relationship to God and this world. They are not a revelation of facts whose knowledge is ordinarily based upon a study of psychology and anthropology. Just as little as the expression *nephesh* as applied to God is meant to supply metaphysical wisdom, just so little does the Biblical usage of this word as applied to man communicate psychological insight. The term is a means to an end, not an end in itself.

For example, the question whether *pneuma* and *psyche* are two different substances is not relevant to the interpretation of Scripture no matter whether both terms are used of God or of man. Rather it is the vitality of both man and God which is expressed in different respects by either term. Neither expression is designed to communicate a special metaphysical knowledge concerning God, nor a special anthropological nor psychological knowledge concerning man.

Similarly it happens that a multitude of expressions are used to designate the spirits of God, for instance, "rulers . . . powers . . . forces," etc. To interpret these different words as referring to a hierarchy of spirits would be to make the same mistake. Any attempt to establish such a hierarchy is bound to fail, because the terms change and the meaning of different terms is often identical. These terms do not present to us a hierarchy of spirits, but rather they express the entire multitude of the spirits of God, that is to say, the diversity of their work in the universe. It is true that Scripture differentiates between "angel" and "archangel," not to distinguish the latter one from other spirits, but merely to indicate that archangels rule over a realm of greater importance than angels.

Furthermore, it is a mistake to use II Cor. 12:2 to prove that there is a multitude of heavens, or to ask whether there are three or seven heavens. The "third heaven" is part of a vision which is merely a reflection of reality. Likewise, when in Eph. 4:10 it is said that Christ was exalted "above all heavens," it is utterly erroneous to ask how many heavens there are. The Apostle uses this expression in order to exclude any attempt to confine Christ in some spacial limitation. The gravest error would be to use such statements as found in I John 1:5 or Tim. 6:16 for theosophical purposes. In that case the interpretation of the passage would become utterly estranged from its original intent.

In all these instances something in Scripture is considered certain and infallible which is beyond natural knowledge and experience yet has not been made the object of faith through the revelation of Holy History. Similarly, facts of human history, reported on the basis of natural knowledge, are considered infallible simply because they are reported in Scripture. All this is the evil consequence of a merely rational doctrine of Inspiration, and creates many conflicts with the actual world.

The list of nations in Gen. 10 must not be understood as teaching the number and names of nations at the beginning of history. Its purpose is rather to trace back the multitude of nations to Noah and his sons. It is an attempt to show how the original unity eventually resulted in the variety of nations. It is quite possible that the enumeration of the various branches of the nations, which is the result of the author's own investigations, may contain gaps. It is evident that certain tribes are discussed in greater detail than others. Some tribes are called by names familiar to the reader, though they were not the names used by the tribes themselves, etc. The reliability of the record depends, in this respect, upon the ability of the author to obtain the necessary information.

When we read for instance in Numbers 13:22 that Hebron was built seven years before Zoan, we must realize that the certainty of this historical information depended upon the ability of the author to gather such knowledge. The 40, or 2 times 40 years, which are used for the chronology of the age of the Judges, are not necessarily years. The "forty years" may designate the life span of a generation.

There is nothing wrong with examining the chronology of the Kingdom of Judah and the Kingdom of Israel in the light of the results of Egyptology and Assyriology, or with recognizing differences based upon errors. Likewise, to give a New Testament example, we read in Luke 2:1 that Caesar Augustus gave an order to conduct a world wide census. But it is not easy to harmonize this information in its actual form with historical research. In order to gain a correct view we will have to conduct an investigation in other places as well. The historical reality of this decree may demand another context than the one given by the evangelist. If this should prove to be the case it would not be necessary to do violence to the text of Scripture nor to ignore such a result of historical investigation. The evangelist's concern was to show that the fact that Jesus was born in Bethlehem happened in connection with the execution of an imperial decree.

When in Matt. 23:35 Zechariah is called a son of Barachias it is an obvious error. Likewise when Paul claims in I Cor. 10:8 that 23,000 died while Num. 25:9 says that 24,000 died, his memory played him a trick.

The phrase "when his father was dead," in Stephen's speech in Acts 7:4, is not compatible with Gen. 11:32. And when it says in Acts 7:16 that Jacob and our fathers "were carried back to Shechem and laid in the tomb," we have a confused combination of information concerning Jacob's and Joseph's burial (Gen. 49:30 and 24:32) on the one hand, and the purchase of the place by Jacob and Abraham (Gen. 33:19 and chapter 23) on the other.

These errors are due to the fact that the author of Acts did not record verbatim the speech of Stephen and the other speeches. We should not forget that the facts which are reported here should be gathered from the historical reports of Genesis rather than from the Acts of the Apostles.

What has been said concerning the non-literal recording of the speech of Stephen is equally true of the speeches of Jesus in the Gospels. If their text differs in the different Gospels, it is not only because those who heard them did not remember them in the same way, but also because they were used in different ways by the evangelists.

Thus in Matthew we find certain things in one speech of Jesus which Luke reports as having been spoken at a number of different occasions. It would be impossible to find a method that would mechanically remove these differences. The harmonizers became so perverted as to ask for instance, whether Jesus merely said "repent" (Matt. 4:17), or "repent, and believe in the Gospel" (Mark 1:15).

We also find numerous liberties and inaccuracies in the historical narratives, because the evangelists are using them for different purposes and from different viewpoints. We find that the New Testament authors, when quoting the Old Testament, will quote the Septuagint* even in those passages where its text is incorrect. This is particularly the case with the author of Hebrews, since those to whom he wrote knew only the Septuagint. Compare for instance the quotation from Psalm 40 in Heb. 10:5, or from Genesis 49 in Heb. 11: 21. In the course of a discussion on Psalm 95:7 the author of Hebrews says in 4:7 that these are the words of David. It is true that in the Septuagint this Psalm is ascribed to David, but in the original Hebrew the inscription is lacking.

Finally, the New Testament makes use of non-canonical Old Testament traditions, for example, the prophecy of Enoch, and the struggle between Satan and Michael over the body of Moses in Jude 9 and 14. The mention of the names Jannes and Jambres in II Tim. 3:8 rests on a tradition which has no historical verification whatever.

---

* i.e. the Greek version of the O.T.

The Bible is more than an errorless book. The errors that are found in it do not injure in any way that quality of the Bible which makes it different from all other books. If one intends to make the fact that the Bible is the Word of God dependent upon the belief that there is no error of any kind in the Bible, even in information derived from natural knowledge, scientific research, or memory, then one measures the work of the Holy Spirit, not according to the purpose for which it was performed, but according to the nature of God.

On the other hand, it is just as much of a mistake to hold that the Bible is not the Word of God but only contains the Word of God, and thus to differentiate between that which is religious truth and therefore is the Word of God, and that which is not religious truth and therefore is not the Word of God. This view implies a mechanical separation which assumes, as far as inspiration is concerned, a psychological impossibility. The Spirit of God did not work in a piecemeal manner, rather the whole man who wrote under the inspiration of the Spirit of God was thereby affected. Therefore, the question should rather be, what is the relationship of those matters which can be learned from natural knowledge and investigation, to Scripture as the authoritative witness to the saving truth?

What Scripture says about the creation of the world is not meant to satisfy idle curiosity, but is of religious significance. The latter consists in the fact that the creation of the world was a realization of the Word of God, and that it reaches its climax in the creation of man. The six days are followed by a seventh, which brings the divine work to its conclusion. This work of God is divided into two periods of three days, so the world of vegetation is the result of the contrast between light and darkness, heaven and earth, ocean and dry land, which were called into existence in the first three days. The creation of man is the completion of creation of those things which move, as the stars of the heavens which continue in their eternal courses, the birds and fish which move in the air and in the water, the animals of the dry land. Man, called to be free and Lord over his environment, completes creation.

This means there is no "eternal world," and the world as it is, is willed by God. Man is not merely part of nature, but the world has been created for his sake, and he is the goal of its creation. Creation is not an eternal process, but an act of God which has been concluded and which is followed by the history which goes on between God and the world. Thus only can there be a history whose goal is the coming of the Son of Man, and the establishment of a world united and governed by Him. Thus the creation story is not a substitute for scientific research but the expression of a truth to be apprehended by faith.

Nowhere in Scripture do we read anything about the creation of the spirits. They do not belong to the world that was created with man in mind. Yet all of Scripture presupposes that there is a world of spirits. But what is a mere supposition in other religions is here an established fact because it is connected with Holy History.

The miracle of divine participation which alone makes Holy History possible rests upon the fact that there is a world of spirits. Otherwise history would move altogether within the unchangeable context of nature and its eternal laws. Furthermore, since human sin did not have its beginning in man, because that would make salvation unthinkable, it must have originated in the world of spirits.

Scripture does not deal with man in such a way that we can derive from it the same infallible certainty in matters of anthropology and psychology that it gives us in connection with the saving truth. Nevertheless the manner in which Scripture speaks of man is in harmony with the saving truth, and therefore shares in its certainty. Scripture teaches for instance, that out of earthly material man was made into a bodily being which has life because the Spirit which is the breath of divine life dwells in it. Man is not a spiritual being which has been debased to a life on earth nor is he a purely material being which can develop a mental life. Living in an earthly material body, man can suffer death, but since he lives through the Spirit of God he can stay alive as long as this Spirit dwells effectually in him. He did not have to die, nor does he have to remain in death, once he has become sinful through his own guilt. Were he a finite spirit, as is held by the spiritualists, his sin would be Satanic. Were he merely a material being as the naturalists teach, his sin would not be guilt. Since the life into which he was created is the life of a physical being, the condition in which he finds himself on account of sin is passed on by natural heredity. But since he has personal life through the Spirit of God, he is capable of receiving a divine power which enables him to oppose his inherited nature and thus return to harmony with the will of God. And since he was created to be a physical living being, this restoration into communion with God cannot take place without a physical resurrection or a transfiguration by which his physical nature will be brought into accordance with that communion. Thus the manner in which Scripture speaks of man corresponds to the saving truth. This would not be the case if Scripture spoke of him in a different way.

What Holy Scripture teaches concerning the history of the origin of mankind rests upon a tradition which may not agree with actual facts. But whatever tradition or the narrator may have contributed to the story of the first sin, the fact that is essential for the saving truth is that it was the transgression of God's manifest will and that it was caused by a temptation that came to him from the outside. That the first generation was destroyed by a flood and that only one family was saved for a new age as a result of their faith is of essential significance to the saving truth. A constitutive element of the post-diluvian time of sacred history is the fact that a special redemption community now exists. At first this is a potential and eventually an actual nation which lives a life of its own as distinct from mankind outside of Holy History. This is the second stage of mankind's development toward salvation. This stage made its appearance only after the history of mankind, which was based upon the family, had ended in a perversion, which had to be stopped by means of a judgment of destruction. This judgment is the type of the second one which will settle the issue between the holy community and the hostile world. It is of the very nature of Holy History that it was by an act of obedience and faith that the new history of mankind was ushered in, and that the saving community which had its beginning in Abraham rested upon obedience and faith.

The history of Israel's origin rests upon tradition and it is questionable how much of it is exact reproduction of what actually occurred and how much of it has been altered in the course of transmission or by the historian. But that it is the history of a family is based upon the prerequisite of Holy History that the first beginning of this nation should be a personal act of obedient faith. So also the fact that there was a sequence of father, son and grandson prior to the moment when the sons of the grandson became the ancestors of the tribes of Israel, depended upon another necessity of Holy History, namely that the history of the origin of this nation must represent the law of Holy History. Whatever sons Abraham had before and after Isaac had to be neglected so that it might become clear that the special nature of this people depended exclusively upon the divine promise. And of Isaac's sons the first born had to be eliminated so that it might become obvious that the promise to Israel was not based upon any merit of her own (Rom. 9).

It is a matter of debate at which date the laws and ordinances of Exodus, Leviticus, Numbers received their present form and how their summary in Deuteronomy is related to them chronologically. But the institution of the Holy Tabernacle and the resulting position of the organized priesthood is so much the expression of the relationship of a nation which as a nation is the congregation of God, that it must be simultaneous with the beginning of this relationship. Anyway, the legal order of this nation, allegedly instituted by

Moses, cannot be the gradual product of its historical development but must have governed it from its beginning,
so that Israel was to differ from the other nations just as the
Savior differs from the mankind which He has redeemed.
Consequently it was necessary that the sacrifices, when they
were transformed from voluntary oblations into statutory
institutions, should be given a legal order that would be
valid for all times. For in them prayer was to be given an
expression that would be in agreement with Israel's relation
to God. Such an order had therefore to be the basic rule for
the offering of sacrifices; it could not be gradually developed
out of sacrificial practice.

In the history of David's youth there are probably two
parallel reports, and the question is how to harmonize them.
However, the manner of his appointment as king and the
fact that he did not receive the throne without first being
persecuted by Saul and suffering the things mentioned in
Psalm 22, is essential if his kingdom is to be a figure of the
manner in which the New Testament king was appointed.
He also had to suffer before he could achieve his royal glory.

The history which precedes the public ministry of Jesus
is often characterized as mythical or legendary, and it is
likely that it was molded by tradition and the narrator in
such a way that it would differ from a mere chronicle or a
transcript of the events. But its basic features are closely
related to the saving ministry of Jesus. Mary must have
received a message, as reported, if Jesus' entrance into the
world was to be conditioned on nothing else than the
obedience of faith of her who conceived Him and gave birth
to Him. She must have given birth to Him in Bethlehem—
not Nazareth, a place never mentioned in prophecy—since
Israel had to prove its faith by accepting the Nazarene as
its Savior without knowing that He was really born in the
prophesied place. Neither was Bethlehem to be the voluntary
domicile of Joseph and Mary at the birth of the Savior, nor
the city of Galilee after His birth. It had to be by the guidance of God that the promise was fulfilled and yet that the

fulfillment was hidden. Thus the narratives of both Matthew
and Luke are true, although in some details they are not
easily harmonized.

According to John the Apostle, the Baptist speaks the same
language as Jesus, and both speak the language of John.
Expressions, sentence structure, and thought in the speeches
of the Fourth Gospel are therefore freely reproduced by the
evangelist. But it is not equally open to question whether
John the Baptist called Jesus "Lamb of God." If he had seen
in Him only one who would baptize with water and fire,
there would have been such a breach between his witness
and that of Jesus, that it could not be said of the Baptist that
he had come to reveal Jesus.

Equally, what John reports of Jesus' words concerning the
destruction and restoration of the Temple, and to Nicodemus
concerning the serpent in the wilderness is not questionable.
For John uses these sayings to show that Jesus knew from
the outset what His end would be, and that it did not dawn
on Him gradually.

Matthew seems to indicate that Jesus sent out the Twelve
immediately after their calling, while Luke separates the
two events. But one thing is certain: that He called them for
Himself, and just these, and that He called them all at once.
This indicates both that He was concerned in advance for
the continuation of His work and the organization of His
followers as a congregation and also that He deliberately
added to their number the one who was later to betray Him.

Granted that the narratives of the appearances of the risen
Christ cannot easily be harmonized. One thing is sure, however. He appeared to His own in such a manner that they
knew that He lived in the same body which had been crucified, yet in a bodily life in which the body served merely as
a means for His revelation and spontaneous activity and
was no longer a barrier. Thereby the disciples obtained the
assurance that Christ though living an exalted and super-
natural life with God, had also communion with them.

It is doubtful whether the various narratives of Christ's

appearance to Saul on the Damascus road can be harmonized. Nevertheless, one thing is sure: he saw Jesus with his own eyes. Upon this fact rests the uniqueness of his conversion which agrees with the uniqueness of his apostolic calling.

While subjects of natural knowledge described in Scripture do not possess the absolute certainty which applies to the matters of faith set forth therein, nevertheless they do share that certainty to the extent to which these matters are related to the message of redemption. Thus the interpreter will examine those matters with an open mind and in an unprejudiced way and he will subject them to the same tests as all other subjects of natural knowledge. Yet at the same time he will keep in mind the connection which these matters may have with that truth of which he is certain by faith, in order to have them verified or to see them in the right light.

2. The Diversity of the Biblical Proclamation and the Unity of Scripture

The saving truth which the Scripture proclaims authoritatively to the Church does not consist in a series of doctrinal propositions, but rather in the fact that Jesus has mediated a connection between God and mankind. In the assurance of this comprehensive truth the interpreter of Scripture approaches his task. And since he firmly believes that the Church has the documentary proof of this truth in Scripture, he starts his work with the expectation that everything in Scripture will be an aspect of this truth. This, correctly understood, is what is meant by the rule that Scripture must be interpreted according to the analogy of faith.

This rule is not really applied however when similar passages are merely compared or differences harmonized. Rather every detail must be understood in the light of the comprehensive truth. If one should discover passages which did not agree with the saving truth, the canonicity of the portion of Scripture where such ideas were found would have to be called into question. Thus Luther judged books such as the Epistle of James according to their concern for Christ. We can formulate this rule as follows: every single passage of the Bible has to be interpreted in the light of the fact that Christ is the subject matter of the whole Scripture.

At first sight it looks as though the Old Testament taught a way of salvation totally different than that of the New Testament. In Lev. 18:5 for instance we find Israel admonished to keep God's statutes and ordinances because in doing them man will have life. Similarly, in Deut. 27:26 those who do not keep the words of the law are accursed. Such passages seem to indicate a path to salvation entirely different from the one we find in the New Testament, especially when we compare them with Romans 3:28, that "a man is justified by faith," etc.

However, we must understand these Old Testament passages in the light of the fact that the giving of the Law is preceded by the saying, "I am the Lord thy God who brought you out of the land of Egypt." The presupposition which makes the law valid for the Israelite is that his faith is in the God who, as he knows, saved Israel from Egypt and thus is the only true God.

Since this salvation out of Egypt was the fulfillment of the promise given to Abraham, it had to be recognized as such in gratitude. This means that faith in God is belief in His plan for salvation, for whose realization Israel was called. The promise of life applies to a keeping of the law in which that faith is actualized.

In Galatians 3:12 and Romans 10:5 Paul uses these passages in an entirely different sense because he is confronted with people who separate the law from its connection with Holy History and interprets them as divine demands apart from the promise which required faith. In other words, they considered the fulfillment of these demands an activity apart from faith rather than faith in action. When the law is used in a manner which is in contradiction to Holy History, then it is true that it kills and condemns (II Cor. 3:6).

How utterly different is the way in which the author of Psalm 19 understands the law! When he describes the law of the Lord as "reviving the soul and rejoicing the heart," he means by "law" that witness of God's holy will which includes the divine promises and the election of Israel, that is, the whole basis of Holy History. Thus the witness of salvation sheds its joyful light even upon the commandments of the law.

When the author of Psalm 9 says in v. 17, "The wicked shall depart to Sheol, and all the nations that forget God," this passage taken in isolation would make it appear that Israel expected to be the only nation to be saved, while all the rest of mankind would perish. But the psalmist must be understood in the light of the promise given to Abraham: "in you all the families of the earth will be blest." What both statements have in common is the contrast between Israel on the one hand and the Gentile nations whose historical development is determined by their sinfulness, on the other. But the end of history, the stage of which will be Israel according to God's election, will bring to non-Israelitic mankind both blessing and judgment. The Gentile world will be judged on account of its enmity against the people of the true God, but all those will be blessed who were willing to be led to the knowledge of God (cf. Ps. 22:27). The promise given to Abraham stated that no generation on earth will receive a blessing except through him and his descendents. The psalmist knows that enmity against Israel can have no other end than the destruction of her enemies. Thus Isaiah 41:16 comforts his nation by contrasting it with the other nations by which it is being persecuted. While he foretells their destruction to the nations of the world he calls to Israel: "And you shall rejoice in the Lord, in the Holy One of Israel you shall glory." This passage has to be understood in the light of the fact that it belongs to the part of chapters 40-66 where the contrast between Israel and the Gentile world is discussed. In this connection the comforting news of better times was designed for Israel as the congregation of God. Entirely different however is the message in that part of this prophetic book which deals with the contrast between the believers and non-believers. For example Isaiah says in 65:9, "I will bring forth descendents from Jacob, and from Judah inheritors of my mountains," and in 66:24 which deals with "transgressors," he says, "Their worm shall not die, their fire shall not be quenched." Salvation comes to Israel not because they are Israel, nor judgment to non-Israelites because they are non-Israelites, but judgment separates those who fear God from those who have forgotten Him. But it is through Israel that salvation comes. This fact points to the condition under which salvation is granted, namely faith. It is a misunderstanding to see in the "ungodly" of the Psalms only non-Israelites.

Ecclesiastes has been called the strangest book in the Bible. Its message is summed up in the sentence "all is vanity" (Eccl. 1:2). The life of man is described as nothingness and change. The only thing certain is that nothing is certain and nothing endures. But what is the final conclusion of the man who has written this? He does not recommend enjoyment of life as much as possible, nor melancholic resignation, nor both. On the contrary, his answer is that all the deeds of men will be judged by God whether they are good or evil. Therefore, he admonishes in 12:13, "Fear God, and keep his commandments."

This conclusion is reached by a man who for argument's sake ignores Holy History. Only in Israel, whose mentality is completely controlled by God's revelation in Holy History, is such a result of the analysis of human life possible.

It is true that the "wisdom" of the book of Proverbs is indeed common sense but it is not the vulgar cleverness of egoism, because human life throughout is lived under the fear of Jehovah. Similarly in the Song of Songs the relationship of man and wife, which by the will of the creator is sexual love, is glorified with full devotion to natural beauty, but it never descends from the enjoyment of that which God has created to the vulgarity of mere sensuality. Thus Solomon's joy in his wife agrees with the creation of woman on the one hand and prefigures like Adam's joy in his wife the relationship of Christ to His Church on the other. There is no need for interpreting all the details of this poem allegorically. We can see that this song of love originated in the life of a nation which did not share the degeneration of a mankind left to its own devices. In order to retain their place in the canon, neither the Song of Solomon nor Psalm 45 have to be allegorized. Such portions of the canon have to be looked at in comparison with similar products of the non-Israelitic world. They show how human life in its trifles and in its beauty, in the moods which it calls forth and the activities which it demands, is bound by a moral law which in one way or another will be transgressed by a nation whose life has not been molded through Holy History.

The New Testament does not contain such features because in it the community of salvation is no longer a nation in its dealings with other nations, rather it is the congregation of Jesus which has been molded by the saving event itself. Thus the saving truth has here a different kind of diversity. The truth manifests itself in a number of ways. Scholars are wont to speak of doctrinal ideas, but it would be erroneous to regard the various books of the New Testament merely as literary products in which each author gives his own personal version of the saving truth. Just as in the historical writings every detail has to be understood from the contribution it makes to the execution of God's redemptive plan, so also in the Epistles we must study the reason and purpose of each letter and ascertain how its content was determined thereby. It is not true to say that Peter considers hope, Paul faith, and John love the center of their respective views of salvation. Likewise within the New Testament things do not move from a spiritualized Jewish legalism to Paul's universalism of salvation which is by faith in Jesus, and finally to a synthesis from which the extremist views have been eliminated.

In Matthew 5:19 the righteousness demanded by Christ is characterized as doing the commandments of the law in contrast with abrogating them. The language used here creates the impression that in this passage Christianity is but a spiritualized legalism. However, we ought to keep in mind that in this passage the Lord speaks to people who believe in Him. They are enjoined to obey not only the letter of the commandments, but also the purpose of the divine lawgiver as revealed by Jesus. Apart from this kind of obedience, confessing Christ will not assure participation in God's kingdom.

Thus James speaks later of keeping "the whole law." But this law is both a "law of liberty" for Christians, since it has become one with the will of him who is to obey it, so that he will do freely what it demands, and it is in its content "the law of love" (Rom. 13:10). This love through which faith is active (Gal. 5:6) has the same origin according to Paul and to James, for the latter says, "He brought us forth with the word of truth" (James 1:18). Through His word of truth God has granted us a new life of His own, in which we enjoy freedom (cf. Rom. 5:5). While James does not indicate the content of this word of truth, he speaks to people who have "the faith of our Lord Jesus Christ, the Lord of Glory" (James 2:1), and admonishes them in 5:7 to "be patient until the coming of the Lord." He defines the "word of truth" as the "implanted word, which is able to save your souls" (1:21), and he continues in v. 22, "Be doers of the word, and not hearers only." He combines hearing and doing because it is the task of that "Word" to exhort people to live according to their Christian calling. Thus, the word which proclaims the Lord Jesus Christ implies also the works of faith, it does not merely provide an intellectual knowledge. Therefore James says in 2:14, "What does it profit, if a man says he has faith but not works? Can his faith save him?"

Though Paul states in Romans 2:6, "He will render to every man according to his works," he will also state with emphasis in Romans 3:28, that "man is justified by faith apart from works of law." Here he had to explain how a man may come into such a relationship to God that his sins are forgiven and he is justified in the eyes of God. Paul denies that there is anything besides faith in Jesus that is required, or another way that can secure the goal. In the former passage (2:6) he emphasizes that a person will not be acquitted in the judgment of God because he "knows" what is right, but because he "does" what is right.

Therefore when James says in 2:24, "a man is justified by works and not by faith alone," he is not discussing what is necessary for a sinful man to be judged favorably by God, but what is necessary for his conduct to correspond to the will of God. He uses the verb "to be made righteous" in the sense he uses the adjective "righteous," and the latter condition cannot be reached by a faith which lacks works. Though this would indeed be another faith than that of Abraham of whose faith it is said: "He reckoned it to him as righteousness," his certainty was not a faith without works either. If one does not approach the interpretation of Scripture with the presupposition that it testifies to the unified saving truth, the letter of James will be read from a different viewpoint than James expected the addressees to read it.

It has been claimed of the letter to the Hebrews that it used another concept of faith than Paul does in Romans or Galatians, because justifying faith is not mentioned here. However, in Romans and Galatians the way is described in which man through the forgiveness of sins would obtain a favorable judgment from God. That way is nothing else than faith in Jesus who has atoned for the sin of the world. However, Hebrews is directed to people who doubted whether Jesus was the fulfillment of Old Testament promises, because they were being threatened on account of their faith in Him who was not with them in the world. Their faith had to be strengthened in this respect so that they would persevere in the hope that Christ would bring to completion the salvation already granted to them. Thus they were shown that the very death of Jesus, which gave them so much offense, had in fact enabled Him to return to God and thus carried with it the fulfillment of the promised salvation. There was as little reason to speak of justifying faith in this context as there would have been to discuss the return of Christ in the Epistle to the Romans or Galatians. For these letters fought the Jewish claims of the primacy of Israel and the Jewish demand that everyone ought to submit himself to the Law.

Some have found in the synoptic Gospels a different teaching of Jesus than in the Gospel of John. The latter allegedly emphasizes the pre-existence of Jesus which is not found in the other Gospels. But how could one be conceived by the Holy Spirit and thus start his existence from that act unless he had his origin in a self-propagating mankind? If it was to be demonstrated that in the person and history of Jesus the Old Testament history and Scripture were fulfilled even where it seemingly contradicted them, this could be done only by referring to the history of the man Jesus.

Luke, who wanted to show the beginning of the New Testament proclamation of salvation, had to describe what we read in Hebrew 2:3 about the "salvation which began to be spoken by the Lord" (a.v.).

The Gospel according to St. John, on the other hand, tries to show what it means to believe in Jesus, namely to confess him as the Son of God upon the word of the witness and in accordance with that witness which he had borne of himself. Therefore, John prefers to speak of Jesus as "the Son of God," and the others speak of Him as "the Son of Man."

Is it reasonable to assume that the author of the Gospel of John rejected the miraculous conception of Jesus because He does not mention it? He is the one who says, "the word became flesh." John presupposes a knowledge of the miraculous conception in his readers, just as Matthew and Luke presuppose that their readers know that Jesus' existence did not begin with His conception. When we assume that Scripture bears a unified witness to the saving truth it is unthinkable that everything that is not expressly stated in a New

Testament book was not known or was rejected by its author.

It has been said that none of the genuine letters of Paul teaches the pre-existence of Jesus, and that therefore Colossians cannot be genuine and that Hebrews could not possibly have been written by Paul. But not only do we read of Jesus in I Corinthians 8:6: "through whom are all things," and of the Father: "from whom are all things"; but we read also in Galatians 4:4, "God sent forth (i.e., from himself) his Son" and "the Spirit of his Son" (4:6). This sheds further light on the phrase in Romans 8:3, "God, sending his own Son." Jesus is here called the Son of God in contrast to those who are the offspring of a self-propagating mankind.

Likewise in Hebrews 3:2 we read, "He was faithful to him who appointed him," while in 1:2, "Through whom also he created the world." Furthermore what is said in Psalm 102:25 of Jehovah, namely, that He was "before all," is applied in Hebrews 1:10 to the Son. Where the faithfulness which He has shown to God in the fulfillment of His calling is discussed, He is spoken of as the man whom God has called into this life for this purpose; however, when the greatness of Him through whom God has spoken to us is mentioned, it is by expressions such as in Hebrews 1:3, "He reflects the glory of God and bears the very stamp of his nature." The idea that Christ is the mirror or the image of the Father is not introduced here as a new doctrine, but it is rather presupposed as commonly believed.

Similar statements are also found in Colossians. This letter was written against people who held that faith in Jesus and baptism were not sufficient to escape the power which evil spirits had over the nations. It is therefore emphatically stated that everything, including the world of spirits, was created through Him. So also in Philippians 2:6 when Christ's existence before the Incarnation is characterized as being "in the form of God," this implies that He shared in the glorious power of Him whom after His incarnation He calls Father.

In Romans and Galatians no mention is made of Jesus'

return. Does the apostle not know of it, or does he object to the idea? In I Corinthians 15 belief in the return of Christ is presupposed just as much as in I Thessalonians. When Paul deals with this hope in Thessalonians he does so both in order to comfort people bewailing the members of the congregation who had died before this event, and to correct the erroneous belief that the Parousia had already taken place.

In I Corinthians 15 the return of Christ is mentioned in connection with Paul's refutation of those who thought they could dispense with the doctrine of the resurrection of the dead. Again when we read in I Peter of the "revelation of Christ," and again in II Peter 3:10 of the "day of the Lord" which will bring the dissolution of this world and the bringing forth of a new world, the latter statement is made against those who believe that everything will remain as is, and the revelation of Jesus Christ is promised as the end of the "sufferings" of the Christians.

Finally, Hebrews 12:27 speaks of a "removal of what is shaken," in order to remind us how much is at stake in listening to him who speaks to us. The writer does not explain how this "removal" is connected with the fact that "Christ will appear . . . to save those who are eagerly waiting for him," which according to 9:28 is the culmination of the process which started with His death and departure. Both are not taught here specifically but are only hinted at as common beliefs.

In Galatians the death of Jesus is mentioned constantly, His Resurrection only in 1:1, and His Ascension not at all, though both are presuppositions of the "revelation of Jesus Christ" which is mentioned in 1:12. Paul wants to stress in this letter the fact that Christ did not die in vain (Gal. 2:21). I Corinthians 15 on the other hand does not only discuss Jesus' Resurrection and return, but also His kingly rule which begins therewith, and which will last until all the powers that are hostile to God even death will be destroyed, "at which moment he delivers the kingdom to God the Father" (I Cor. 15:24). This statement has only one parallel, namely

Revelation 20:6 where reference is made to the millennium. The Apostle mentioned this kingdom in I Corinthians 15 not because he wanted to teach a startling doctrine but in order to underscore the importance which the belief that the present state of death will not remain forever, has in the context of Holy History. Finally, when II Peter 3:10 speaks of a judgment of fire which will destroy this present world, this doctrine of a world conflagration is not peculiar to this letter, but rather it rests upon teachings with which readers of the Old Testament were familiar.

By means of a number of examples we have tried to show how the unity of the saving message of the Scripture is to be interpreted, if the diversity of its witness is to receive its proper due. This correlation of diversity and unity of Scripture is closely related to the miracle of its origin for which it offers corroborative evidence. On the other hand those things in Scripture which can be apprehended by reason or experience share the certainty of faith to the degree in which they are related to the saving truth.

To conclude. The miraculous nature of Scripture, its Israelitic character, and its unity as the document of salvation, form the theological presuppositions with which the interpreter approaches Scripture. With these in mind, the interpreter deals with the Bible as an integral whole in the sense in which it is recognized by the Church as the authoritative proclamation of the saving truth. It is as a member of the Church that the interpreter does his work. This does not mean however, as a member of this or that Christian denomination, but rather as belonging to that one Church of the Lord whose faith he shares because it has been confirmed to him by his own experience.

Apart from these presuppositions, the interpretation of Scripture is of little avail. It may be grammatically and historically correct, but neither the language nor the content of Scripture are then understood with reference to the goal for which it is given. For through its exegesis a particular church is to be enabled to use Scripture as the rule of its life of faith, and as the Word of God present in its midst. Only then is a grammatico-historical interpretation of Scripture certain to understand this document as it is meant to be understood.

So far we have looked at Scripture in its unity, as the present possession of the Church, and at the interpreter who approaches it as a member of the Church. The question arises, what is his equipment for this task? Furthermore, Scripture comes to him from the past, as something inherited by the Church. The question arises now, what does the fact that it is a document of the past require of him for its adequate understanding?

Thus far we have discussed Scripture with reference to the characteristics which it shares with all the other works of the Spirit operating in the Church, namely that they all participate in the Word of God. Its distinction lies in the fact that Scripture is not a momentary Word of God issuing now and then from a particular church but rather the Word of God which is given once for all and is the rule for the Church at all times and in all places.

Now we want to look at those features of Scripture which it has in common with other literary products of antiquity, always keeping in mind however that the history from which it comes in Holy History. Thus it is not simply a matter of applying general hermeneutical principles to a particular case.

Having regarded Scripture so far as a unit, we must now study it as a sum of all its parts, with the following three questions in mind:

1. What was the original condition of Holy Scripture?

   a) As far as the canonicity of its various books is concerned?

   b) As far as the text is concerned?

2. What is the relationship between the original language in which each of the books was written, on the one hand,

and the various translations by means of which Scripture has been made useful for the particular churches?

3. How did all the individual books of the Bible originate? When, by whom, and for whom, and under what circumstances were they written?

In all these respects, investigations into the history of Holy Scripture and knowledge of the pertinent facts are prerequisites of exegesis. What influence do they have upon interpretation?

CHAPTER TWO

The Bible in History

A. THE ORIGINAL CONDITION OF SCRIPTURE

1. The Limits of the Canon

There is no ecumenically determined canon of Holy Scripture to guide the interpreter nor has the Lutheran Church defined its limits in its confessions. If the exegete finds portions of the canon of the ancient Church which can not be integrated into the framework of a unified truth of salvation, he must not force them into this unity, or accommodate the saving truth to them; rather he is entitled to doubt whether they truly belong to the Holy Scripture of Christendom. On the other hand, sections may have been incorporated into Scripture by some particular church, whose presence in the canon cannot be justified on purely historical grounds. The interpreter must pay special attention to them because he has to investigate whether their intrinsic value makes them fit to be part of the canon.

As far as the Old Testament canon is concerned, it is of little importance for us to ask how it was formed, since very little is known about it. For us as Christians the important question is: what was the Holy Scripture used by Jesus and the Apostles? For on that basis the Old Testament has become Holy Scripture for us. It is an established historical fact that at the beginning of the Christian Church

Holy Scripture consisted of no other writings than those which we find in our Old Testament canon. However, in the Septuagint, to which the writers of the New Testament frequently refer, there are some writings and portions of writings which are not found in the Hebrew Old Testament. However, it cannot be proved that these elements were ever held in equal esteem with canonical Scripture.

For instance when Hebrews 11 refers to events that are reported in the books of Maccabees, these references are to historical occurrences, and the books of Maccabees are used merely as historical documents. The Epistle of James may show certain similarities to the Wisdom of Solomon or Ecclesiastes, but these references do not claim Scriptural authority. It is true that later on in history the difference between canonical and non-canonical writings was obliterated, and the Roman Catholic church declares that the apocryphal writings are of equal authority with the canonical writings. Consequently the interpreter has to deal with the apocryphal writings too, constantly keeping this difference in mind however, and investigating whether the denial of the difference is in any way justified.

Matters are entirely different when it comes to the New Testament writings, because the development of the canon is known to us. In the earliest times of the Church, only the Gospels, Acts, those Epistles of Paul which bear his name, I Peter, and I John were considered canonical. II Peter, II and III John, Epistle of James, Jude, and Revelation were accepted only by sections of the Church. The Book of Revelation, even when it was considered as written by John, and II Peter, were not generally accepted until a relatively late period. In the west Hebrews was not officially accepted until the fourth century. The so-called Epistle of Barnabas and the Shepherd of Hermas were used in some parts of the Church as canonical. However, these last two were never generally received into the canon and therefore need not concern us.

But the interpreter should keep in mind the difference between those writings which were part of Holy Scripture from the beginning and those which were accepted gradually. He must investigate whether the latter are indeed to be considered of equal value with the former, and he must examine the difference between the early-canonical and later-canonical writings to see if it is of such a nature as to affect the authority which the latter have for the Church as portions of Holy Scripture.

There are also portions of the canonical books which are demonstrably not part of the original writings, for example, the first verses of John 8. The manuscript evidence clearly indicates that the narrative of the Adulterous Woman does not belong to the original Gospel of John. The same is true with respect to the verses of the Gospel of Mark which are usually found after the words, "they were afraid" (Mark 16:8). It is also questionable whether Romans 16:15-17 is in the right place and even whether it is a part of the original letter. It is likely that John 5:4 is an interpolation, and it is certain of I John 5:7.° On the other hand, though John 21 is not part of the original work of John and never claimed his authorship, but rather is introduced as an addition, the Gospel never circulated without it.

In all such cases there are facts which the interpreter must know in order to take them into account when he deals with them in his exegesis, lest he accept as a portion of Holy Scripture that which is not warranted by historical fact. In the light of exegesis he must also be ready to admit that certain portions of Scripture have been misplaced and sometimes added to a canonical writing.

It is quite possible, for instance, that Zechariah 9-11 or 12-14 was written by another author than chapters 1-8, or that the speeches of Elihu in Job were later additions. But that would not affect their place in the canon.

However, if the prophecies in Isaiah 40-66 were written after Cyrus, or the revelations of Daniel after Antiochus

---

° A comparison of the text of the King James' Version with the Revised Standard Version will show that in the latter the passages mentioned here have been either relegated to footnotes or omitted.

Epiphanes, then they would not be prophecies in the sense in which they were received into the canon. Or if II Peter is not written by Peter, then chapter 2 is not a prophecy but a reproduction of the Epistle of Jude, and the reference to the author's own experience in 1:12f. and to the Epistles of Paul is less than worthless because it is mere fiction.

On the other hand, if Solomon's authorship of Ecclesiastes were merely a literary device, that fact would not make its content less fitting for the canon. In this case the authorship is of little significance.

2. The Text of Scripture

Turning to the text of the Bible, we remind ourselves that that of the Old Testament goes back to the time when its various writings had been collected into one document. It is quite possible that the text as it was accepted at that time had already deteriorated or was intentionally altered. But ever since these writings had been collected into the Old Testament canon, the text was preserved with such care that even between the Eastern text of the Petersburg manuscript of the latter Prophets, and the western text, there are very few variants. Obviously the scribes preferred to leave manifest mistakes of the parent manuscripts unaltered. The variants in *Kethib* and *Keri* are not true variants.*

To correct the Hebrew text according to the Septuagint is rarely advisable. Its deviations from the Massoretic text were sometimes intentional alterations and sometimes due to a misunderstanding. It is also possible that they sometimes had a corrupt text, or misread the unpointed text of that day. It is worth investigating however, whether in some instances the correct text was preserved by the Septuagint. For example in Genesis 47:31 the Septuagint could read correctly "the staff," which would mean that in Hebrews 11:21 "over the

---

* Kethib means "the way it was actually written."
Keri means "the way the scribe thinks it should be read," i.e. Keri are marginal corrections by the scribe.

head of his staff" is the correct text of the Old Testament. Similarly in Psalm 48:14 we should read "for ever," instead of "unto death."

Quite apart from the Septuagint text, changes may be necessary. For example, in II Samuel 8:13 a comparison with Psalm 60:2 and I Chronicle 18:12 shows that the text has been corrupted in many places.

In Zechariah 14:17 the Hebrew text reads, "If they go not up and come not," which makes no sense. Perhaps it should be read, "And if they go not up, the rain does not come." (RSV: "If they . . . do not go up . . . there will be no rain . . . .")

It is also possible in some instances that the verse division is erroneous. For example, in Psalm 95:10 "for forty years" belongs in the preceding verse, as it is quoted in Hebrews 3:9, which in turn was quoted from the Septuagint. So also in Psalm 110:3 "in the beauties of holiness" (A.V.) probably belongs to the first half of the verse.

It would be going too far to demand that the text should be read as though it were unpointed.* But at the same time it should be read with the thought in mind that the pointing might be erroneous. To change the text overzealously simply because it doesn't seem to fit is dangerous. And yet the interpreter must constantly be aware of the possibility that the text might be corrupt.

As far as the New Testament is concerned, it is fortunate we have such a wealth of material to secure the correct text; but unfortunately we have such a large number of variants. The writings of the New Testament were used in a very small circle. Since they were addressed to individual congregations and individual people, they were copied more or less incidentally. There was no unified supervision as was the case with the Old Testament. That made it possible for the text to become corrupt in many ways before the forma-

---

* Since the Hebrew language has no vowels, it became necessary to indicate the pronunciation by a system of "points" (i.e. dots and dashes) under the consonants.

tion of the New Testament canon had begun, and especially before the Church had agreed on the whole content of this canon.

Here it is indeed necessary for the interpreter to read the critical text in the manner in which it appeared in the original manuscripts, that is, without division into words, and without punctuation, accents and breathings. There are many cases where this method leads to the correct interpretation. . . .

It is a task for the textual critic to present the results of the collation of manuscripts, versions, and patristic quotations. Were it possible to establish on this basis the oldest text, the task of the textual critic and that of the interpreter would be far more clearly separated. However, this task, as proposed by Lachmann, can never be solved completely. Therefore, the textual critic has to become more or less of an interpreter, and the interpreter cannot dispense completely with the work of textual criticism. He must keep in mind the respective age of the manuscripts, and their families, as well as the value of the versions and their mutual relationship in order to judge which text has the best attestation. In this connection he has to ascertain which variant has probably developed from some other, and which variants are the results of intentional changes. In the oldest uncials, for example, that which was considered superfluous was often omitted. Sometimes one section of the Church has accused another of intentional textual changes. But the manner in which Marcion manipulated the text is conceivable only in the case of a heretic.

One cannot lightheartedly reject the text which has been established upon these critical considerations even though it may appear at first sight less suitable or unsuitable. For example, in Philippians 2:1 the interpreters usually reject the reading, "if anyone" in favor of "if any"; yet such eminent critics as Lachmann, Tischendorf, and Tregelles, accept it, and closer examination will prove it acceptable.

On the other hand, a certain reading may have been

generally accepted because it seemed to fit into the context, without being the original one. For example, it is customary to read I Timothy 5:16, "If a believing man or a believing woman has (the care of) widows." But here the newer textual criticism has decided unanimously for the seemingly much less suitable "If a believing woman has (the care of) widows."

In Luke 6:1 the reading "on the second Sabbath after the first" is commonly accepted in spite of its difficulty. Yet according to Tregelles it should be read, "on the Sabbath." Indeed, all efforts to make sense out of this "second after the first" is in vain. Obviously "first" was added at one time because another Sabbath is mentioned in v. 6, and then because 4:31 refers to another event on the Sabbath, "second" was added, which later became combined with "first."

It is also possible that in some instances the original text has been lost, and has to be rediscovered amongst the various readings. This is the case, for instance, in Hebrews 11:37, where the expression "they were tempted" does not seem to fit. However, there is hardly any reason for adopting conjectural readings which have no basis in the variants. Just as the interpreter's canon is not fixed by denominational confession, so is there no edition of the Greek or Hebrew text of the Bible that enjoys absolute authority. In both respects the interpreter must attempt to go back to the original conditions on account of the historical character of the Holy Scripture. For this reason it is also necessary to deal appropriately with the languages of Holy Scripture.

B. THE LANGUAGES OF HOLY SCRIPTURE

The interpreter is not bound by any particular translation which would once and for all determine the true understanding of the original text, as is the case in the Greek church with the Septuagint and in the Roman church with the Vulgate. He has to translate the original text according to the rules of the language in which it was written.

As far as the Old Testament is concerned he must keep in mind three points.

  a) The Hebrew language is a branch of the Semitic language.
  b) During the making of the Old Testament its language had an historical development.
  c) It was influenced by foreign languages.

a) The fact that the language of the Old Testament is a branch of the Semitic languages is of particular importance for lexicography. Take for instance the Hebrew word for "God": *Elohim*. On the basis of the vocabulary of the Old Testament and perhaps its later development in Rabbinical Hebrew one will be inclined to derive its meaning from a root found in the Old Testament Hebrew, for instance *allah*, meaning "strong." Then we understand *elohim* in the sense of *el*, "the strong one." However, *elohim* is used in passages like Genesis 31:42, 53 interchangeably with a word which means "object of fear," which is translated in II Thessalonians 2:4 with the Greek word which denotes "an object of awe." This justifies us in assuming for *elohim* a corresponding meaning. This we gain from an Arabic root, *aliha*, which has the basic meaning "to shudder, to be afraid."

The fact that Hebrew is a branch of the Semitic languages is misapplied if one goes back to roots or meanings which are found only in non-Hebrew dialects of the Semitic languages, when a correct meaning can be obtained within the framework of the known Hebrew.

b) During the period in which the Old Testament came into being, its language has undergone an historical development. This is more noticeable in the formation of its words than in its syntax. The assumption that it developed from original simplicity to increasing complexity, or from an original awkwardness to a greater facility, seems unwarranted. It is quite possible that different styles existed simultaneously and that the same author used more than one style. Thus the Blessing of Moses in Deuteronomy 33 sounds aggressive and rough compared with the Song of Moses we find in chapter 32. But the latter one was intended to be understood by everyone, whereas the former is intentionally enigmatic. A similar difference can be seen between the last saying of Bileam and the preceding ones, because the last one is an oracle. Psalm 8 is considered as written by David because of its simplicity, yet Psalm 18 is attributed to David because of its difficult language.

The fact that Psalms 22 and 40 are written in a broad style does not make them psalms of Jeremiah. Because Psalm 68 is rough in style and Psalm 62 is a smooth prayer it does not follow that centuries have passed between this writing. Among the prophecies in Jeremiah 47-49 are some that because of their bold and terse manner of expression make an archaic impression. This may indicate that they are older prophecies re-worked by Jeremiah.

That Zechariah 12:14 differs linguistically so much from chapters 9-10 is due to the fact that the latter chapters repeat older predictions in their original language. The interpreter should not jump to conclusions concerning the time in which a passage has been written, merely on the basis of the style in which it was written. Things are different in the book of Isaiah. If the section covered by chapters 40-66 differs from the first twelve chapters not only in style but also in its historical character—some even claim to find Aramaic influences in it—its interpretation must adopt a historical perspective of its own.

On the other hand, the age of an idiomatic expression may determine the interpretation. Thus, for example Genesis 6:3 can be interpreted variously according to whether the terminology used there is considered as agreeing with the date of this particular section of the Pentateuch.

c) The influence which foreign languages, whether Semitic or non-Semitic, had upon the Hebrew must be taken into account because it serves to determine the date of the parts of the Old Testament. In this respect we have to make a threefold distinction:

1. Whether there are remainders of the original common Semitic family prior to the formation of its various branches.
2. Whether elements of foreign languages have been used intentionally for artistic purposes by an author.
3. Whether as a result of contacts with non-Israelitic nations, the vernacular language has adopted certain lexicographical and syntactical idioms from their languages.

Examples of the first kind are found especially in the oldest parts of the Pentateuch, examples of the second kind in Job and the Song of Songs. The third development is illustrated by literary works like Jeremiah, Daniel, Ezekiel, and Ecclesiastes. One has only to look at Ecclesiastes to realize how important it is to investigate whether its Aramaisms are of the second or third kind. Futhermore, is the striking similarity with Rabbinic Hebrew which characterizes the language of much of this book to be attributed to its late date or to the nature of the subject with which it deals? If its language is to be explained by a late date, the book would have contacts with the beginning of Rabbinic learning. If by the nature of the subject, the book could be a product of the time of Solomon, like the Song of Songs. Depending on the answer to this question, the details of this book will take an entirely different appearance. This will have a profound influence upon its interpretation.

The study of Biblical Greek requires a somewhat different approach, because unlike the Hebrew Old Testament, the making of the New Testament did not extend over a period of a thousand years. Rather for an understanding of the New Testament writings, and of the Septuagint including writings which are not part of the Old Testament canon and are found only in the Septuagint, we must study the history of the Greek language before it became the language of the New Testament. We see how, after the death of Alexander the Great, a new literary language, the so-called *koine,* developed from the Attic dialect, and how, simultaneously in many sections where the Greek language spread, a common popular language came into being which contained elements of the various Greek dialects, yet developed new provincial and national differentiations. The literary language was used by Philo, Josephus, and on the whole by the author of the Book of Wisdom though with an admixture of Hebraisms. Compared with the literary language of their time, their language had no distinctive features except those which resulted from the nature of their subjects and their particular outlook. On the other hand, we encounter the Judeo-Greek popular language in the Septuagint, for instance in Ecclesiasticus which was translated from Hebrew, the two books of Maccabees, Tobit, Judith and Baruch. The authors of these writings learned their Greek not from books but from daily life.

There are no translations from Hebrew or Aramaic in the New Testament. The Gospel according to St. Matthew is not a translation, even though there was an Aramaic Gospel of Matthew and there is no reason to doubt that it was written by the same author. This only means that the same author wrote the same book twice, in two different languages, just as Josephus did with his book on the Jewish War. However, it is true of all the authors of the New Testament writings, even of Luke, that theirs is a Hebrew mentality. As a result their Greek has a more or less Hebrew or Aramaic tinge.

If an author was familiar with Greek literature, this fact will be noticeable because the literary language will show through. For instance, in Luke we find passages side by side which are written in the literary *koine,* and others which show the characteristics of the Jewish popular language. Thus the first words of his Gospel for instance have all the characteristics of the *koine,* and yet immediately following are passages in the most outspoken Jewish-Greek.

This fact determines the extent to which the interpreter of the New Testament must compare its language with the usage of classic Attic Greek, or that of the *koine,* or that of the apocryphal writings of the Septuagint. Classical usage is relevant only insofar as it is continued in the *koine*, and that of the *koine* only insofar as it influenced the New Testament writing beyond and above the popular usage.

For example, the Greek term in Matthew 23:39 *ap'arti*, translated variously: "from now on . . . henceforth . . . again" is not Attic. In Attic Greek the term *aparti* means "exactly, just." In its later development it has a temporal connotation, and means "now, immediately." In this sense it has continued in the *koine* and we find it in John 13:19 and Revelation 14:13.

In Hebrews 2:17 the Greek expression originally means, "to reconcile the sins of the people." This sounds very strange from the point of view of Classical Greek, where it is said, "to reconcile the gods." But that must not mislead us to understand this New Testament expression elliptically, as if "God" had been omitted. It would never occur to a Greek speaking Hebrew to say, "to reconcile God," provided he had remained within the religious mentality of his nation. From the Old Testament he was accustomed to speak of an atonement for sin, and this concept he associated with the Greek verb "to reconcile" and thus would say "to reconcile sins." It is clear, therefore, that this New Testament expression must be understood in the light of the Hebrew idiom.

Furthermore Colossians 2:18 would be interpreted in an utterly false way if the Greek verb *thelein* were understood according to Classic Greek usage or even that of *koine* Greek. In Classic Greek its present participle means "gladly." This is not, however, what Paul means. He uses the language of the Septuagint, and thus the passage means "finding pleasure in." Some of the Hebraisms of the New Testament agree with Greek idioms, as, for example, the instrumental use of the Greek preposition *en*, which, in addition to its original local sense of "in" also means "through." This usage, however, is found more frequently in the New Testament than in Classical Greek.

It would be erroneous to draw conclusions concerning the

author of a book from the amount of Hebraisms used in the text. Luke, for instance, uses the language of the *koine* in his Preface. But in chapters one and two he employs Hebraisms as much as possible. The content determines here the linguistic coloring of the narrative, which is more strongly influenced by the Old Testament than the subsequent chapters of the Gospel.

It is the same in the Book of Acts. As long as a narrative moves in Jewish lands, his expression is strongly influenced by the Hebrew. At the end of Acts, in describing the trip to Rome, there is no reason to Hebraize so Luke uses mostly the language of the *koine*. Similarly, on Mars Hill he has Paul speaking a different kind of Greek than in the synagogue of Antioch in Pisidia.

The strongly Hebrew tinge of Revelation and its curious grammatical irregularities do not prove that it could not have been written by the author of the Gospel and Epistles. In the Gospel and Epistles the author writes with care and remains within a narrow confine of expressions and thoughts. In Revelation he is under the urge to express quickly what he has envisioned, and this he does depending throughout upon Old Testament prophecy. Thus while he writes a very unGreek Greek, he employs a very rich vocabulary.

During the period in which the New Testament books were written, the language of the New Testament did not pass through a historical development, as was the case with the Old Testament. Among the New Testament authors, Paul alone might perhaps show a development of his language. Yet the second letter to Timothy is more closely related to the Epistle to the Romans than some portions of II Corinthians. The long sentences of the letters to the Ephesians and the Colossians are used as evidence against Pauline authorship, and similarly the well constructed sentences of the Epistle to the Hebrews. But in Romans 2:7-28 there is also such a long and well constructed sentence, and in Ephesians 4:13-16 we find an entirely different sentence than in 1:3-14 where one sentence is strung on to the next.

The varieties of linguistic expression in the letters of the Apostle can be attributed to their respective destination and purpose, with all their attendant mental and emotional implications. Great caution is therefore needed if one is trying to use these expressions to ascertain on such a basis what he wrote earlier or later, or what is written by the Apostle himself and what by somebody else.

Now that we have seen what it means to interpret Holy Scripture on the basis of its original composition, text, and languages, we still have to deal with the origin of the individual writings.

C. ORIGIN AND MAKING OF THE INDIVIDUAL BOOKS

Since Holy Scripture consists of writings which come to us from antiquity, the interpreter has to investigate when and for whom and by whom they were written, and what were the circumstances and purpose of the writings.

In this respect too the Old Testament is different from the New Testament. In the Old Testament canon we find collections whose parts originated at different times, for instance, Psalms and Proverbs. Psalm 90 claims to be a Song of Moses, whereas the last collection of psalms contains much post-exilic material.

From Genesis to II Kings and perhaps even including Ruth we have one coherent literary work which is not homogeneous but rather a collection of works which was not concluded before the end of the exile. It is doubtful how far the individual parts can be separated from each other and whether it is possible to ascertain the dates of their origin. Furthermore, in the Old Testament there are writings by unknown authors, for instance Job, where the only question can be concerning the date of their origin, while tradition assigns authors to the New Testament writings of the same type, for instance Hebrews and the historical books, so that the correctness of these traditions can be examined.

In studying collections of writings one must keep in mind the period from which the individual part may have come, and also when the collection was made and edited by one individual, whether and to what extent he reworked it, and to what extent his influence is felt. For instance in Deuteronomy 2:10-12, 20-23 we find notes which interrupt the flow of the report, and deal with the former inhabitants of the Moabite, Ammanite, Edomite, and Philistian territory. These notes were added by a later redactor. In the words of Judges 18:30, "until the day of the captivity of the land," we also recognize a later interpolation.

But the problem in this historical work is not merely that of interpolations. For example, in Genesis a distinction has been made between the so-called Elohistic and Jahvistic sections, which are attributed to different authors and traditions. But the unity of the narrative resists such a mechanical separation.

However, it seems quite obvious that materials originating in different times and by different authors have been united in the Torah. For example, Deuteronomy 1:1 begins a type of narrative which is dissimilar to the preceding one and yet is continued in the Book of Joshua. Of course we are not bound by the division of this historical work into the five books of Moses, Joshua, etc. For instance Judges 2:16–16:31 is a complete work, namely the "Book of Judges" from Othniel to Samson. It has no connection with what follows afterward and is only loosely connected with what precedes it. In turn, the section Judges 17:1–21:25 contains a number of individual narratives from the so-called time of the Judges, among which we must include the Book of Ruth.

The picture in II Samuel is similar. From I Samuel 1 to II Samuel 20 there is a fairly coherent narrative describing the history of Samuel, Saul and David, whereas chapters 21-24 consist of individual sections by a different author. In II Kings 4:1-–8:15 we discover a series of narratives from the life of the prophet Elisha which have been interpolated in their original form by the redactor who collected this whole section. In order to judge the historical value of the individual parts one has to ascertain in what manner the work as a whole has come into being. The result of the interpretation must be a view of the whole work which reflects the differences of its parts. An interpretation of the Book of Psalms, for instance, is not complete until the individual groups within the collection and their mutual relationship have been identified and the problem of the order within the individual groups has been clarified. It would contribute considerably to the evaluation of the individual psalms if it could be established that the beginning of the work was a collection comprehending Psalms 2-41, to which other collections were later added.

It has been suggested that the synoptic Gospels, too, are the result of the rewording of original documents or the combination of various documents. Is it possible to discover within them flaws and gaps which would indicate that materials of various periods and authors have been put together? Similarly, what is the relationship of the three Gospels to each other: Do they depend on each other? If a unified theme is found to dominate a book, it is not likely to be the work of an editor.

However, in the case of internal unity, increased attention has to be given to the question how this unity agrees with the possible dependence of this Gospel upon another. For example, beginning with 6:14 the Gospel of Mark becomes ever more similar to the Gospel of Matthew, while the very beginning of Matthew presents a basically different idea of history. In what sequence did these Gospels originate? And to what extent did their authors have independent knowledge which might enable them to apply different ideas of history to their materials? The answer to this question will help us to decide whether the traditional authors could have been the real ones. The Gospels themselves do not name their authors, though they give us some hints, for example, when the author of Matthew's Gospel emphasizes the calling of Matthew by Jesus, or when the author of the second part of the work which is ascribed to Luke (i.e. Acts) uses "we" when reporting these things which he saw himself, or when in the Gospel of John the name of John is carefully avoided.

There are also parts of the Old Testament which do not name their authors, as for example, Job. All that can be done here is to investigate the date of its origin. But it is quite possible that a later hand added to such a book, and that these accretions must be removed in order to recognize the original theme of the book. For example, the beginning and end of Job are alleged to be later additions, and the speeches of Elihu are said to have been inserted in order to round out the idea which the author had in mind. Once these questions have been settled the interpreter has to ask himself at what time such an idea might have been carried through in this particular manner. For instance, if the book dates from the time of Solomon, the theme would be different than if it dated from the time of the catastrophe of the Jewish people, in which case the latter would be symbolized in the person of Job. The same is true of the anonymous portions of the Book of Psalms. If Psalm 132 for instance comes to us from post-exilic times it must be interpreted in a different way than if Solomon is its author, for the prayer that Jehovah should fulfill the promises given to David would have entirely different undertones in Solomon's time than in that of Zerubbabel. The conclusion whether one or the other is the case has to be reached on the basis of its content.

Since the superscriptions of the Psalms are of questionable value, we must also ask in the case of those psalms which name an author, whether they could possibly have been written by him. When we read in Psalm 44:17, "All this is come upon us, though we have not forgotten thee," this cannot be fitted into the Chaldean or Macabbean times to which this psalm has been assigned, and therefore the accuracy of the superscription is confirmed. But in Psalm 74: 7-8, "They set thy sanctuary on fire . . . they burned up all the meeting places of God," seems not to fit in with the superscription which ascribes this Psalm to Asaph.

In some instances a book of prophecy may contain parts which have been erroneously added. Can we understand for example, Isaiah 13, 14 and 19 from the same viewpoint which dominates the rest of the book?

Furthermore, we must investigate whether the various portions of a book of prophecy can be subsumed under a common idea. For example, does Isaiah 1-35 reveal such a unity that it is necessary to assume that the author of the individual sections arranged them into a whole? This common theme must then be made explicit and the details have to be appraised in their relation to it.

In the New Testament also the possibility must be granted that originally unrelated materials have been added to a book. For example, if the greetings in Romans 16 should not fit into a letter to the Roman congregation, this section must have been erroneously added to this letter of Paul. Similarly, if II Corinthians 6:14–7:1 should interrupt the context or if the content of chapters 10-13 should be incompatible with the preceding chapters, one must question whether these originally formed part of this letter. The Epistle to Colossians is said to be thoroughly interpolated. In view of this assertion, the interpreter must pay special attention to whether the letter can be properly understood without the "interpolated" passages.

Furthermore, the possibility must be left open that pseudonymous writings have crept into the New Testament. For example, in reading II Peter one must ascertain whether the point of view from which chapter 2 prophesies, and from which chapter 3 refers to Paul and his letters, can be attributed to Peter. Similarly I Timothy and Titus must be studied with the view of finding out whether the situations which they presuppose can be accommodated in the life of Paul.

But quite apart from such possibilities, the date of origin is important for the understanding of the New Testament writings. Each of its books should be studied with the question of its date in mind, and from its date the book as a

whole and its details should be interpreted. If the Epistle of
James for instance precedes the Pauline letters, and the
events recorded in Galatians 2:1 f., this fact would preclude
once and for all the possibility that its concern with faith
and works is a direct polemic against Paul. Above all, this
discussion ought to be interpreted on its own merits without
prejudice concerning the date of origin of the letter. If it
should be discovered that the Epistle is of a very early origin,
light would be shed upon the circumstances of its writing
and the peculiarity of its content, namely, that it does not
discuss doctrine.

If Revelation was written in the time of Domitian, it will
be impossible to interpret chapter 11 as referring to the
Jewish War. (This is impossible for other reasons too.) Also
the interpretation of the "Beast" of chapter 13 as referring
to Nero would have a more solid basis if the book had been
written in the period between Nero and Vespasian, because
in the time of Domitian the idea of the return of a "still
living Nero" would be unthinkable. In Revelation 11:8 the
seer calls Jerusalem not only the city where the Lord was
crucified, but also the spiritual Sodom and Egypt. This
designation makes sense if these visions were seen after
judgment had befallen Jerusalem. These epithets would then
indicate that the congregation of Jesus was saved out of
Jerusalem as Lot out of Sodom and Israel out of Egypt.
However, if the book was written during the Jewish War, we
must seek another interpretation of this passage. The date
when the book originated must be derived from the Letters
to the Seven Churches, which depict a peculiar type of
church life.

A similar case may help to elucidate: In order to interpret Jesus' prophecies in Matthew 24 or Luke 21 correctly,
it is of considerable importance to know whether they were
written down before or after the Jewish War. To make this
problem relevant it is not necessary to go so far as to say
that in the latter case it would be a prophecy fabricated after
the event. Each detail will be interpreted differently accord-

ing to whether one thinks that it was transmitted by one who had gone through the Jewish War, or by one for whom the judgment is still in the future.

Thus each book of the New Testament must be read with the problem of its time of origin in mind. In this light the historical significance of the book as a whole and its component parts are to be evaluated. The interpretation of details must not be dominated by preconceived opinions concerning the date of the book.

When in cases where the author is known beyond doubt or has been discovered with certainty, the investigation must be directed toward his historical position, and to the manner in which the outlook of the book is determined thereby. For example, if Psalm 2 is a psalm of David, the content of verse 7 is explained by that fact. The "sonship" mentioned there is that of the king whom Jehovah has called to rule over his people. Likewise if Psalm 110 is by David, there can be no question about the meaning of "the Lord," for then the author was one who had no lord over himself. The divine word spoken here cannot be directed to anybody else but to him who will be also his Lord, whom he will have to serve: the future King of Israel (i.e. Messiah). If Psalm 40 is a psalm of David, the meaning of verse 7, "Lo, I come; in the roll of the book it is written of me," in contrast to v. 6, "Sacrifice and offering thou dost not desire"; has a special meaning when it comes from the mouth of the King of Israel who was anointed by Samuel to take the place of Saul (I Sam. 15:22).

The mission of Isaiah is described in the story of his call in Isaiah 6 as one in which he could not expect his proclamation to succeed among his people until its situation had become desperate. With this revelation in mind we must read the prophecies in 7-12. Then they have an entirely different significance than if we suppose that the prophet proclaimed them or perhaps merely wrote them down at a later date in the hope of averting the impending judgment.

We learn concerning Amos that he was called to prophesy

in Bethel, one of the two official sanctuaries of the ten-tribe kingdom. This makes it clear why his prophecies are directed against the kingdom of Jeroboam, while Micah directs his threatening speeches against the Kingdom of Judah to which he himself belongs.

The Book of Zechariah consists of many parts which have been attributed to a number of different authors. One should consider, however, that the opening visions of the book belong to a time when it was the task of the prophet to work with Haggai for the reconstruction of the Temple in Jerusalem. Once this immediate purpose had been achieved, he could prophesy in an entirely different manner, as is evidenced, for instance, in chapter 9 ff. where he takes up older prophecies and interprets them from the point of view of his own time.

James' position in Holy History differs essentially from that of Paul. He was the head of the local congregation at Jerusalem and therefore the highest authority for the Jewish Christians of the Holy Land. He views Christendom from Jerusalem and that makes it appear primarily a Jewish Christianity. This we recognize in the moral faults against which he inveighs in his letter, the peculiar faults of the Jewish people.

If Paul wrote the Epistle to the Hebrews, he would stand in an entirely different relationship to them than he did to the congregations which he founded in the pagan world, and this would affect his attitude to the addressees. He would not have to assert his Apostolic calling and yet make a claim to be heard. This gives a clue to the locality of the Jewish group to whom this letter was directed. Similarly, Paul had a different relationship to the Roman congregation from that to the church at Corinth. The fact that the former had come into being without his participation explains the peculiar content of the Epistle to the Romans.

If Peter wrote the letter ascribed to him, the very fact that this man should address himself to Gentile Christians is of central importance for our appreciation of their value. No less significant, however, is it that Peter should refer to Paul and his letters by saying, "which have now been proclaimed to you by those who preached the good news to you" (I Pet. 1:12) thereby acknowledging Paul's authority. The Petrine authorship of these letters is denied because of a supposed antagonism between Peter and Paul. If there should be no reason for denying Peter's authorship, these documents would illustrate the concord between Paul and Peter, which is attested also in Galatians 2.

In some instances, we know the situation in which a certain portion of Scripture originated either because specifically mentioned, or by inference. In such cases it is necessary to find out how this situation is reflected in this particular passage of Scripture. Thus, the song in Exodus 15 corresponds to the great moment which is said to have produced it. Similarly, Psalm 90, if written by Moses, has an entirely different meaning than if it were written at some later time. This psalm then gives expression to Moses' realizing that he was living among a people which was about to die within a certain period of time. For this reason he asks, in view of the promise under which Israel left Egypt: how long will God's wrath continue to cut off the people? He would not ask this question merely in view of the fact that man is mortal, and he would not pray as he does at the end of the psalm, for this petition refers to the promise that was given to Israel at its Exodus.

The superscription of Psalm 60 designates the only situation which can make this psalm understandable, namely, after a victory and before a new battle which will bring Moab, Edom, and Philistia under the rule of Jehovah. Psalm 22 is described simply as a Song of David. Is there a special situation in the life of David which this psalm memorializes? The one who is praying complains that he is "poured out like water," and he laments, "I can count all my bones." His enemies rejoice at his calamity and cast lots upon his vesture. This must have been the mood of David when Saul caught up with him and he seemed to be the certain victim of his enemies. He had every reason to expect that if he should fall into the hands of Saul, all the things which he here envisions would happen to him. It is obvious that this psalm originated in the situation described in I Samuel 23:26.

That the mood of the prophecies in Joel 2:19 suddenly changes, can be explained as the result of the effect which the prophet's call to repentance (v. 17) brought about among the people, as well as of Jehovah's gracious acceptance, v. 18.

It is of significance for the understanding of the Revelation of St. John that the Apostle was on the island of Patmos when he saw his visions. There he had been exiled, and thus he could call himself one who shared with those to whom he wrote, both the Kingdom and the tribulation. He was to learn what the end of time would be in which such tribulation had to be suffered.

And if II Peter is actually a work of the Apostle, it is important that it was written in view of his impending death and his desire to let his readers have something which would preserve their faith when the "heresies" and "scoffers" which he envisions will come to pass.

We distinguish between the letters of Paul which date from that arrest in Rome which was the result of the accusations of his own nation, and others which date from a later arrest. The former one lasted for many years. Thus when he writes as a prisoner to the Gentile Christians in Ephesus, one has to keep in mind what this arrest meant to him and to the congregation which he had gathered. He who had been called to convert the Gentiles was in chains for such a long time! This explains why he asks, "So I ask you not to lose heart over what I am suffering for you" (Eph. 3:13). It is from that same period of arrest, but at a time when release seemed imminent, that he wrote in his Epistle to the Philippians, "I know that I shall remain with you" (1:25). It has been said that the pseudo-Paul, who is supposed to have written this letter, put words of presumption in the Apostle's mouth. But such a remark would not be made if one were willing to let the situation described in the letter speak for itself.

The situation of the Apostle in II Timothy is entirely different from that in the Epistle to the Philippians. The complete change in scene is indicated by the fact that he is now jailed as an evil doer, accused of a crime against the laws of the pagan state. In view of his approaching death he exhorts Timothy so urgently in order that after his death the preaching of the Gospel proclaimed by him would continue.

We have seen how the life situation in which a certain part of Scripture originated must be kept in mind. From the writings which had their origin in some particular situation we must differentiate those which came about from a desire to give adequate form to the accumulating material. These are genuinely literary products. However, among the New Testament books some have been erroneously numbered in this classification, since they were written for a specific purpose.

Among the Old Testament writings, Job, Song of Songs, Proverbs, Ecclesiastes, belong to this group; also the two historical works, the great one reaching from Genesis to II Kings, on the one hand, and the Books of Chronicles and Ezra on the other, and finally Jonah and Lamentations.

The task of the interpreter is now to bring to light the main theme which the author is elaborating, whether ethical, poetical, or historical. The great historical work from Genesis to II Kings was compiled from documents which the author had at hand, and which reached back to the earliest times, and whose oldest part was a condensation of the tradition which embraced the beginning of the world and of mankind. These documents were arranged in such a way that they present a history which took place between God and man and which points to the eventual restoration of the created order perverted at present by sin. This history was brought to a conclusion at a point when it seemed as if the promised result would never be reached, and when the only tangible hope that things would ever change was the fact that Nebuchadnezzar had released Jehoiah from prison and restored his royal rank. The traditions of the earliest time form not only the nucleus around which later informations accrued but they also determine the line which all subsequent writing of history is to follow.

On the other hand, the contemporary situation in which this historical work was concluded exerted an influence on its execution and determined the mood of its presentation, particularly the presentation of those events which had taken place since David and Solomon. For the man who concluded this historical work was also the author of this particular section, even though he utilized existing documents.

The historical idea developed by the author of the other historical work of the Old Testament is essentially different. The situation is that of a restored politico-religious Jewish commonwealth. From this viewpoint its past and its far distant roots are traced. This is the reason that this work begins with a geneology of the twelve tribes, going back to the beginning of the human race. The historical narrative itself, however, begins with the death of Saul and the rule of David. It is confined to the history of the Kingdom of Judah, which is continued until the time when after the exile the new settlement was established and the Temple restored, the religious and legal order renewed and the national purity of the new commonwealth secured. The selection of material, the tone and color of the narrative, are entirely different from the other historical work. It is Jewish rather than Israelitic, and the exaggerated character of the stories which is so offensive to some, as well as the meticulous description of the ritual are explained by this fact.

The Book of Job is the poetical development of an idea which would be entirely missed if only the speeches of Job and his friends were taken into consideration. Its subject matter is the riddle of life which finds its supreme expression in the misfortunes of the just and the fortune of the unjust.

The poem shows both that the problem has its origin in God and that man cannot find peace unless God takes his side and speaks to him. For this reason the sections which are inappropriately called the prologue and epilogue are essential parts of the book. This is also true of the speeches of Elihu, who utters purely human wisdom. While Job refuses to answer him he does not find the peace of submission. To this he attains eventually when God turns to him, in spite of the fact that God, too, does not provide the solution for the riddle of his suffering.

The Song of Songs is a lyrical song depicting in its full natural beauty the relationship of man and woman as willed by the creator. The Book of Ecclesiastes, in turn, sets forth the vanity of all human and worldly endeavor, when seen in their earthly perspective. In Lamentations an Israelite pours out his profound sorrow at the downfall of Zion. The Book of Jonah, regardless of whether it is history or a poem, shows that a prophet cannot dodge his calling, and also that the prophet has no right to demand that his prophecy should be fulfilled.

All these are literary works. They were written without regard to any special occasion or purpose for no other end but to present a certain subject. The interpreter must try to put himself in the place of the author. However, there is a difference between writings like the Song of Songs (into which Solomon poured the abundance of his joy) and Lamentations (in which Jeremiah expressed his personal sorrow) on the one hand, and the Book of Job and the Book of Jonah on the other, which are intended to teach the reader a lesson; or the Book of Ecclesiastes whose author wants to share with others an attitude towards life which has grown out of his own experiences.

It is different with the prophetic writings of the Old Testament. Whether they are individual prophecies like Obadiah, Nahum and Habakkuk, or are collections of prophecies like Isaiah, Jeremiah, Ezekiel, they are destined for their contemporaries. In their case we must know the attitude of these contemporaries. Zephaniah, for instance, has nothing new to say. But to those who in his time said of Jehovah, "The Lord will not do good, nor will he do ill" (1:12), he repeated things that had been prophesied earlier. He begins by saying, "I will utterly sweep away everything from the face of the earth" (1:2), in other words with the threat of a judgment which will destroy all men and animals from the face of the earth, and then passes on to the threat of a judgment which will exterminate the godless from Judah. He admonishes them to take this threat seriously, especially in view of the fact that Jehovah will vindicate the cause of Judah and restore its former honor.

When Isaiah added chapter 1 as a preface to his book of prophecies (chapters 2-35), his contemporaries were people who by their attitude provoked the judgment of God. This is the reason why he proclaims promises only after announcing the imminent divine judgment. On the other hand, chapters 40-66 were written for the sake of people who needed the comfort of Israel. Thus he begins immediately with consolation, which changes into scoldings and threats only with reference to the ungodly.

Not a single one of the New Testament books owes its origin exclusively to the desire to give a literary form to a given material. This is true even of the Book of Revelation. It is not the work of a man who wanted to present certain ideas concerning the future and the end of all things, in the form of visions. Neither his vision nor his writing were the result of his own initiative. He is given to see things and at the very beginning of his visions he is told to write them down. For it is God who desires that the congregation of Jesus should receive these revelations concerning the final outcome both of contemporary events and all future ones. The purpose for which this book is destined is quite different from the Book of Daniel. We read in Daniel 8:26 that with reference to the vision reported in this chapter Daniel is told: "seal up the vision," to which was added: "it pertains to many days hence." And again after the vision reported in chapters 10-12, it is said to Daniel, "The words are shut up and sealed until the time of the end" (12:9).

Unlike all these revelations which are destined for a distant future, we read in Revelation 22:10, "Do not seal up the words of the prophecy of this book, for the time is near." The whole content of these visions could immediately be used. John did not leave his book to Christendom as an heirloom, but rather published it in order that the Christians might study it.

The Epistles are mostly the result of the relationship in which the writer stood to a definite group of readers. We must therefore gain a picture of that circle of readers. For example, in order to understand the content of the two Epistles to the Corinthians, one must previously obtain a picture of this congregation and the contemporary conditions. If one has a clear idea of the spiritual life of the congregation and of its relationship to the Apostle, it will be easier for instance to understand why in I Corinthians the Apostle waits until chapter seven before he answers the questions which the congregation had asked him. The presence of factions within the congregation as well as their pride, which had led them to an exaggerated notion of their own spiritual growth, induced the Apostle first to humiliate them and then to call their various moral deficiencies to their attention so that they might be in the right mood to receive appropriately his answers to their questions.

The same is true of II Corinthians. The development of his thought is determined by the intention of the Apostle to move the congregation in a certain direction. It is therefore imperative for the interpreter to gain a clear view of the condition of the congregation, for only then can he understand why the Apostle wrote at times in a winning way though criticizing them, while in other places he proceeded with all sternness. The reason was that in general the Apostle was pleased that the congregation had received his former letter in the right spirit. However, the same congregation is not yet clear as to its right relationship to the

Apostle. It is still under outside influences, and many of them still persisted in their defiance which had characterized their attitude for some time, and continued in the sins for which he had chided them. This is the reason why, opening on a friendly note, he will soon discuss in great detail the nature of his office and the manner in which he discharges it. He puts them to shame in regard to the collection which he had arranged, yet he does so in a restrained and considerate manner. Abruptly with "I, myself" in 10:1 the tone changes entirely. He personally attacks those who are opposing him, turns upon them with cutting sternness, and concludes on a threatening note.

The situation is similar in the Epistle to the Galatians. From the letter as a whole one has to gain an idea from the confusion which the adversaries of the Apostle have caused in that congregation, before starting the interpretation of the details. Then only will it become clear why the Apostle begins with the factual report in chapters one and two, why, after the explanation of justification by faith he continues with such a moving speech, and why he unexpectedly employs the allegory of the relationship between Isaac and Ishmael, and Hagar and Sarah. Above all, this will help us understand what he is trying to say in chapter 5, writing in numerous brief sentences which give only hints of what he wants to convey.

In order to understand the Epistle to the Colossians, one must know in advance what it was that threatened the Colossian congregation at that time, and caused the Apostle to write this letter. From the very beginning, everything he says is determined by the particular danger that threatens the inner life of this congregation. From the initial thanksgiving with which he begins, and the specific petitions which he makes for them, to the ensuing development of the central idea—namely the person and work of Christ and the significance which his death and resurrection has for us—everything is said with the purpose of preparing the ground for the refutation of the inventors of a self-made piety.

Quite a few people believe that I Peter was written for Christians of Jewish origin, or what seems even less likely, for Jewish proselytes who later became Christians. Whether one holds this erroneous opinion or sees correctly that this epistle was written to a Gentile Christian group of readers scattered over a wide area, is of the greatest importance for the correct understanding of the letter as a whole as well as of the details. When the Apostle says in 1:21 concerning his readers that through Christ they have become believers in God, namely the God who raised Christ from the dead, this means something entirely different if it is said with reference to people who had already believed in the true and living God and had hoped for Christ, or to people who had worshipped idols and who, to use the Apostle's words, had been in this world "without God." Similarly when the Apostle Peter writes in 4:3 of his Epistle, "Let the time that is past suffice for doing what the Gentiles like to do, living in licentiousness, passions, drunkenness, revels, carousing, and lawless idolatry." This has an entirely different meaning if it is said to Jews who could not be accused of having formerly committed idolatry, than if it is said to Gentiles, who dwelling among their pagan compatriots, had to adopt an entirely different conduct than before. If one notices that the Epistle in its entire conception, but especially in its opening section, shows great similarity to the Epistle to the Ephesians, this fact gains a new significance and appears in a new light if the letter is directed to Gentile Christians—a number of whom lived in the same territory as the Ephesians—than if it was directed to a scattered group of individual Jewish Christians living in Gentile Christian congregations. The entire outline of the Epistle to the Ephesians is determined by the fact that it is directed to Gentile Christians who had to be reminded that Christianity is not a purely personal matter and that the Christian Church is not a sect or philosophical school. For this reason the Apostle intends from the very beginning to remind his readers that their Christian faith has its eternal ground in God's gracious will, and its historical ground in the person of Jesus Christ whom God had raised from the dead and exhalted to heavenly glory. Thus the fact that they were Christians was not due to any merits of their own but was given to them as a free gift of grace, the greatness of which was underscored by the fact that they had not even belonged to God's chosen people but were made members of it through the atoning death of Jesus Christ.

The particular group of Gentile Christians to whom this letter was directed is of little importance for its understanding. However, in the case of the Epistle to the Romans, the fact is of basic importance that it was addressed to the Gentile Christian congregation in the capitol of the world. This congregation, though not founded by Paul, would be of the greatest importance for the continuation of his work in the West. From the beginning to the end, everything said in this letter was designed to bring this congregation in Rome, with whom he did not have any direct personal relationship, to an understanding of his proclamation of the Gospel ahead of his visit in the hope that they would serve him as a base for his operations in the West.

For a correct understanding of the Epistles to Timothy and Titus it is not sufficient to say that in a general way the Apostle is giving advice for the Christian ministry. Especially one must not overlook how different in I Timothy and Titus the specific problem of the office of the two men is, in spite of certain similarities. It was the particular task of Titus to organize congregations among the Christians of Crete. Timothy on the other hand had to guide and supervise a congregation which had been in existence for some time. In both cases it is important to note how great the danger was at that time that Christianity should be reduced to a matter of abstract knowledge by people to whom Christian teaching was merely a source of income.

But in this respect there is another difference between the two letters. From the hints thrown out by Paul in I Timothy one must form an impression of the state of mind of

Timothy, because it was in view of it that the Apostle deemed it necessary to give such exhortations and reminders as would otherwise be strange in this letter. This is particularly true of II Timothy, for in that letter Paul no longer deals with the temporary ministerial task of Timothy in Ephesus, but he attempts to win him back to his teaching office which he had fled in fear of persecution. Furthermore, special attention has to be paid to the manner in which the Apostle writes, in order to learn not only those dangers which threatened the purity of Apostolic Christianity in the environment of Paul and Timothy, but also those which threatened Timothy himself. Not until we achieve a clear picture of these two facts is it possible to comprehend the apparently confused course which the letter follows.

A knowledge of the intended readers seems less important in the case of the Gospel of John and the First Epistle. As one who has seen and heard the Lord, John writes for people who believe in Him as a result of the Apostolic preaching. There is nothing in the Epistle which does not concern believers at any time. It is written in such a manner that every Christian at any time can read it as if it were written especially for him. The Epistle declares in the simplest possible way what the Christian life and its opposite are like.

In the Gospel we have a selection of those incidents from the life of our Lord which show Him as the Son of God and thus as the object of the Christian faith. The Gospel records the witness of the Baptist, as well as the witness which Jesus bore to Himself in word and deed. At the same time we are shown what it means to believe in Him and how His disciples believed in Him, in contrast to the unbelief of the people who remained outside of His fellowship. This contrast explains why His enemies were called "the Jews."

However, even here a knowledge of the group for whom these writings were destined is not entirely worthless to the interpreter. In I John this may explain what the author writes about "false prophets" and the "anti-Christs" which had arisen among them. Even in the Gospel it is evident

THE BIBLE IN HISTORY 121

that the selection of the material was made with regard to certain contemporary views which were incompatible with the nature and the basic content of the Christian faith.

The Gospel of Matthew was written with greater concern for the contemporary audience than the Gospel of John. The author collected those passages which were suitable to show that from now on the congregation of Jesus Christ is the rightful congregation of God, as opposed to the Jewish claims. For this reason he demonstrates that Old Testament history and Scripture is fulfilled in Jesus, even in those aspects of the life of Jesus which seemed to the Jews to contradict the promises. Such a book was of greatest value for the congregation of Jesus which had just evolved out of Israel, as well as for the Jewish people of that time who maintained that they were God's true congregation.

The situation is similar with the case of Luke who wrote a book which was dedicated to a Gentile Christian, and thus destined for all Gentile Christians. His purpose is expressed in rather general terms in 1:4 by the words: "That you may know the truth concerning the things of which you have been informed." But this objective is accomplished by explaining why the New Testament proclamation of salvation, which began in connection with the Old Testament promise among the Jewish people and in the Holy Land, had transcended these limits; and why it was that predominantly Gentile congregations were established in Gentile lands when the Jewish people everywhere rejected that message, and why their center was shifting from Jerusalem to the capital of the Roman Empire. This picture of the historical development filled a need of Gentile Christianity. They needed to know both that "salvation is of the Jews" and that the Kingdom had been delegated to the Gentiles, and that the latter fact was based upon the former one.

Finally, if we look at the Gospel of Mark we can see that the fact that it is different from the Gospel of Matthew in spite of striking similarities, and the fact that it was designed for an entirely different circle of readers explains this. That the Gospel of Mark was not written for Jewish Christians is evident from certain remarks which would be utterly superfluous for Jewish readers. Some clues seem to indicate that this Gospel was originally written for Gentile Christians in Rome or Italy.

Whether a book was written for literary purposes or because of contemporary conditions and in order to meet some particular needs, it must always be read in the same way that the original readers read it. This is true even for formal characteristics and material details. One must know them as they were known at that time. For example when we read in Psalm 69:22, "Let their own table before them become a snare," it is important to know how people used to eat in those days. When it is said in Song of Songs 8:6, "Set me as a seal upon thine heart, as a seal upon thine arm," this requires knowledge of how a signet ring was carried. The original reader of the opening words of Psalm 110, "sit at my right hand" would not think of a group of people sitting in a row where the seat at the right is the seat of honor, but of a ruler sitting on a throne at whose side the next in honor would be placed while all the others stood in front of him. When explaining Zech. 14:16 one must know something about the meaning of the Feast of Tabernacles. Furthermore, when Mark speaks of the Herodians while Matthew speaks of the Sadducees we must realize what the political role of the Sadducees was. One must be familiar with the practice of foot-washing if I Timothy 5:10 as well as the foot washing of Jesus are rightly to be appreciated. Similarly, the passage in John 1:39, "It was about the tenth hour" can be understood only if one knows which hour was counted as the first one by the readers. It is also necessary to know how a Jewish home was arranged in order to understand Luke 5:19.

More than anything else, however, one has to apprehend emphatically the understanding of Holy History which the writer assumes in his readers and shares with them. This understanding may be gained from a study of Biblical

Theology, provided that its perspective is an historical one as is required for its special task. Of course any particular exposition of Biblical Theology must in turn be examined on the basis of the Scriptures. But this is equally true of the relationship between Biblical exegesis and all the other branches of Scriptural study. In each case there is a reciprocal relationship, since the interpreter will be guided at any given time by the ascertained results of the other fields, while in turn the results of his work will form the basis for their re-examination.

This applies also to the relationship of Biblical Theology and exegesis. The subject matter of Biblical Theology is the historical development of the revelation and recognition of the saving truth. The interpreter can rely on the general results of Biblical Theology, but he may reach a point where the result of his interpretation clashes with certain details of the traditional Biblical Theology. If his interpretation is confirmed by the further progress of his work, he will revise the traditional Biblical Theology. But in order to do that he must have a general idea of the historical process in which the divine Word witnessed by the Scripture revealed itself. Thus alone he can ascertain the degree of spiritual knowledge which an author writing at a certain period of Holy History had in common with his readers and which he took for granted on their part. This is a must for an interpreter who wants to read a Biblical book in the way the author expected it to be read. The exegete who fails to form for himself such an idea will be apt to espouse erroneous interpretations by starting from presuppositions which lacked an actual basis at the time when the book was written.

For instance, Isaiah 9:6 lists among the names of the Messiah, two which are usually translated "mighty God, everlasting father." Christian interpreters who believed that the former title contained the proper name of God, accordingly rendered the latter one "everlasting father" meaning "Father of Eternity." In analogy with Isaiah 10:21 however, the former term means "outstanding hero." Accordingly, "everlasting father" is to be understood as meaning one who is always the father of his people, so that these two names stand fittingly beside the other ones: "outstanding hero" beside "wonderful counsellor," and "everlasting father" beside the similar "prince of peace."

Some interpreted "God" in Psalm 45:6-7 as being addressed to the Messianic king; but a trinitarian relationship is not even thought of in that place. In verse 6 the psalmist does not mean "thy throne, O God" but rather, "thy divine throne"; and accordingly in the following verse "the Lord thy God" instead of "O God, thy God."

It is just as wrong to discover in the words of Micah 5:2, "whose origin is from of old, from ancient days" the eternal origin of the Promised One, or to interpret Zechariah 12:10, "when they look on him whom they have pierced," as meaning that he who is pierced is Jehovah, and thus the Messiah, since God appeared in Christ, and Christ suffered a violent death.

Furthermore the final words of Psalm 17:15, "when I awake, I shall be satisfied with beholding thy form," will look quite different to an interpreter who is certain that those for whose benefit David included this prayer in his collection of psalms, hoped firmly for a resurrection of the just to life eternal, or at least were familiar with such a hope, than it will look to one who thinks that this was not so much a hope as rather a notion or intimation which originated with the post-Davidic time and became part of the popular religion perhaps as late as during the exile. In the latter case it would be indeed preferable to explain the concluding words of the psalm from the fact that it was an evening prayer of David. This would be better than to imagine that there was just one single Israelite who through some unknown operation of his inner life had an intimation of an awakening from death to eternal life.

Similarly the so-called prologue of Job will look one way to the interpreter who is sure that the author could consider the idea of a spiritual being who opposes God as commonly accepted by his readers, but quite another way by one who believes that the idea of such a being came to the Jewish people much later, under the influence of Parsism. In that case it would indeed be advisable to consider the prologue and the epilogue of this book to be later additions. For if they are considered original parts of the book, then the main message of the entire book is this: the righteous man is surrounded by suffering and temptation, which God uses for man's good, the devil for his destruction.

Or in Romans 3 and 4 where justification by faith is discussed, we will read these passages with an entirely different expectation, and will interpret both details and context in a different way if we believe that Paul presents here his own peculiar doctrine of justification, than if we are sure that he assumes in his readers a knowledge of justification before God, and also of faith in Jesus, and of their relationship to each other.

In the former case it will be hard to understand how Paul could pass over the most important elements of this doctrine in such a hurry, or else we will try to put too much into every word that refers to this doctrine. If we follow the latter case, we will understand that he was only concerned with asserting what he presupposes among his readers, partly against those who might deny it, and partly against misunderstanding and wrong application on the part of his readers. The basic error which hinders a correct understanding of Scripture, in innumerable instances, is that Scripture is regarded as a collection of individual doctrinal propositions which successively came into being and which had to be communicated and accepted step by step. On the basis of this erroneous approach, scholars are surprised that Paul should include in his elementary teachings such things as II Thessalonians 2:2-6! Precisely because of this erroneous approach de Wette finds in I Corinthians 15:52 a dogma concerning the trumpets of the final times! Compared with this it will seem like a minor matter that some believed that the doctrine of the high-priestly office of Christ was invented by the author of the Epistle to the Hebrews.

Neither in the Old Testament or New Testament times did Scriptural teaching originate in this way. Facts of the past, present, and future were taught which formed a continuous historical process. There was no special doctrine, for instance, concerning the existence of Satan, rather it was implied in the history of the origin of sin. Likewise there was no special teaching that Jesus was High Priest. This expression of the fact that in the person of Jesus the sin of the world had been atoned was formed for a special occasion. Jesus coming from God into this world and His going from this world to God formed the eternal fact which we express by the doctrine of the Trinity. The fact that people believed in the person of Jesus because His coming was a divine gift and work, implies what we call the doctrine of justification by faith. For the proper response of man to Him whom God had given was to believe in Him, and this implied that it was a belief in the reconciliation of the world with God. For God had given Jesus to a sinful world, and He had destined His life and death for the sin of the world.

We must also keep in mind that the Holy Scripture was in the hands of the New Testament believers. This meant that even those who had been Gentiles knew Holy History, which is presupposed in the appearance of Jesus, and they knew the prophecy concerning the end of all things, which had only to be reinterpreted in the light of Jesus' appearance, exaltation, and final manifestation.

If it had been the task of the Apostle Paul during the few weeks he spent at Thessalonica, to give to that congregation instruction in Christianity which would cover all the traditional dogmas in their proper sequence, the question would come to mind at once, how could Paul possibly have come to eschatology, that is, the last chapter of dogmatics, in such a short time? The fact is that Paul converted the pagans by preaching Jesus whom God had raised from the dead.

There was good reason for speaking of the final manifestation of this king who was now hidden but who would transfigure the believers into the community of His glory. By referring to the prophecies concerning the end of things, especially to Daniel, he enables them to learn of those things which, as he intimates in his letter, they should have known from the Scriptures. What the Epistle to the Hebrews said concerning the high-priestly office of Christ was nothing spectacular to the Hebrew Christians even if they had never heard it put just that way before. They knew what the Law taught concerning the atonement of the chosen people with God, and it was their belief that the congregation of Jesus was God's people of the New Covenant. Though they had scruples because their membership in the congregation of Jesus had excluded them from participation in the worship of their people, they were able without having heard of a sacrifice of Christ or of His high-priestly office to understand immediately what was meant thereby, and why the author of this epistle wrote that Jesus was the High Priest of the New Testament congregation who had offered the true atoning sacrifice. They understood that they were thereby reminded of the fact that the person and life of Jesus was the perfect antitype of the Old Testament atonement.

Just as the authors of the Old Testament books started from the basic assumption that Israel was the people of God, so those of the New Testament writings took it for granted that their readers believed that Jesus was the Savior of the world, and that His congregation was the congregation which lives in perfect relationship to God.

This did not have to be proven. Even for those in Israel whom Jehovah reprimanded as apostates it was not necessary to prove that Israel was the people of God. They had merely to be led back to the moral truth of this axiom and thus to be converted. Likewise it was not necessary for the readers of the Epistle to the Hebrews, who were tempted to slide back into Judaism, to be given proof that Jesus was the promised Messiah or the Son of God, and that His congregation was the true people of God on earth. In these two facts everything was implied which was necessary for the understanding of the books which had originated in Israel for Israel, and in Christianity for Christianity.

To sum up. We have seen the importance which the historical origin of Biblical writings has for their interpretation and the influence which the knowledge of this historical background exerts upon the work of the interpreter. Our analysis has indicated the role which the text, the original language and the historical origin of the Biblical books have for the exegesis of Scripture. That analysis was preceded by an investigation of the subjective factors of exegesis, that is, the recognition of the miraculous character of the origin and the content of the Bible, the understanding of its Israelitic character and the assurance that the Bible bears witness to the same salvation that the believer holds as his property.

But there are also intrinsic differences in Scripture by which the interpretation is affected. One of them concerns the successive stages in which God's redemptive salvation is carried out. Thereby Scripture is divided into two halves. The other difference concerns the manner in which salvation is evidenced, and it runs through both halves. The former is the difference between the Old and the New Testament. The latter is differentiated according to the temporal order of the events of Holy History. We prefer the differentiation of past, present and future stages of salvation to the traditional distinction between historical, poetical, and prophetic books. That distinction is unsatisfactory because both poetic and prophetic writing, as also prophetic and historical writings, overlap. Furthermore, an historical book may contain poetic and prophetic portions, while a poetic book may include historical sections. For this reason we deem the traditional division impractical.

Interpretation is affected not so much by differences in the general character of a book as by the nature of its component parts. If in one and the same book we find historical materials as well as poetic and prophetic ones, three different kinds of interpretation must be employed within this

book. Above all, the poetic form is not on the same level as
the prophetic or historic forms of narration. Thus we prefer
differentiations which are grounded in the nature of a document of salvation, in that it speaks of salvation as either
present or future, either evidenced by an historical event, or
experienced as present. Thus by differentiating between
testimony to past, present, and future events, we shall show
how the task of interpretation is thereby affected. It is only
proper that we should first deal with the difference which
is rooted in the nature of salvation itself, that is, the difference between the Old Testament and the New Testament. Once this distinction has been clarified we can consider the significance it has for exegesis.

Part Two

THE DIVERSITY

OF

SCRIPTURE

CHAPTER THREE

The Difference Between the Old and the New Testaments

The salvation in which the interpreter believes has been completely realized in the person of Jesus. The interpreter discerns the evidences of this salvation everywhere in the New Testament. Its witness, in turn, originated in the Church of Jesus, especially in its Israelitic branch. In the Old Testament we see a process moving towards this complete salvation, of which the people of Israel, as the national community of the God who sent Jesus, is the witness.

This recognition, which is implied in the Christian's certainty of salvation, will prompt the exegete to take different viewpoints of the Old Testament and New Testament, with the result that the method of Old Testament exegesis is distinctly different from that of the New Testament. This is due to the fact that both the salvation experienced and the origin of the testimony born to it are of a different nature.

A. THE DISTINCTIVE FEATURES OF OLD TESTAMENT INTERPRETATION

The Christian interpreter finds in the Old Testament evidences of the same salvation which he knows, yet given in a different mode. Hence he will read the Old Testament as bearing witness to his own salvation while at the same time taking into account the fact that the Old Testament considers salvation as something completely to be realized in the future. He therefore reads and interprets the Old Testament with spiritual discernment and historical sense.

Since this spiritual understanding was of such primary importance to the church, historical interpretation lagged behind for a long period of time. The damage caused thereby was by no means as serious as that which resulted when the situation was reversed. This happened when historical interpretation predominated to the point where the spiritual understanding was lost.

By "spiritual understanding" we mean an interpretation based on the premise that the Old Testament Scripture is the work of the same Holy Spirit who is effectively at work in the New Testament Church. The Christian is particularly qualified to adopt this view because he is aware of this activity of the Holy Spirit and is moved by Him. He is therefore also able to identify in the Old Testament the same salvation which he personally experiences.

But since we are concerned with scholarly interpretation, a certain scientific qualification, particularly for the spiritual understanding of the Old Testament is also necessary. For this the theologian is prepared by Biblical history and Biblical theology.

For the Old Testament Scriptures record on the one hand a continuous series of events in which through a reciprocal relationship of God and mankind, the coming of Jesus and the formation of His Church were prepared. On the other hand we find therein statements concerning salvation which gradually realizes itself in those processes and tends toward its full actualization. That is to say, it offers a knowledge of salvation which is completed only in the New Testament proclamation of present salvation.

Hence we divide the study of the Old Testament into two different subjects, Old Testament History and Old Testament Theology. The former reproduces the series of events recorded in the Old Testament as a continuous history. The latter describes the history of the proclamation of salvation implied in that history. The former one teaches the intrinsic connection of the revelatory facts, the latter one that of the divine revelation by word.

While in both disciplines the understanding of the Bible as the document of salvation must precede its historical interpretation, yet the latter cannot be dispensed with either. The records of those events demand to be read as the record of the realization of actual salvation, yet of one which tends towards its full realization. Similarly the theoretical statements concerning salvation must be read as speaking throughout of one and the same salvation, according to the knowledge people had of it in the time prior to Christianity.*

1. The Theological Interpretation of Old Testament History

The history recorded in the Old Testament is the history of salvation as proceeding towards its full realization. Hence the things recorded therein are to be interpreted teleologically, i.e., as aiming at their final goal, and thus as being of the same nature as the goal yet modified by their respective place in history. Since the course and the events of that history are determined by their goal, this goal will manifest itself in all important stages of its progress in a way which, though preliminary, prefigures it.

These manifestations are like the joints of a plant which develops towards its flower and fruit, namely, the salvation which will be fully realized in Jesus and His Church, but

---

*In this statement Hofmann differentiates his own view both from that of Protestant orthodoxy and fundamentalism according to which there is no difference at all in the presentation of salvation as found in the Old Testament and New Testament, and from a purely historical approach to the Old Testament on the other, according to which the Jewish religion is but one of the historical antecedents of Christianity while the subject matter of the Christian proclamation differs essentially from that of the Old Testament.

which has not yet reached the full fruition of that salvation. In order correctly to understand the details of this history, four things are required:

1. I have to know that the history of the Old Testament is the provisional stage of that salvation which in the New Testament is realized and moves towards its consummation.

2. I must know the facts of this process and their intrinsic connection.

3. I must perceive the respective place which each fact occupies in that process.

4. Finally, I have to appraise the typological* significance which each fact possesses with reference to the New Testament salvation on account of the place which it occupies in this process.

If we proceed according to these rules we preclude those arbitrary interpretations which caused the typological interpretation to be discredited.

The salvation proclaimed in the New Testament is an historical reality, since through faith in Jesus Christ the human race has found its rallying point in his righteousness and thus is destined to share in His glory. Hence the very beginning of history points toward Him. History starts with the fact that the first couple which as a result of their sin had lost that life in which they had been created, was in need of the remission of sins. They obtained forgiveness because Adam accepted by faith the word of divine punishment. For this implied also the promise that mankind would be able to procreate itself and that it would eventually prevail over the tempter. God indicated that forgiveness by giving them something to cover their nakedness which as a result of their sin had become an occasion of mutual shame. This corresponded on their level to the remission of sins which in the New Testament is granted for Christ's sake.

---

*The author is here referring to the practice of regarding Old Testament characters and events as typical (i.e. as prefigurative, therefore prophetic) of New Testament characters and events. See pages 145, 165-7 below.

For when that which had become to them an occasion of shame had been covered it was practically nonexistent. This form of forgiveness agreed with the initial stage of mankind just as did their sin. For they ate something which had not been given to them for the nurture of that life in which they had been created, but rather against which they had been warned because it would make them lose this life. The bodily manifestation of their consciousness of sin consisted in the shame which they felt, for the latter is the conscience of the body. Thus God gave them something to cover their nakedness. This would calm their conscience because it was given by Him against whom they had sinned. There is a long way between the death of the animal whose skin became the garment that covered their shameful nakedness on the one hand, and the death of the Son of God whose righteousness covers our sin, on the other. Yet they are like the beginning and the end of the same journey.

Let us also consider the death of Abel. What is its place in the context of the Old Testament History of redemption? When for the first time after sin had entered this world the contrast between the righteous and the unrighteous is mentioned, it is God's will to hand the former over to the latter.

That the righteous one should succumb to the unrighteous one is a riddle whose solution is found only in the death of the Son of God. To the first man the victory of the woman's generation over the originator of sin and death had been promised. In Christ that victory is accomplished in such a way that he who brings salvation is handed over to the enemies of God's redemptive work and suffers death at their hands. Thus the death of Abel, the righteous one, prefigures the death of Jesus. Hence we judge the story according to the significance which that death had, namely, as the first instance of the conflict between righteousness and unrighteousness. However, the sacrifice which Abel offered should not be compared with the sacrifice of Jesus and does not prefigure it, for Abel made a sacrifice for himself and not for others.

The conflict between righteousness and unrighteousness increases to the point where Noah and his family are confronted with a world which was perverted beyond remedy and hence doomed to be destroyed. That judgment does not take place however until God has called and appointed Noah to save himself and his family. The deliverance corresponds to the final end of things, namely, to a judgment and a Savior who, once the measure of sin of the human race has been filled, will save the righteous ones into a new world. To compare the church and its members with the ark and Noah's family sheltered in it is a legitimate typological interpretation of that fact, not a mere analogy.

As contrasted with the world of nations left to itself, a specific community of salvation is started with the call of Abraham. In his call we discern the law which presides over the development of this commonwealth of salvation. It is not from Ishmael who was engendered according to the common course of things, but from Isaac alone that the family grew which was destined to become this commonwealth. In the same way later on it is not Esau, notwithstanding his being Isaac's son, but he whom the promise had pointed out. The whole development is exclusively the realization of the divine promise and every claim on the part of man is precluded.

The way Paul uses that fact in Romans 9 and Galatians 4 to demonstrate that the community of salvation is rooted exclusively in the divine promise, is based upon the typological interpretation of those facts. Membership in that community is founded merely upon God's promise, not upon anything that man is in himself or that he does, and all those are excluded from it who think they have a claim of their own.

The promise attached to Isaac cannot be fulfilled however apart from his sacrifice. Upon God's behest Abraham must surrender him to death and receive him again as though from death. He must give evidence of the fact that he believes that even his son's death will not thwart the promise.

Such things had to happen at the beginning of the common-wealth of salvation in order that it should agree with the full realization of salvation. For he through whom this realization is accomplished will pass through death, and the Savior will be one who out of death returns to a new life. In that way the divine behest to sacrifice Isaac and the willingness of Abraham to act accordingly prefigured the only begotten Son of God as one who was surrendered to death and was brought back from it.

But before Abraham saw how the fulfilment of the promise was to begin in Isaac, he encountered Melchizedek, priest of God the Creator. He recognized and acknowledged him as one who in relation to him was a priest, though he did not belong to the generation to whom the promise had been given but rather to a prior one. Abraham considered this priest of God as being of superior dignity to himself, notwithstanding the promise he had received. Therefore when the one comes in whom the promise will be fulfilled, he will not only be the son of Abraham but also be like Abraham, because his priestly office was superior to the ancestor of the family to whom the promise was given. For this reason the king of the nation is called in Psalm 110 a priest of God after the order of Melchizedek. He who as the anti-type of Isaac is doomed to die is also the anti-type of that priest who blest the recipient of the promise, and under whose blessing hand the ancestor of God's people bowed down. The fact however that Melchizedek offered bread and wine to Abraham is in this connection without significance since it was not a priestly ministration. It does not point to the Lord's Supper. Melchizedek's significance lies in the fact that he is a priest who blesses, rather than one who sacrifices.

Out of Isaac there grows the promised family. This takes place in such a way that in the house of Isaac, in Jacob and Esau the same thing repeats itself as with Ishmael and Isaac. The story of Joseph on the other hand describes only an instance of the divine providence as a result of which the family of the promise grew in Egypt into a nation and then was redeemed out of that country. While nothing therefore is prefigured in Joseph and his story, the redemption out of Israel which God accomplished through one taken out of the midst of Israel, whom he appointed as the mediator of his work, has typological significance. Through the mediation of this man his nation was later brought into such a relation to God, that it became God's people and God its God. When God establishes the community of the New Testament this also will be done by way of a redemption from slavery.

The redemption out of Egypt implied the judgment over Egypt. But Israel was to know and to confess that the reason why she escaped that judgment was merely that God wanted to redeem her. Hence the redemption did not take place without the Passover. The blood of the animal slaughtered at God's behest, which was on the homes of the Israelites, saved their occupants from the judgment, and its meat strengthened them for the migration for which they prepared themselves because they believed that now their redemption was about to come.

With reference to that fact Paul says in I Corinthians 5:7, "Christ was sacrificed as our Passover." It is through Christ whose life is given for us into death, and through the hope we put in the forgiveness of sins thereby accomplished that we are saved from the judgment of this world. Similarly through His self-giving He strengthens us for the way to that place where God will truly be our God and we shall be His people. The prerequisite of the former redemption prefigures also that of the New Testament community of God.

The migration of the redeemed people through the desert corresponds to that of the congregation of Jesus on its way to its rest. God provides food and drink, He guides them and dwells with them, yet faith is required lest they go astray or murmur against Him and thus should not arrive at the goal. (I Cor. 10; Heb. 3.)

But it is Israel as a nation that is God's congregation. Hence its priestly office belongs to a family singled out of its own midst. Its sanctuary and the ministration therein are in agreement with that fact. Its worship gives expression to the actual relation of Israel and God, but at the same time and through that very fact the relationship of the New Testament Church to God is thereby prefigured. As a result of the sinful nature of the people, sacrifices are required. For that purpose there is the altar of the burnt offering where sin is atoned for through the priest who alone ministrates in the interior of the sanctuary. There is also the altar of the incense from which the fragrance ascends to the place in which the presence of God is symbolized. Furthermore, there is the table of the shewbread which is the image of the commonwealth as dedicated to God, and the candlestick which provides light in the place where God is served. Again, it is out of the priesthood that the high priest is singled out for the annual sacrifice of atonement. His office starts from the altar of burnt offering and ends before the throne of God.

In this symbolic presentation of the relationship between the national community and God is prefigured the relationship between the Church of Christ and God. In Christ it has Him who has atoned for their sins once for all through His self-offering, as a result of which He was lifted up to God. For this reason the difference between laity and priesthood, and between the holy and the holy of holies has here been abolished. It is the community of the sanctified which as an anti-type serves God in the light of truth through self-dedication and prayer. The congregation itself is the house of God. Yet in that function God both dwells in it and at the same time transcends it. Its high priest is present just as Jehovah was present in the holy tabernacle and yet is above it in heaven. While the church has free access to Him it nevertheless waits for Him to return to her. Thus the relationship of the New Testament Church to God is the anti-type of Israel as symbolized by its sanctuary and its service, yet in the same manner as the Church of Jesus is prefigured by Jehovah's people. We must not forget that in the Old Testament we are dealing with an arrangement for the worship of God given for a national community. Hence it

was in the outward forms and the order of this worship that
expression was to be given to the relation in which this national congregation stood to God. On the other hand, the
relation of the New Testament Church to God as mediated
by Jesus Christ is prefigured by that externally organized
and regulated worship. The New Testament Church is not
a form of natural social life. Rather it is nothing but the
community of those whose salvation has been accomplished.

Just as Moses was the mediator who established Israel's
relationship to God, so now the priest, and particularly the
high priest, is the one who does this. He is the mediator who
protects and actualizes that relationship by restoring the
holiness of the community when that relationship is disturbed by sin, and by ministering in accordance with its
holiness. The functions separated in the old covenant are
united in Christ. In Christ we find connected in an antitypical way both the sacrifice offered by Moses, the blood
of which served to establish a relationship between Israel
and God, and also the annual sacrifice of atonement by
means of which that relationship was continually healed from
the disruption caused by the sin of the people. By sacrificing
Himself once, Christ has sanctified the Church once for all,
thereby establishing its permanent relationship to God.

But the congregation of God was also destined to become
the people of a realm of God on earth. This Israel became,
through the kingship. The intervening time was only a time
of transition in which no typologically significant facts
should be sought, as some have done with regard to Gideon
or Samson. For the occupancy of Canaan was but the beginning of a period in which the people was led toward the
kingship. The kingship toward which that historical process
pointed was that of David and his house to whom a promise
was given similar to that received by Abraham. Just as Abraham was destined to become the ancestor of that nation in
which all families of the earth should be blest, so the kingship which was destined to lead Israel toward the completion of its calling was tied up with David and his family. The

king is the mediator of the power of God as he establishes
his kingdom and makes Israel the people of his kingdom.
Thus in the beginning of that kingdom we can already see
the law both of its own growth and of the development of
God's kingdom. In the same way one discerns the law of the
development of God's people in the family from which the
Jewish nation originated.

David was appointed as king through a prophetic proclamation in which God's revealed will was actualized.
Thereby he was related to Jehovah like a son to his father,
and thus typified Christ the Son of God in His relationship
to the mankind into which He had entered. However, on
his way to the throne David suffered from the enmity of
Saul. Again, when he had become king, he had to overcome the enmity of those nations who plotted against Israel.
Later on when Absalom and the whole nation rebelled
against him, the rebels' counsellor was Ahitophel, his intimate friend. In all these things He is the type of that king
who came into the world to bear witness to the truth and
to have as His subjects those who would obey the truth. His
rule is opposed by Herod who seeks to kill Him, by Pilate
who as the representative of the pagan empire sentences
Him, by the Jewish people who hand Him over into the
procurator's hands, and finally by Iscariot who betrays Him.
While His victory takes place in His Resurrection and Ascension, He will complete His rule only in His future manifestation.

Through David the kingship became a hereditary institution. The rule of the "prince of victory" is continued in
that of the "prince of peace." Analogously Christ, once He
has in His Parousia completed His victory over the enemies
of God's kingdom, will reign in this world with His transfigured Church. The work of the "prince of peace" consisted
in transforming the tent of the tabernacle into a solid sanctuary. In the same way after Christ's Parousia His congregation will be restored to imperishable glory.

But things did not continue in the same way as they

began with David and Solomon. Rather, through the fault both of the nation and of the family of David the disintegration of a kingdom whose throne was the throne of Jehovah began, developed and progressed to the point where the national existence of Israel seemed to be doomed. In that period the history of the kingdom has no typological significance. Yet then the prophetic office began its mediatorial function. What had been one office for Moses is now divided into the mediatorship of priest, king, and prophet. Prophecy as it emerges in this period of the disintegration of the kingdom consists in convicting Israel of her guilt, yet it also keeps alive the continuous promise of God as the hope of the believers in Israel, and bears witness to the fact that that promise would be fulfilled in a glorious restoration of the divided kingdom. The prophets performed that mediatorial function by enduring with Israel the misery into which she had brought herself, by suffering under her lack of repentance and her unbelief, and by being mistreated by the rebellious people.

That mediatorship too corresponded to that of Jesus, who as a prophet was a minister of the circumcision for the truth of God (Rom. 15:8). Though He gathered from them a group of disciples who accepted His message, He was killed by His own people on account of His witness. Jesus is a prophet in that He gathered a community prior to transforming (text: transfiguring) it into a kingdom, just as the restoration of David's kingdom, of which it is the anti-type, did not take place prior to the intervening office of the prophets.

Finally, a restoration of God's people and a rebuilding of the temple took place. It was erected by Zerubbabel of the family of David, and Joshua of the family of Aaron was its priest. But it was the prophetic word of Haggai and Zechariah which encouraged the people to complete it. This activity prefigures the work of Jesus as a work of restoration. He is Zerubbabel to whom Haggai reaffirms the promise given to David, the Branch whose example Zechariah sees in

Joshua, and the prophet the bringer of the spirit of God of whom it is said that it is through him that the work will be accomplished. It is he who built the temple of God in which he officiated as priest and he fulfilled Haggai's prophecy that the glory of that house would be greater than that of Solomon's temple. Thus he restored in a more glorious way what had been done by David and Solomon. At that point the typological history of the Old Testament comes to its close.

The typology of the Old Testament is not confined, as was formerly held, only to those instances which happen to be referred to in the New Testament. Taken by themselves and in isolation it is not feasible to interpret the facts of Old Testament history in a typological way. It is necessary always to interpret a single fact as part of the whole history of the Old Testament. By proceeding in that manner there is no danger that we should arbitrarily single out certain facts. Rather we scrutinze the whole history of the Old Testament for those basic elements which are typical. There is no danger either that with this method individual features of an Old Testament event should be given a wrong interpretation as a result of isolating them. This method resembles the interpretation of a parable. What matters above all is that the specific significance of the total story should be recognized. By doing so its individual features will be given a typological interpretation merely in as much as they are related to the story as a whole. No individual feature will be interpreted in isolation.

2. The Theological Interpretation of the Proclamation of Salvation in the Old Testament

Old Testament history is intertwined with the spiritual interpretation of that history as seen in historical perspective by the Old Testament writers. They are to be understood as bearing witness to the same salvation which is revealed in the New Testament, yet they do so in their historical situation. Thus the spiritual, but historical, understanding of Old Testament history is the prerequisite.

1. I must know that Old Testament manifestations of salvation tend towards those of the New Testament as their goal in which they are integrated into a unity.

2. I have to know their intrinsic development and mutual relationship.

3. I have to discern the place that the individual fact occupies in that process.

4. Finally, I have to ascertain in what respect the content of the New Testament manifestation of salvation has been given a preliminary expression in the Old Testament.

The starting point of the Old Testament manifestation and recognition of salvation is found in the words by which Jehovah addresses the serpent (Gen. 3:14-15). Although in Revelation 12:9 Satan is called "the old serpent" nevertheless in the Old Testament context the word of Jehovah was not addressed to Satan but rather to the serpent from whom the tempting stimulus proceeded, no matter how we interpret that fact. The fact that the serpent crawls on the ground as contrasted with the erect posture of man is meant to indicate to man that the tempter is destined to be subjugated by the man who was tempted by him.

However, it was the woman in the first place to whom the tempter addressed himself. Hence it is said of her that there should be enmity between her and the serpent, between her and his children, and that finally the seed of the woman would crush the serpent's head, while the serpent would merely be able to injure the heel by which its head will be crushed. Hence there will be enmity between the mankind descended from the woman and him through whom by way of deceit the woman was tempted to sin. She will be able to destroy him, and the fact that he will harm her will not impede her from doing so. "The seed of the woman" does not designate an individual but rather the human race descended from her. But just as it was ordained that the temptation should come to the woman rather than to the man, so the woman's seed will triumph and repair the harm done by the woman. This will ultimately be fulfilled by the "one born of a woman." In his birth the destination of the woman was fulfilled in a way necessary for one born of a woman to win the victory over Satan. In this word of God concerning the serpent man has been told once for all what his right attitude must consist in, namely in finding his comfort in the divinely revealed prospect of human life and in believing in the word of promise.

These are the first manifestations of that faith:

1. In Genesis 3:20, the man calls the woman "Eve," that is "life," on account of the promise given to her.

2. The woman exclaims at the birth of her first son, "I have gotten a man from the Lord" (Gen. 4:1). This word taken by itself and apart from its context in the whole body of the Old Testament witness looks as though it did in no way refer to that salvation which will be proclaimed in the New Testament. It appears to be merely an expression of joy over the birth of a son, though one that implies gratitude toward God and thus religion. One further element might be the joy over the fact that this boy was the first child ever born. But it should be remembered that the conception and birth of the son was preceded by God's promise. It is in that connection that her exclamation has to be interpreted. Since as a result of their sin the first pair was doomed to die, their salvation and that of mankind was tied up with the fulfilment of that promise. Now Eve sees the beginning of this fulfilment in the son to whom with the help of God she has given birth. Hence the joy of the exclamation was not so much over the birth of a son, as it was over the fact that the promised salvation of the whole human race had started.

The New Testament witness of salvation states what the final fulfilment of that original promise of God was. It became real in the person of Jesus Christ. In retrospect it is evident in what respect Eve's exclamation referred to the

New Testament manifestation of salvation. With the birth of Jesus that salvation is fully present which started with the birth of the first son of man. We do not say however that Eve rejoiced in the future birth of Jesus or that she believed that in her first son she had already received him who would repair the harm done by her. Rather she rejoiced over the birth because it commenced the realization of that same salvation which according to the New Testament reached its completion with the birth of Jesus.

Similarly Lamech hoped that Noah, that is, the tenth generation, would bring to mankind reprieve from the misery in which it found itself because of the curse which sin had brought over the earth (Gen. 5:29). This hope is fulfilled in the fact that Noah saves mankind by transferring it across the judgment into a new age. Its new life begins with an act of worship in which he became sure that God had determined to place no further curse upon the earth nor to exterminate mankind again. The new generation is newly blest and its life is rendered more easy because it is placed under the order of law. Now life can be more greatly enjoyed. Until the promised end of time history will never again be interrupted as was done by the flood. Rather the generation descending from Noah will see that final end. Noah's relation to Christ is the same as that of the flood to the final judgment. Christ will in fact accomplish what Lamech had hoped that Noah would do.

When Noah says "blest be the God of Shem" and "he shall dwell in the tents of Shem" (Gen. 9:26f.), he knows which of his three descendants will be the one whose history will be crowned by God's dwelling with him. This will be marvelous because having banished man from that place where God was present with him, God has become a God beyond and above man, and the "God the most high." This prophetic blessing commences its fulfilment with the call of Abraham. It is continued in the building of Israel's sanctuary, makes its full appearance when Jesus comes from the Father, and reaches its conclusion in His return. Yet it cannot be said that in verse 26 "Jehovah" designates Christ.

It is in this connection that we must understand Abraham's call (Gen. 12:1 f.), and the word of God that came to him on that occasion. He was told that he would become a great nation and that in him all the families of the earth would be blest. Taken in isolation this word might seem to indicate that Abraham was merely promised to become an ancestor in the same way as other individuals had become the ancestors of other nations. However, in that case the only peculiar feature of the promise would be that he could become an ancestor in a different way than in other instances, and that he would grow into a big nation in a specific way. Nevertheless these features would not lift him above the natural order of things. Once this word of God concerning Abraham had been understood in such a way, the blessing which should be brought through him to all the families of the earth would also be evaluated accordingly. It would result in a kind of happiness belonging to the earthly order of things, and no matter how refined this happiness would be it would nevertheless not be a spiritual one. It would certainly not be the blessing of spiritual salvation which forms the content of the New Testament witness.

However, interpreted in connection with the preceding promise this word of God to Abraham indicates that the fulfilment of the promise is tied up with Abraham, whereas all natural nations live by an intrinsic development. Similarly the nation into which Abraham is to grow is meant to be the place in which that salvation will find its full realization, and to which the New Testament bears witness. It is from this nation that Jesus, the spiritual salvation of the world, went forth. The promise given to Abraham is to be judged in the light of that fact. Furthermore, it is evident now what is the specific aspect of the New Testament history of salvation to which reference is made in this promise. As above mentioned, the future salvation implied in that divine word

lies in Jesus who descended from that nation whose ancestor
Abraham was destined to become.

In the same sense we must understand the revelation
given to Abraham according to which his family should live
in Canaan. That refers not simply to a country in the same
sense as any other nation has a country in which it lives.
Certainly as a nation it needs a country. But in accordance
with its destination that country will not only be its dwelling
place but also the place where God will live in its midst.
What this means can be seen from the New Testament proclamation, both in its reference to things which have already taken place, and in its promises of future things. The
incarnate word lived among men so that they saw His glory.
But that same Jesus will be revealed again in this world
and He will transfigure the community which believes in
Him into the likeness of His glory, so that it will be with
Him and He with it in full union. These two facts realized
in the New Testament were the purpose of the word that
God spoke to Abraham. This does not mean that the family
of Abraham is to be interpreted as designating the church
of Christ, or that Canaan stands for the eternal bliss. Rather
it refers to a real nation, yet one which is the place in which
the blessed communion of God with man is to be restored.

Things are similar with Moses' song of triumph, Exodus
15:1 f. Therein we hear him praising God who has thrown
horse and rider into the sea, and he finds comfort in the hope
that that same God will bring Israel to the mountain of his
property (i.e. Canaan) and will plant her there. Detached
from the total context of the Old Testament witness, this
song seems to be concerned only with the ruin of an enemy
of whom Israel was greatly afraid, and the joyful hope of
this song seems only to indicate that the nation which thus
far had been in a foreign country would obtain its own
land. But we interpret this song of triumph in connection
with Israel's hope which was rooted in the promise given
to Abraham. Consequently the song is not dealing with the
earthly well-being of this specific nation but rather with the

realization of the salvation of mankind inasmuch as it is tied up with that nation. For that same reason when the king of Egypt refuses to accede to the miraculously accredited demand of Moses he opposes thereby the saving will of God. Even a gentile like Pharaoh was able to recognize this, since the word of God manifested itself in his heart and in this case it had also been affirmed through miracles. Hence Moses does not simply rejoice over the ruin of an oppressor of his nation and he does not simply hope that his nation will obtain a dwelling place. Rather, in the fact that his nation had been brought safely through the sea and that its enemies had perished, he sees realized the beginning of that salvation which God would bring about in the midst of that nation, and he rejoices that this salvation will not be confined to that nation but rather will be granted to all the families of the earth.

Yet the hope uttered by Moses in his song of triumph was not fulfilled in the generation which left Egypt. Rather it is said of them in Psalm 95:11, "They shall not come to the place of my rest," meaning the place where God's work in the history of redemption would come to rest or reach his goal in the same way as his work of Creation had been completed. A new generation was destined to arrive there. But difficult times are in store for them too. As foretold in Deuteronomy 32 they would be unfaithful to their God, and not until having received their punishment at the hands of the hostile gentiles, would they finally experience God's help. Since the congregation of God is organized as a nation its enemies too are nations. Likewise when Jehovah finally comes to the assistance of His people, it is, as it were, in a war which He fights for them against their enemies. Consequently we read in Deuteronomy 32:41-42, "I will render vengeance to mine enemies, and will reward them that hate me. I will make mine arrows drunk with blood, and my sword shall devour flesh."

Similarly the king of God's people has been promised that "Thou shalt break them with a rod of iron" (Ps. 2:9), and

He says of Himself in Psalm 18:37, "I will pursue mine enemies, and overtake them; neither will I turn again till they are consumed."

If such words were uttered by a carnally minded person they would express nothing but the hope to obtain a victory over His personal enemies. But He who pronounces them is the king whom God had appointed for His congregation and whose royal power has reached its full realization in Jesus Christ's kingly rule over His church. Since it is evident that the hope of the psalmist extends towards the future completion of that kingdom and of the reign of Israel as promised to Abraham, the hope here expressed is not a carnal one. For whoever opposes God's Annointed opposes the salvation of the world, the saving will of God, who has chosen Israel as His congregation, and hence that man incurs divine judgment.

Once David had established Zion as the center of a kingdom tied up with him and his house, Jehovah too made His dwelling place there. Thus Zion is now the center of the world. This explains why in Psalm 68 the survey of the future course of history sounds like a survey of the world made from Zion. We read there that He whose throne is established upon Zion governs the people of Israel and its land in order to protect it against its enemies until at last all the nations of the earth will render homage to Him (Psalm 68:16-36). Likewise, when David describes the king of the future who brings Israel's kingdom to its full realization and who is called by him "his Lord" (Psalm 110), he sees Him reigning from Zion at the right hand of Jehovah, while all the enemies which now encircle Him will be subjected to Him. This corresponds to David who had triumphed over the nations aligned against him and then was reigning from Zion. In a similar way Solomon in Psalm 72 borrows the image of the ruler, the "son of the king" to whom he addresses his prayer from his own royal office. He reigns from sea to sea; nations and kings serve him; he administers the law; the land under him is blessed with abundant fertility. Similarly in Psalm 45 the glory of Solomon is extolled by means of features which refer specifically to him but which are introduced as describing the glory of the king of God's people whose throne is that of Jehovah. In this psalm it can be seen with special clarity how inappropriate it would be to interpret the details of the description as referring to the king of the New Testament. Rather the total picture of Israel's king, with the features derived from the reigns of David and Solomon merged into one, is to be interpreted as referring to the New Testament salvation, yet without ignoring the fact that it has grown from an historical soil.

In order to illustrate the spiritual interpretation of the Old Testament proclamation of salvation it will be helpful to give two instances which seem to be rather removed from the context of Holy History and in general from that which is the specific subject matter of Holy Scripture, namely Psalm 8 and the Song of Songs. In Psalm 8:6 we read "Thou [God] hast put all things under his [man's] foot." The joy expressed here by David can easily be understood as though he rejoiced merely over the fact that man occupies such a great and exalted position in the universe; yet such joy would have no moral value even if God were recognized in it as the one who had assigned to man such superior power over all the living creatures. Our interpretation will already be modified when we consider what precedes that exclamation, namely, "What is man that thou art mindful of him," etc. For then his joy implies the recognition of that divine grace by which man, who in comparison with the radiant luminaries of the sky is so inconspicuous, has nevertheless been endowed so richly and granted such superiority. The ethical value of the psalm is increased further when we turn to its opening sentence. In it God's glory is found in the fact that out of babes and sucklings he has ordained strength (see Psalm 8:2 A.V.). In other words, he makes them grow in order that they might incapacitate and annihilate that which is opposed to him. It is with reference to this destination of man that David rejoices in the fact that God has endowed man so richly and given him such a high position.

The objection might be raised however whether this fact is connected with the real subject of Scripture, namely, the salvation in which the Christian finds his comfort? We are in a position to answer this question in the affirmative. He who speaks of an enemy and opponent of God whom man is destined to incapacitate and destroy, is one who is familiar with the original promise given by God, according to which the seed of the woman should crush the head of the serpent. For then only is the task of man with which the psalm deals brought into connection with God's forgiving grace, and then only is it related with Holy History, i.e., with a history which starts with the sin of the first man and culminates in the victory of Him who annihilates the enemy by whom man was tempted to sin. We do not contend that the enemy and opponent designates merely and without qualification Satan. Rather when opposition to God is mentioned this rebellion must be interpreted in the light of that primeval fact. Apart from this Gentiles too might refer to their God in the same way. A Parsee, for instance, might state that the good God who had created him had destined him to annihilate God's enemy. But Jehovah, who glorifies himself upon earth in man, is the God of that promise and He will do as, in His forgiving grace, He has promised in the beginning. The psalmist rejoices in man's endowment and superiority because he sees them in the light of that victory which Jesus has won and which He will bring to completion. The fact that God had destined man to annihilate what is opposed to God has been brought to full realization in Jesus. Hence correctly interpreted, Psalm 8 does not simply proffer a truth of the so-called natural religion; that is to say, one which would have been possible outside of Israel too.

Things are different and yet in a way similar with the Song of Songs. Undoubtedly this poem gives expression to the happiness which Solomon and the Shulamite find in each other. The poet describes the glory of that love of man and

woman which is based exclusively on that which they are
for each other as representatives of their sex. Nevertheless
already at this point it should be taken into consideration
that it is King Solomon who describes this happiness.
Though possessing everything, enjoying the most glorious
position and the wealth of life in all its diversity, he nevertheless finds the climax of earthly happiness in this relationship notwithstanding the fact that it is rooted merely
in creation and based upon its order. Hence when he speaks
of his happiness he thereby confirms by means of his own
experience the truth of that which the first man spoke when
he saw the woman.

   But again the question might be raised, does this song
bear witness to salvation? The answer to this question will
be derived from a consideration of the condition of him who
is speaking here. He is the king of God's people. Yet he ranks
all the goods of his kingdom which belong to the natural
order of things behind the happiness which he finds in his
wife and his wife in him. In other words, he subordinates the
glory of his kingdom to a happiness which originates from
the order of creation, that is to say, from the relationship
of man and woman as implied in creation and thus ante-
dating all the diversifications of human status.

   Since he speaks as the king of God's people we must also
consider the prospects of his kingdom. We keep in mind that
he uttered in Psalm 72 the request for a king who would
be in full measure what he himself was only in a typological
and preliminary way. When that future kingdom is realized
it will be the antitype of that happiness in which Solomon
rejoices and which he recognizes as the climax of earthly
happiness. In the same manner as the kingdom of that future
king for whose coming he asked is related to his own, thus
the happiness which that king is to enjoy will be the antitype of his own. In that case however the happiness of love
will no longer be just one detail side by side with others.
Rather the joy which the future king will have in the congregation of his people will imply everything that formed

Solomon's happiness and joy. Since the latter was clinched by the love of man and woman as rooted in the order of creation, the relation of that future king to his people, will be an antitype of that human love. As the antitype of this relationship of man and woman, the relationship of the king to his people will reach its culmination. Hence the Song of Songs must be interpreted both in reference to the union of man and woman as implied in the order of creation, and also in reference to that future completion of the kingdom which was prefigured only in David and Solomon. Interpreted in such a way, the happiness of love which joined Solomon and the Shulamite deserved, according to Solomon's judgment, to be the subject of the Song of Songs. Hence the Song of Songs does not exclusively deal with experiences of natural life, notwithstanding the fact that its subject was chosen from it. But neither the Song of Songs, nor Psalm 45, is an allegory, and we must not expect to find corresponding features for every detail of their text in the New Testament.

In Solomon, Israel's kingdom had reached the climax of its earthly glory. When this glory was destroyed the prophets foretold that the promise would be fulfilled by way of a restoration of that kingdom. God would bring about a change in which Israel would be vindicated as his people over against the hostile world of nations. This final end is envisaged in its relation to the historical circumstances of the prophet and thus the language of the prophecy is shaped by that relationship. Obadiah for instance prophesies against the Edomites who had ransacked Jerusalem. The threat of vengeance is enlarged into this prophecy: "The day of the Lord will come upon all the nations" (v. 15). The whole world of nations will act in the same way as Edom did to Jerusalem, but for that same reason it will be destroyed; but upon Mt. Zion there shall be "deliverance" (v. 17).

Since at that moment Israel was divided it is foretold that as a united nation it will possess not only its own land but also the territory of those who at that time were his enemies, the Philistines and Edomites. Equally since many of the Israelites had been carried into captivity it is said that they shall be brought home again. The prophecy concludes with the words, "The kingdom will be the Lord's" (v. 21).

The prophecy of Joel was given in view of a plague of locusts which was so terrible that the prophecy concerning it becomes the warning that the Day of the Lord is coming. But the prophet also promises that Jehovah will bring about a change. The barns will be full again and that which the locusts devoured will be replaced. This is due to the fact that Jehovah has given to the people "the early rain for your vindication" (Joel 2:23) through which it has been called to repentance.

In chapter three is added the promise of that which shall happen "afterwards." As Jehovah has presently given the prophet, so He will then pour out His spirit over the whole nation and all of them will prophesy. When the terrors of the Day of the Lord will arrive, then, as prophesied by Obadiah, there will be "deliverance" upon Mt. Zion and in Jerusalem, namely, as defined by Joel: "all who call upon the name of the Lord shall be saved" (2:32).

Similarly, the word of Obadiah concerning the return of those carried away, and the judgment over the whole world of nations, is repeated in Joel 3:2, where it says that Jehovah will gather the nations together into the valley of "Jehoshaphat" where His angels will execute judgment. The prophecy terminates with the promise that the land of Israel will flourish in rich abundance, whereas Egypt and Edom, the land of its enemies, will lie waste.

The nations over which David had reigned have now again become Israel's enemies. Therefore Amos resumes the word of Joel: "The Lord roars from Zion, and utters his voice from Jerusalem," in such a way that the tempest of destruction will pass over those nations, but also over Judah, whose palaces will be devoured by fire, and over Israel, whose kingdom though still powerful at present, will perish. To this however Amos adds the promise (9:11-12) that Jehovah

will erect again the fallen tabernacle of David and that He
will build it up again as in the days of old, "that they may
possess the remnant of Edom and all the nations who are
called by my name," that is, those who once had been part
of David's dominion.

Micah, the younger contemporary of Amos, turns his
prophecy against Judah because he was to punish her very
heads. Thus he announces in chapter 3:12 that "Zion shall
be plowed as a field," and that "Jerusalem shall become
a heap of ruins." But in contrast with this he intimates in
4:1 that in the "last days" Zion will be the center of the
world, where all the nations will seek justice and from which
the law will proceed over all the lands. He indicates however
that prior to that event the inhabitants of the city must
emigrate to a foreign country and be captives in Babylon.
This seems to terminate Israel's existence as an independent
nation. In 4:11 Micah also repeats the prophecy of Joel concerning a day of battle in which the army of many nations
will attack Jerusalem, yet will perish in the vain attempt.
This will not happen however until the people of Zion has
been brought to Babylon and again has been redeemed from
that place. At that time Assyria was the dreaded enemy,
consequently it is not only said in 5:2 that a ruler will come
from Bethlehem as David did formerly and that under him
the whole of Israel will be gathered together again, but also
that when Assyria comes, leaders will not be lacking, and
that they will carry the war into her territory. In that time
Israel will be among the nations what the lion is among the
beasts of the forests (Micah 5:8). What happened when
Jehovah brought Israel from Egypt into its land will then
be repeated. God will restore Israel while the empire of
the world of nations will be its servants (Micah 7:12 f.).

Isaiah 1-35 has its parallels in Micah 1-5. There too it is
foretold to the people that they will be brought to extreme
distress before the prophecy will be fulfilled. Let us consider chapter 7 first. The issue there is this: Will Ahaz seek
support against his enemies from God or from Assyria? As a

result of his choosing the latter one the promised salvation will be realized—so the prophet says—in the midst of a distress caused by this foolishness on the part of the house of David. When in this connection it is announced in v. 14, "Behold a virgin will conceive and give birth to a son," it is bad exegesis to see in this prediction a direct reference to Mary and her Son Jesus. It is true that Matthew (1:23) finds the fulfilment of that prophetic word in Mary's conceiving and giving birth. But the right to use that passage in such a way is not impaired when we first interpret it as we did above, i.e., in its historical context. Just as little as the words "butter and honey he will eat" can be literally applied to Jesus, so little can the pregnancy of the "young woman" and the name "Emmanuel" given to the new born child be interpreted directly in the New Testament sense.

The child will feed on milk and honey because, as the prophet says in v. 15, the land has been laid waste during the war between Egypt and Assyria, and is no longer cultivated. The salvation designated by the term "Emmanuel" will not arrive until just such a complete destruction of the Holy Land and its people has taken place and the salvation will proceed from it in the same miraculous way as the miracle of a virgin's conceiving and giving birth would be. This is a sign that Jehovah Himself will give, since the sign which the prophet had offered to Ahaz in confirmation of his message had been rejected. Now the nation must be brought to extreme distress until the situation will change. Hence what is said in a prophetic passage concerning a virgin conceiving and giving birth is not meant in the literal sense but rather is an image chosen to express the absolute miracle of the coming of the promised salvation.

When Isaiah says (9:6) however, that "a child has been born to us," the statement is to be interpreted in the literal sense. It refers to Him who sits "on the throne of David" and whose coming will make an end of all war and break the yoke lying upon the shoulders of the nation. The realization of this salvation is likened to a light seen rising above it by a people that walks in the darkness. But the significance which this Son has for the people is expressed in terms of the consequences which His sitting upon the throne of David carry with it. He is a miraculous counsellor, a strong and mighty one, a prince of peace, and one who is eternally the father of His nation. In Him the promised king will then be present, as requested in Psalm 72.

It is similar in Isaiah 11:1 f. In contrast with the judgment over Assyria which is now the scourge in the hand of Jehovah, and in contrast with the cutting of the proud forest of her power, the prophet speaks of a branch which will come forth from the cut stem of Jesse. This signifies a ruler like David who will proceed from the family of Jesse which at the present moment has been reduced to the low status of its pre-kingly position. The rule of that king is described in a manner similar to Psalm 72. Isaiah also says that the wild beasts "shall not do any damage on my holy mountain, for the whole land is full of the knowledge of the Lord as the waters cover the sea" (11:9). In this context the "land" in parallel with "my holy mountain" designates the Holy Land, which has now become a "resting place" (v. 10), i.e., a place of undisturbed peace embracing both the human and non-human creatures, because its people have arrived now at a full knowledge of God. The rest of the world is contradistinguished from that land. In the branch proceeding from the root of Jesse they will discern the banner around which they will gather. Of this prophecy too it should be said that it is the picture in its totality rather than its details which prefigures the future. One should not interpret the details in an allegorical way. Where one goes so far as to refer the prophecy to the expansion of the Christian faith, "the holy mountain" is transformed into the church and the physical state of peace into a spiritual one.

Parallel with events in the Holy Land is the return of the exiled people. This is the case here too. Since at that time Judah and Ephraim are arrayed against each other as enemies, the cessation of that enmity is foretold. Likewise since the nations who were formerly under David's dominion and who acknowledged the sovereignty of the people of God are now its enemies, the restoration of the united nation will imply the regaining of dominion over them. When the nation will return from the foreign country, its way will be prepared in the same miraculous way as was done when they were redeemed out of Egypt. In chapter 13 the judgment over Babylon as brought about by the Medes is first described as the fate of a conquered city which is rendered forever into a wilderness. But then it is enlarged into the picture of the day of Jehovah when sun and moon and stars will lose their light and all evil things on earth will receive their punishment. Yet this picture of the final end of things changes again into another one in which Jehovah restores Israel in her land. The nations will bring her back and serve her as man servants and maid servants in Jehovah's country in the same way as Israel had formerly served them.

Conversely, in Isaiah 24 f. the judgment over the whole earth alternates with a judgment over Assyria which will collapse under the sword of Jehovah. This is the prophecy as uttered prior to Sennacherib's invasion into the Holy Land. Afterwards it will assume a different form.

The outlook which characterizes Isaiah 44-66 is succinctly indicated in the saying in 40:1, "The Lord will say, comfort ye, comfort ye my people." The passage deals with the comfort which Jehovah will prepare in the future for His vexed people. He will vindicate himself over against the pagan deities and his people over against the idolatrous nations. He foretells the things to come, in order that when they take place he should be known as the God who had appointed these things in advance and known them. He calls upon a non-Israelitic sovereign through whom as his servant he executes these things. In advance he mentions his name, namely Koresh (Cyrus). Having destroyed Babylon the capital of the empire which keeps Israel captive, he will give orders to rebuild the house of Jehovah and the city of Jerusalem. God also appoints a prophet for His people, who

through the word of His witness will restore Israel and teach
the nations the law of Jehovah. Yet that man will suffer to the
fullest the fate of a prophet. He will be misunderstood by
His people and die like a criminal. But after these things
He will be glorified. Not only His people but all the other
nations too will recognize Him and the rulers will bow
before Him. In both instances Jehovah is glorifying Himself: in the fact that Cyrus serves Him by executing His
judgment over Babylon and by restoring His house and city,
and that His witness is exalted to a place of honor from the
humiliation into which it had been abased by the people
in their ignorance.

The events that are described here conjointly were not
fulfilled simultaneously but rather in succession. When Cyrus
came, the servant of Jehovah was not yet present. Babylon
fell and the commonwealth of Israel was restored; but that
redemption and glorification of Israel which is the prophecy
had been coupled with the ruin of Babylon, did not take
place. This reminds us of the prophecy in Jeremiah 29:10.
Therein God announced to the exiles in Babylon that He
would come to them when Babylon's seventy years were
over, and that He would fulfill His promise. Yet the prophecy
continues in Jeremiah 29:14, "I shall gather you from all the
nations and all the places to which I have driven you."
Since the promise refers to the final goal of the present eon,
one would expect that together with these things the promise
given in 31:31 f. would be fulfilled too. There it is predicted
that in the new order of things the will of Jehovah would be
written upon everybody's heart. But later on Daniel is informed that in lieu of the seventy years of Jeremiah, seventy
seven-fold times must elapse until the final fulfilment of the
promise will take place (Dan. 9:24-25).

In Haggai the fulfilment of the prophecy, which in other
respects is identical with the former one, is connected with
the new temple. The whole world will be agitated and as a
result the treasures of all the nations will come to the
temple. Then Jehovah will fill His house with glory and

grant peace to that place. The prophet connects the realization of the promise not only with the restoration of the temple but also with Zerubbabel. When by that upheaval of the world the thrones and empires have been overthrown, God will use Zerubbabel and do with him as one does with a signet ring. The restoration of the Israelitic commonwealth is the guarantee that that which has been restored will be brought to its final destination.

Zechariah too repeats the former prophecy. He starts from the misfortune which had befallen the territory which was formerly David's kingdom. Continuing he speaks in 9:9 about Zion. He announces that her king is arriving, not one who will ride on a war horse, for no horses and chariots will be found under him in Ephraim and Jerusalem. Rather, he will reign in peace "from sea to sea and from the river to the ends of the earth." Yet side by side with that prediction we are also told that in Jehovah's hand Zion will be like a hero's sword against those of Javan, and that God will help His nation win the victory over her enemies. As is shown in Zechariah 10:3-5, this is not only a prediction of the Maccabees' war but also of a final victory; yet one to be interpreted in the light of the corresponding revelations in Daniel. Both ideas are legitimate: that the judgment of ruin will not affect Zion, and also that Israel will win the victory over her enemies.

An entirely different picture of the future is given in Zechariah 11. The 30 shekels which the speaker receives as his wages (Zech. 11:12), remind one of Iscariot. Would it therefore be correct to say that he who speaks is Jesus? No; the prophet is speaking of himself. Yet he refers to the mission of the prophet in general, which in his person he represents. He introduces himself as one who is commissioned by Jehovah to tend the flock of humanity which is destined for slaughter. He has abandoned the world of nations which he has delivered of three nefarious shepherds within a month. Yet from Israel, which he continues to supervise, he receives thirty shekels, i.e., the wages for one month. In other words, Israel feels grateful only for that protection which she enjoys in common with the world of nations. After having broken one of the two staffs with which he had tended his flock, and thus having dissolved his connection with the world of nations, the prophet breaks also the other one in order to "dissolve the brotherhood between Juda and Israel" (Zech. 11:14).

The latter act has been interpreted as referring to the separation of Christ's church from the Jewish people remaining outside of it. While this interpretation is not wrong, yet in the context of the prophetic saying Zechariah merely predicts a national mishap more serious than the separation of the two kingdoms. Thus from this picture of the future we learn that the gravest guilt and the most terrible misfortune are still ahead of the prophet's people. They will become guilty before him who at that time will be their shepherd and whom the prophet symbolizes, since in him the prophetic mission in general is portrayed.

A different picture of the future is found in chapters 12-14. Here the prophet envisages the ultimate settlement of the conflict between Israel and the world of nations. In these chapters the salvation of the oppressed Holy City begins with an act of Jehovah in which He pours out the spirit of humble request over the oppressed ones. As a result they begin to bewail one who has been slain just as they had bewailed the slaying of Josiah, whose death they considered as the climax of their misery (Zech. 12:10). In John 19:37 the slain one is Jesus. Yet within the context of the prophecy He is one who was killed by an enemy of the nation just as Josiah had been. Similarly when they bewail Him, they do so as a result of the pouring out of the spirit of prayer, with which Jehovah has started the extermination of the enemies. The passage in Zechariah 13:7 should be compared with this. There Jehovah calls for the sword to kill the shepherd of the flock of Israel whom He had appointed, in order that they should be a flock without a shepherd to be purified in misery until the remnant would call on God again. How is it that John recognized Jesus in that slain one? Significant for this interpretation is a feature which we find in Luke 18:32, "He will be handed over to the gentiles." It is through the Gentiles that Israel is deprived of her Savior. Yet when they lament the fact that they have lost Him, that will be the beginning of their salvation.

In Malachi, finally, the Day of Jehovah which the people desire impatiently appears as a day of terror. Since everything that is evil will then be removed from Israel, that day would lead to Israel's complete ruin unless Jehovah would send ahead of Himself and the Mediator of the new order a Messenger like Elijah who would call them to repentance. According to Matthew 11, John the Baptist is that Messenger. Nevertheless Jesus whose coming he prepares, states that He did not come to judge the world. The explanation is that what is called by Malachi the Day of Jehovah is differentiated in its historical fulfilment as the appearance of Jesus in humility on the one hand, and His glory on the other.

It will be the day when Jehovah will establish the promised new relationship with His people Israel, because they repent. Therefore He first calls them to repentance as He actually did through John the Baptist. He will give another call before he returns for judgment. In the meantime Israel will be converted to Him.

It should be evident by now that in our spiritual understanding of the Old Testament witness of salvation we differ essentially from those who dispense with the arrangement indicated by us, and who transpose all individual features of the Old Testament directly into those of the New Testament. This procedure as applied to the proclamation of salvation is as illegitimate as is that typological interpretation of Old Testament history in which every detail of an event has its analogy in the New Testament. We reject that kind of typological interpretation of the Old Testament because in it the statements are not truly interpreted but rather so to speak transposed into the New Testament like an interlinear

translation. Yet the application should be similar to a translation in which the mentality of one language is substituted
for the other one. The former method fails to interpret the
Old Testament Scriptures in an historical way. Yet there can
be no correct spiritual understanding of the Old Testament
when the historical interpretation is omitted. The historical
interpretation of the Old Testament requires two things:
The events of Old Testament history must be taken as pre-
figurations (that is the prerequisite of their interpretation);
and the salvation to which the Old Testament bears witness
must be understood in a spiritual way. Yet in both cases
the historical conditions in which they are found have to be
respected.

Our spiritual understanding of the Old Testament implies
its historical interpretation. For instance, notwithstanding
the fact that Melchizedek is mentioned in Hebrews 7 we did
not misinterpret that passage, e.g., by seeing in him an appearance of the Logos or the Angel of Jehovah or something
similar, but rather we described him in accordance with the
narrative as the king of a Canaanite city who was the contemporary of Abraham.

Similarly we did not interpret the tabernacle which was
commanded in the law as a copy of the tabernacle already
present then in heaven, nor as a prefiguration of the body of
Christ, but rather took it in the way Moses was told to build
it, namely, as the holy tent in which God was dwelling in
the camp of His people Israel. It was on this basis that we
interpreted the institution of the tabernacle. We consider
the difference between the national commonwealth of Israel
and the Church of Jesus Christ. Yet while the dwelling of
God with men was entirely different there than in the New
Testament where Christ is with God, nevertheless the Old
Testament tabernacle prefigures Christ.

We interpret each single event of the Old Testament in
the context of the whole history of the Old Testament, and
the details of each event in relation to the event as a whole;

and we discover their typological significance on that basis. By this method it was not necessary to contend that it was impossible to interpret certain events in their proper sense because that would be unworthy of Holy Scripture, whether the narrative seemed purely superficial or if it contained sinful features. The ancient interpreters proceeding in that manner maltreated the stories of the Old Testament until they finally forced upon them an interpretation in which they believed to have gotten rid of the purely natural or sinful nature of the narrative. This was done, for instance, by Hippolytus with the story of Jacob's betrayal of Esau. He changed it into a story worthy of Holy Scripture by interpreting Isaac as God the Father, Rebecca as the Holy Spirit, Jacob as Christ, Esau as the Jewish people, the old age of Isaac as the fulness of time, his blindness as the spiritual darkness of the world, and the kids as converted sinners. We understand, however, that not everything that is recorded of Abraham, Isaac and Jacob is to bear witness to their holiness. Similarly when the book of Esther tells of the way the Jews made use of their permission to take measures against their enemies, this is not to be interpreted as a trait recommended for imitation, particularly since in that book the name of God is not even mentioned. Rather, the book is to be read as a record of the origin of the Feast of Purim, offering a picture of the condition in which the Jews found themselves in the land of their enemies.

Although in our days such misinterpretations are no longer customary, similar ones nevertheless are practiced in the spiritual interpretation of the Old Testament proclamation. It is true that in interpreting Psalm 8 the exegetes will no longer ask the question, what was meant by the animals over which man rules? For instance, are the birds of the heaven to be interpreted as the blessed ones and the fish of the sea as the souls in purgatory? Nevertheless Stier is not content with the clear text of the psalm. He holds that the reign of Christ is described therein. Hence he thinks that in the enumeration of the animal world all the powers and beings and bodies of the heavens are introduced as the flock of the great Shepherd Christ.

The reason the spiritual interpretation of the Song of Songs has not yet advanced beyond such allegorizing can easily be seen. King Solomon, with whom the song deals, is e.g., directly identified by Hengstenberg with the heavenly Solomon, and the Shulamite with the Church of Jesus Christ. The skin of the Shulamite, parched by the sun, and its dark color, point to the church's form of a servant and to the consequences of the heat of her troubles. The fact that the sons of her mother are angry with her means the enmity of the nations against her. The watchmen of the city of Jerusalem are the angels and so are the sixty heroes surrounding Solomon's portable throne. The sixty queens are the principal nations of Christianity, the eighty concubines are the subordinate nations, the innumerable virgins the nations which have not yet been converted. In our view however, everything in Psalm 8 and in the Song of Songs retains its peculiar nature and historical character. Yet we interpret it in such a manner that there is no cleavage between them and the true meaning of Scripture.

B. THE SPECIFIC CHARACTER OF NEW TESTAMENT INTERPRETATION

The New Testament proclaims the same salvation as we experience and also the same mode of experience. This witness originates from the Church of Jesus to which we too belong, although it was borne originally by its Jewish members. In view of these facts the nature of the New Testament would not seem to require a further qualification of the interpreter's task, and the events and the message recorded therein would seem to be directly intelligible to the Christian believer, were it not for the fact that the New Testament was intimately connected with the Old Testament. As a

result the events recorded in the New Testament are antitypes of those in the Old Testament and its message is proclaimed in the language of the Old Testament. Just as the
Old Testament would lose its saving significance if its content were interpreted as ordinary history rather than as holy
history, so also the spiritual value of the New Testament
would be diminished by such a purely historical interpretation in which the antitypical character of its events and the
Old Testament forms of expression of its message were not
appreciated. As a result the antitypical character of the New
Testament will thus appear incidental, and the Old Testament terminology of the New Testament irrelevant or the
former is interpreted as a proof of the unhistorical character
of the facts, and the latter one as a result of the Jewish
narrowness of the New Testament writers. While in the
former instance, people fail only to recognize how important
is the fact that the New Testament is related to the Old,
in the latter instance, the value of the New Testament itself
inasmuch as it is related to the Old Testament is also dis-
paraged.

We start with a consideration of the connection which
exists between the facts recorded in the Old Testament and
those in the New, and then investigate the way in which the
interpretation of the New Testament facts is determined by
their relation to the Old Testament.

1. The Typological Understanding of the New Testament

The events of the New Testament are not new as contrasted with the old, which dissolved and vanished as they
came to pass, but are rather antitypes which bring a preliminary history to its conclusion and fulfill a prophecy. New
Testament events belong to the same process as that by
which they were foretold, yet they are not a mere serial
continuation of that process, but rather on the same line
they begin a new series which contrasts with the earlier one.

Hence the facts of the New Testament have to be studied under the following viewpoints:

1) How much does their connection with the history which led toward them and the prophecy which announced them determine the formal aspect of these new things?

2) How far is the fulfilment of the predictive history or prophecy influenced by the newness of the things in which it is fulfilled?

New Testament history begins with the conception and birth of John the Baptist, which antedates that of Jesus by six months. Thus the prophecy of Malachi is fulfilled, although Malachi only predicted that Elijah would precede the coming of Jehovah and of Him who would usher in the new order of things before the Day of Jehovah. Since Jehovah's coming to His people takes place in the fact that the man Jesus enters into this world, the "before me" of Malachi 3:1 is realized in the conception and birth of this Elijah as it precedes that of the man Jesus. Thus John's birth is announced in Luke 1:17 in the words of the prophecy of Malachi.

Again, when John makes his appearance as the prophet of his people, the fact is also recorded as the fulfilment of that prophecy. John, in turn, announces the one who is to come after him as one who has the winnowing fork in his hand, "to clear his threshing floor" (Matt. 3:12), while he says to the Pharisees and Sadducees, "Who has warned you to flee from the impending wrath?"

Jesus makes His public appearance after him. Yet the first manifestation of Jesus was not to be that of a judge. Rather He continues the activity of John in His own way. That fact is indicated by the evangelists, in that the proclamation of Jesus to the people is expressed in the same terms as that of John. For that reason John can ask Jesus, "Art thou he that should come, or do we look for another?" (Matt. 11:3.)

Matthew describes the conception of Jesus as the fulfilment of Isaiah 7:14. That prophecy announced that the manner of salvation would be just as miraculous as a virgin's conceiving and giving birth would be. What was an adequate image there, now becomes an historical fact, which is in accordance with the nature of salvation. Similarly what was said about a salvation to be realized is now applied to the Savior as He actually enters into this world. He comes in a miraculous manner, and not as a result of the natural propagation of mankind. The Old Testament prophecy is retained in its historical context. We do not re-interpret it on account of the manner in which it was fulfilled.

Likewise, Mary was told that Jesus would sit on the throne of His father David, in accordance with the promise given to David and his house. But according to Matthew the genealogy of David terminates in Joseph, the one to whom the angel says, "Joseph thou Son of David." Similarly in Luke 2 only the fact that Joseph was of the family of David is mentioned and emphasized. But how then is Jesus the Son of David? This is done, according to Matthew, when Joseph is induced through a divine manifestation in a dream to receive Mary into his home so that it was in his home where she gave birth to Jesus. In this fashion Mary's child became a Son of David. Just as Jesus was not the product of the propagation of the human race, so also did the house of David not bring Him forth out of itself. He entered the house of David in the same manner as He entered mankind. Just as He became the "son of man," so also the "Son of David." Thus He is "the seed of David . . .the seed of Abraham . . . the seed of the woman," i.e., "the son of man." The whole race to whom the promise was given is present in this single one because the promise is fulfilled through Him and in Him.

Jesus was born in Bethlehem and we read in Matthew 2:5 that the scribes too knew of no other place. They had learned it from Micah 5:2. That prophecy is analogous with the idea of Isaiah 11:1 where the promised one is compared with a branch that would grow forth from the cut down stem of Jesse. The meaning is that the ruler for whose coming Israel waits will not come from Zion but rather from Bethlehem. When He appears the House of David will have relapsed into the low and inconspicuous state in which the house of Jesse was at the time when David was called to become king and prior to it. In that prophecy the emphasis is placed upon the circumstances in which His birth would take place rather than upon its locality. But now He is in fact born in Bethlehem. What in Micah symbolized the low estate in which the House of David would be at the time when the Savior appeared has now become an historical fact. He comes as the Son of David, whose house was then of a humble condition. It was by the decree of taxation issued by the emperor of the world that Joseph the son of David was compelled to go to Bethlehem with Mary, while the man who ruled in Jerusalem, the royal city, was an Idumean who reigned under Roman sovereignty! Luke's record shows clearly that the king promised to Israel was born in circumstances which were symptomatic of the low estate of His people and His family.

When He made His public appearance to His people He came from Nazareth. While Scripture does not prophesy His appearance in such a manner as to indicate the locality, Matthew nevertheless states that Joseph moved to Nazareth in order that the word of the prophet should be fulfilled: "He shall be called a Nazarene" (Matt. 2:23). The latter term is to be interpreted however according to the way it was understood by His contemporaries who gave Him that name. They called Him a Nazarene, thereby refusing to recognize His dignity, because His outward appearance seemed to contradict His claim. That such a thing would happen, had indeed been foretold by all the prophets and not in one passage only. For this reason the evangelist says, "by the prophets." Isaiah 53 should particularly be compared. The thing that matters is the meaning connected with the term "Nazarene" rather than the title itself.

It had not been foretold that the appearance of the Messiah would be preceded by a baptism as was the case when

John enjoined the people to be baptized. It had been said however that the coming of Jehovah would be preceded by "a voice crying" in order to announce that He was about to appear (Is. 40:3 f.). In Isaiah that call is one of comfort for those who desire salvation, in Malachi it is one to repentance. For the coming of Jehovah will carry with it the judgment against sinners who are not willing to be moved to repentance. His coming must be recognized in its twofold aspect, namely, as bringing salvation and judgment. Hence when John the Baptist prepares the way, he proclaims both that sins should be confessed and that the salvation which was about to be revealed should be accepted. His baptism is a baptism of repentance yet it is connected with a promise for those who receive it in the right spirit. This shows that the work of the Baptist was foretold in the Old Testament. He prepares the way for the God who comes to sinners for judgment and to those who repent for salvation. But the manner in which John placed the people under the demand to be baptized by him was not foretold.

Concerning the "servant of Jehovah" who was to execute His work in Israel and in the world of nations it was said in Isaiah 42: "I will give my spirit to him." Since this servant of Jehovah made His appearance in Jesus the spirit of God descended upon Jesus when He submitted Himself to John's baptism. Thereby His life becomes a vocation in the service of God who through Him will manifest Himself to His people. Though the descent of the spirit of God took place within Him, this event was nevertheless rendered visible both to Him and to John. This fact had not been foretold by Isaiah. Nevertheless the event as a whole is the fulfilment of his prophecy.

When the activity of the Baptist had been disrupted by His imprisonment, Jesus continued his work. The proclamation of both men is expressed in the same words on purpose. Thus Jesus became the servant of Jehovah who had been spoken of in Isaiah 53. Yet the fact that He made His appearance in Galilee is told by Matthew as being the fulfilment of the things prophesied in Isaiah 9:1-2. The idea that the light of salvation will rise in the midst of greatest distress is expressed by the prophet in the words that Jehovah would glorify the land upon which He had formerly brought contempt, namely the land of the northern border. What originally was an image used to express the prophetic prediction is now an historical fact which is the appropriate fulfilment of that prophecy. The word of Jesus is proclaimed in the region where spiritual ignorance is greatest. This instance resembles Micah 5:2.

The work of a prophet consisted in bearing witness and in confirming his witness by means of miracles. Such also was the activity of Jesus. Yet His signs consisted in healing. For the fact that He is the Savior of the world has to be manifested by an appropriate activity. Hence when Matthew records the healing work of Jesus he states in 8:17 that that fact is a fulfillment of Isaiah 53:4. The servant of Jehovah takes upon His shoulders the burden of the misery which He finds, not only to bear it but also to take it away.

The people remain indolent towards the activity of Jesus. This according to Matt. 13:14 f., is a fulfilment of Isaiah 6:9. In the latter passage the prophet is informed that the prophetic word will remain without effect until the impending judgment has been executed. At that time it was the judgment through the Assyrians and the complete devastation of the country. Now things will happen in the same manner as in the days of the prophet Isaiah: the word spoken by Jesus the prophet will have no effect upon His people in order that the judgment, namely its rejection, should be accomplished. For not until that judgment has come will the people search their heart. In that way Jesus connects the judgment with the prospect that the people will be converted.

By entering into Jerusalem, the Galilean prophet presents Himself as the son of David. According to Matthew 21:4 f. the prophecy of Zechariah 9:9 is fulfilled in that event. In that passage the prophet tells Zion to rejoice because her king was coming, meek and sitting on an ass, etc. Thereby he indicates the character and nature of that king. Though as the king of His nation He is destined to rule over the whole world He nevertheless shows meekness and kindness, and is peaceful and inconspicuous. This prophetic word was fulfilled in the whole appearance of Jesus. It was not simply a prediction of this special episode of the Messianic entrance into Jerusalem, and its fulfilment is not confirmed to this single event. But Jesus' entry into Jerusalem is characteristic of His nature in the same way as the expression "sitting upon the foal of an ass" characterizes the nature of the future king of Israel whom the prophet announces. The same kind of relation is found between His entry into Jerusalem and His conduct as the Savior and King of Israel. Thus it can be said that in a single event or a special aspect of the outward appearance of Jesus a word of Scripture was fulfilled, although that prophetic saying had in mind His whole appearance and person.

Characteristically Matthew has in 21:5, "say to the daughter of Zion" instead of the original "Rejoice greatly, daughter of Zion." The verb "rejoice" would not be appropriate here because this is not a promise given to Zion, but rather the coming one manifests Himself by his weeping over Zion. Zion is to know that her king is coming and Jesus Himself informs her. By the manner of His entry He calls the attention of those who have eyes to see to the prophecy of Zechariah. But His arrival marks the beginning of His Passion whereas Zechariah states of Him that He will win dominion from one corner of the world to the other. Unlike the New Testament, the prophet does not differentiate between the former and the latter manifestation of the Messiah.

From John 13:18 we learn that Jesus Himself quoted Psalm 41:9 as fulfilled in Him. There David painfully complains with reference to Ahitophel, "He who ate his bread with me has lifted his heel against me." In other words, in the history of the true king of God's people, the same things are repeated which were experienced by David with whom the kingdom of God's people had started. It is not an incidental feature of David's history that His kingdom should be jeopardized by those who had formerly recognized Him as the king appointed by Jehovah. Since that feature is essential for the history of the kingdom which prefigures the true one, it must repeat itself in the history of Him whom David's person and history foretell.

Matthew tells in 27:3 ff. of the end of Iscariot in words which are intended to be reminiscent of that of Ahitophel (II Sam. 17:23). Then in v. 9 he refers to the words of Zechariah concerning the 30 shekels of silver which form the wages of the prophet. The 30 shekels spent by Jesus' people in order to get rid of Him are those of that payment. They do not want a shepherd who will guide them differently than he guides other nations, since they are concerned with their earthly well-being only, and do not care for their redemption from sin. In this respect the two events are in agreement, although there it is the shepherd of the nation who receives the 30 shekels as his wages, and here it is he who betrays Him just as Ahitophel betrays his king. Similarly, while originally the number 30 is associated with the idea of tending for one month the flock destined for slaughter, nevertheless through the historical fact that Iscariot made an agreement with the leaders of his people the same amount is in an analogous way used as the price for which Iscariot betrays his Lord and Savior.

In Luke 18:32 (cf. Matt. 20:19) it is said of the Son of Man that "He will be handed over to the Gentiles." This actually took place because the Jewish people were then under Gentile sovereignty and lacked the authority to execute capital punishment. Nevertheless the fact remains that the Savior of Israel was brought to death through the Gentile authorities (I Tim. 6:13). Notwithstanding the fact that the Jewish people were guilty of Jesus' death, nevertheless the sentence was executed by the Gentile ruler. This explains that in John 19:37 the evangelist quotes Zechariah 12:10, "They shall look upon him whom they have pierced" as referring to the thrust of the spear of the soldier who would have killed Jesus if He had not yet been dead. Here, as well as in the prophetic passage, those who "shall see" are not identical with those who "have pierced." In the context of the prophetic passage the people upon whom Jehovah has poured out a spirit of supplication will look around for Him whom the enemy has pierced. In the same way Israel will in the future look bewailingly at Him whom the pagan authorities gave into death. In Zechariah the two facts of the death through the enemy and the bewailing of the loss on the part of Israel are close in time to each other. In the historical fulfilment of the prophecy however, the bewailing of the slain one is separated from His death by the judgment which Israel will previously suffer for her guilt. It is in the future that they will long for Him whom they had handed over to the Gentiles for execution.

The mocking words uttered by those who were gathered beneath the cross of Jesus are expressed in the words of the 22nd Psalm. In John 19:24 it is also said that one passage of this psalm was fulfilled in the fact that the soldiers divided the garments of Jesus among themselves. Furthermore Jesus Himself prays the initial words of the same psalm. Notwithstanding these facts this psalm is originally a prayer of David, the occasion of which can be found in his history (I Sam. 23:25-26). Yet the mind in which David spoke there, corresponds to that in which Jesus speaks here, and the same relationship prevails between the moment in David's history whose memorial this psalm is, and the moment in which Jesus prays its opening words.

David was in imminent danger of falling into the hands of Saul, and he describes in the psalm what in that case he had to expect of his adversary. Hence he implores God to save him. How different is the manner in which Jesus used the words of this psalm! He asks God that he should deliver him from his suffering through death. He is already doomed to die, whereas David only anticipates death. That Jesus' supplication has been granted can be seen in the fact that a few moments later He passes away exclaiming, "Father, into thy hands I commit my spirit." It is by passing through death that He obtains His kingdom.

Jesus' death and resurrection and ascension as well as His passing to God through death form the end for which He came into this world. In that fact we find the antitypical nature of His life as contrasted with the whole preceding prefigurative history, and the fulfilment of the whole of prophecy. This is the victory of the "seed of the woman" over the serpent whose head has been crushed by the heel which it attempted to bite. Here, the only son on whom salvation depends is brought back to life from the death into which He had been surrendered like Isaac. He is the priest who offers Himself to God as the sacrifice which atones for the congregation. By the death which He suffers for the atonement of their sins He becomes their intercessor in the same way as the Jewish priest who offered the blood of an animal for the atonement of the community. He fulfils the confident expectation of David who stated in Psalm 16:10 that he was sure that he would live on until he could hand over his kingdom to his heir (Acts 2:25 f.).

Similarly when it is said of the servant of Jehovah that "He will lengthen his days" when His people have made His life a "guilt" (asham) as though they thereby repaid a debt to God, this fact is now fulfilled in Jesus. By killing Him the people thought they would render a service to God, yet through His death He entered into a state of unending life. He who "after the flesh" was born out of Israel is now, according to Hebrew 7, in a state of life which places Him into the same relationship to the seed of Abraham as Melchisedek was to Abraham. Like David He has also triumphed over the enemies who intended to destroy Him, and He sits at the right hand of God waiting for the moment when God will subject to Him all His enemies. In the interval between His passing away and the return which is foretold of Him, He is the antitype both of David and Melchisedek, that is priest-king, royal priest (Psalm 110).

Everything that in the Old Testament was foretold for the "latter days" has now commenced to be realized. According to Hebrews 9:26 Christ is revealed at the end of time to remove sin and He will reappear for the salvation of those who wait for Him. In that way there is an interval between the beginning and completion of the realization of the things prophesied. During that period His people living in communion with Him will continue His prophetic work in this world in order to gather a community for Him. In time, He makes of them the community of His spirit, and by the latter they are enabled to accomplish their task. Those who have seen and heard the miraculous pouring out of the spirit are reminded by Peter (Acts 2:16 f.) of the prophecy of Joel according to which the time would come when Israel would no longer need a prophet because Jehovah would pour out His spirit over the whole congregation. In Joel this prediction is succeeded by the description of the terrors which the Day of Jehovah will bring. To Peter the things that he has experienced at that moment are the beginning of the fulfilment of the prophecy. For the spirit had descended upon all those who were gathered together by their faith in Jesus and thus they had been moulded into an integrated community. All the subsequent events are indicative of the never-changing presence of the spirit of God. The end of this period in which Christ will be manifest again and all the consequences of that event will thus be in accordance with the picture of the Day of Jehovah as given by Joel.

Baptism now provides what circumcision had signified as a rite of membership of the people of the Old Testament. Since the congregation existed then as a nation, circumsion was the symbolic purification of the body inasmuch as the body served the procreation of the race. In the same way, baptism symbolizes cleansing from sin as well as reception into the church and sharing in the spirit of Christ. Similarly just as the Passover had reminded Israel of her redemption from Egypt, so does the eating and drinking of the church. In it Christ offers for meat and drink His physical nature as it has passed through an atoning death and has been glorified.

That congregation is no longer confined to Israel, however. The saying concerning "the seed of the woman" referred to the whole human race. The differentiation of mankind into nations is but an interlude. Abraham was called in order that through his seed all the families of the earth should be blest. Similarly when David united other nations with his people into a kingdom under his rule, that was an anticipation of the kingdom of Christ. Accordingly in Acts 15:13 ff., James quoting Amos 9:11 f. sees in David's kingdom the justification of a church of Christ out of the Gentiles which is on a par with that of the Jews. Likewise the servant of Jehovah was destined to be the "light of the nations" and not merely the restorer of Israel. That prophecy was fulfilled when the witness of the risen one transcended the borders of Israel and gathered congregations out of the Gentiles. But the fact remains that the Jewish people will not listen to the Word until they seem to be practically annihilated. For this reason the world of nations which at present is the locale of the church of Jesus Christ will remain hostile to it.

It is in this way that the New Testament history has to be read. One has to notice how the new things which take place therein are molded by the typological connection in which they stand with the history of the Old Testament and the prophetic word, and also how by the fulfilment of the Old Testament history and prophecy is molded by the newness of the New Testament history.

2. The New Testament Proclamation of Salvation

In the New Testament the witnesses of salvation are expressed in terms that are derived from the Old Testament. The Old Testament manifestations must be understood spiritually, however, as witnesses of the same salvation that has been given to us as Christians, if the terminology of the New Testament witness is to be interpreted correctly. This terminology has been chosen in order to emphasize the connection which exists in this respect between the Old Testament and the New Testament. Two things have therefore to be investigated:

1) In what respect is the New Testament witness affected by the fact that it is expressed in terms borrowed from the Old Testament?

2) In what respect is the meaning of that terminology modified by the fact that it serves to give expression to the New Testament witness? We retain the terminology which has been borrowed from the Old Testament but we interpret the things thereby expressed according to the New Testament.

When Zechariah revealed that he had received a promise from the Lord, according to which he would be given a son who would walk before the Lord in the spirit and in the power of Elijah, he praised the God of Israel by exclaiming, "for he hath visited and redeemed his people. . . . That we should be saved from our enemies, and from the hand of all that hate us"; and again, "that being delivered out of the hand of our enemies, we might serve him without fear, in holiness and righteousness" (Luke 1:68, 71, 74, 75).

The fact that the praise of Zechariah is expressed entirely in Old Testament terms is in agreement with the place which it occupies in the history of the New Testament. But the way in which he expressed it points nevertheless to a certain extent to the New Testament proclamation. On the basis of the revelation given to him Zechariah sees the beginning of the fulfillment of the promise given to Israel in the inconspicuous, yet in his eyes, miraculous event that a son has been born to him. The things that he sees now coming for Israel are destined for that Israel only which will serve her God in "holiness and righteousness." Hence "her enemies and those who hate her" are to be interpreted in the same way as in the Old Testament, that is, as those who oppose Israel on account of its special character. The hope to be delivered from them is expressed in terms of the prophetic prediction, namely, as being accomplished by the horn of salvation rising from the house of David. While it is redemption for his people, it is only for the people as they serve God.

Different is the praise of God that comes from the mouth of Simeon. In Luke 2:32 he praises God because he was allowed to behold his salvation which he had prepared before all the nations, "a light to light the Gentiles and a glory to thy people Israel." Here too, we find the contrast between Israel and all the other nations. But we also find the idea that in accordance with Isaiah 42:6 and 49:6 Israel will be glorified before them and that a light will rise by which the truth will be revealed to them. By presenting and manifesting Israel as His people, God not only glorifies Himself, but also brings the rest of the world to the knowledge of the truth. This result Simeon expects of the child of poor parents whom he sees before him. He does not allow the things which the spirit of prophecy has manifested to him to be confused by the things which he has before his eyes. Rather in the power of that spirit he is certain that within Israel herself "this one has been appointed as a sign that will be contradicted," and to his mother he says "a sword will pierce your soul." To him this fact is not incompatible with his hope, because his hope for the Messiah was in agreement with the prophecy concerning the servant of Jehovah.

Later on when John the Baptist makes his appearance in the midst of his people he speaks of a "Stronger One" who with fire and spirit will baptize those to whom John himself offers the water baptism, and who will cleanse the threshing floor by gathering the wheat into the barn and burning the chaff. He is the one who will bring about the final end of history, that is, the final separation of good and evil. John recognizes Him as the "Messenger of the Covenant" whom Malachi had foretold, the Mediator who has come to purge His people.

Describing Him in such terms John nevertheless says of

Him "Behold the Lamb of God which taketh away the sin
of the world" (John 1:29). Thereby he designates Him as
that Lamb of God which as the antitype of the Passover
Lamb has been given to the world to atone for her sins.
John speaks in such a manner of Him who had submitted
Himself to his baptism. In the witness he bears to Jesus he
combines what Malachi had predicted concerning the coming of Jehovah and His Mediator on the one hand, and what
Isaiah had told concerning the servant of God on the other.
The terminology in which his witness is couched is that of
the Old Testament, but the insight expressed thereby is that
of the New Testament.

Jesus bears witness to Himself as being "the Son." As the
"Son of God" and the "Son of Man" He is in an absolute
sense what all other people are in a relative sense only: all
men have God as their father, since their lives as members
of the human race are directly rooted in God, in contrast
with the non-human world; Israel as a whole and all its
individual members from God's people in contrast with all
the other nations; David excels over all the other rulers of
the nations. Jesus' unique position implies that He proceeded from God when He came into the world, that He had
been with God before He entered into the world and that
He had been with Him before the world came into being.
These facts constitute the newness and the unique character
of His divine sonship. He is the Son of God in an exclusive
sense. In view of this relationship, He could call His congregation, "my assembly" (Matt. 16:18). Down to that
moment Israel had been "the assembly of God." On account
of the fact the she recognized God as her head and as the
giver of her law she had been a nation who like a dem-
ocratic community was associated and held together by a
law equal for all. From now on, however, those who confess
Jesus and honor Him as their Lord by recognizing His will
as their law, will form His assembly. This is a novel fact that
a man should call this congregation of God his congregation.
Yet this congregation which he calls his own is but the con-

tinuation of that one which formerly had been formed by the people of Israel.

It has been held that originally the teaching of Jesus consisted exclusively in demanding a right disposition of the heart as contrasted with a purely outward observance of the law. This interpretation was based on such passages as Matthews 5:17-19 where Jesus says that He "did not come to dissolve the law and the prophets but rather to fulfill them" and that "he who would do and teach what was demanded by the law and prophets would have a share in God's kingdom." But it should be kept in mind that in speaking in such a manner He addressed people who believed in Him. In other words faith is the prerequisite of His demand. Jesus demands of those who believe in Him that in consequence of their faith they act rightly by keeping the law of love to God and one's neighbor, because that is the integral expression of the will of God.

In Matthew 5:5 Jesus says of the meek that "they shall inherit the earth." It would be wrong to interpret this statement as referring to the "spiritual dominion of Christianity" over the world as though Jesus meant that the Christian spirit would gradually permeate all human conditions. It is equally mistaken, however, to call this statement Judaistic, and to discover in it the expectation of a political empire of Christendom. In keeping with the Old Testament promise the saying refers in fact to the power which God's church is to have over the rest of the world. The statement would be Judaistic if it meant that the Jewish people would be the recipient of such a promise. But it should be evident that the community of the Holy Spirit will finally hold sway over everything outside of itself. For that result is but the triumph of God over all that opposes Him. Similarly, no evidence of Judaistic materialism is found in the Revelation of John. When it is said, for instance in Revelation 20:6, that the believers will be raised and glorified at the return of Christ in order to rule with Him, it is obvious that their dominion will not be of the kind found before the return of Christ but one that is its result. Matthew 5:5 should be compared with such passages as Psalm 37:11, "They shall inherit the land," and Romans 4:13, "heirs of the world," and particularly Hebrews 2:5 where the author speaks of the coming world as the recipient and the subject matter of the apostolic proclamation.

In Matthew 19:28 Jesus promises to His disciples that in the future they would sit on twelve thrones judging the twelve tribes of Israel. The term "to judge" is used here in the same sense that the heads of Israel are called "judges," that is, administrators. This promise appears reminiscent of the end of Psalm 45. There it is said of the king extolled in this psalm that he would appoint his sons "as princes over the whole earth." But Jesus said characteristically that His promise would be realized "in the new world," when the Son of Man will sit on his throne of glory." His disciples' reign will be of the same kind as His own. Since He is to return to this world which He left to go to the Father, the throne of His glory will be in this world. In it He will exercise His power as the Son of God in such a manner that it will be manifest to all. It is in this power that those who founded His church will share. Then the Church of God will be formed by the twelve tribes of Israel, inasmuch as it will be a church which confesses the Savior who came out of Israel (James 1:1).

When on the eve of His death Jesus celebrated the Passover, He said, "I shall not drink, etc., until I drink it afresh with you in the kingdom of my Father" (Matt. 26:29), and "I shall no longer eat it until it is fulfilled in the kingdom of God" (Luke 22:16). The Passover will be a new one when the things which are spoken of in Luke 22:29 take place, namely, "I appoint unto you a kingdom . . . that ye may eat and drink at my table in my kingdom." Sharing in the glorious life of Him who has returned, is the perfect antitype of the Passover. For in celebrating a redemption which is the antitype of the deliverance from Egypt they enjoy it as their possession. On this occasion Jesus calls His blood which is to be shed for the remission of sins, "my blood of the covenant," for in the fact that His life is given into death and that His church shares in His blood they have the anti-type of the things recorded in Exodus 24.

When Paul contrasts "works of the Law" and "faith" or "obedience of faith" as he does in Galatians 3:2 for instance, the first term is meant in a generic sense, designating "works of the law," rather than "*the* works of the law." Paul speaks of legalistic actions rather than of the actions which are demanded by Israel's revealed law. Nevertheless he thinks of the kind of law which Israel had in the law of Mt. Sinai, and he does not refer to a moral law to be derived from philosophical speculations. He means such a revelation of God's demanding will as was possible only in Holy History. When in this connection he speaks of "faith" as an attitude which is contrasted with the legalistic outlook, he has in mind the faith found in the realm of Holy History, and he does not refer specifically to the Christian faith. The Apostle points out, for instance, that Abraham had such a faith. Nevertheless in Galatians 3:23 he states that prior to the coming of faith we were kept and guarded under the law. Hence though there is evidence that Abraham was justified by such faith as spoken of by the Apostle, nevertheless the period preceding Christ can be called the time where faith was not yet. The novel feature of the New Testament faith is this: In the New Testament it is by faith that the community is formed, whereas the Old Testament community was sub-ject to a law by which it was unified and kept together as a nation.

In Paul's contradistinction of law and faith, the term "law" is not used in the same sense, as for instance in Psalm 19:8. There the term designates the totality of the divine revela-tion and thus the Law appears as a gift of divine grace. This is also the case in Deuteronomy 30:11-14. Yet what in those passages is said of the Law, Paul will predicate of Christ and the salvation revealed in Him (Rom. 10:5 f.).

In Romans 3:24 Paul writes that we are "justified through

the redemption which is in Jesus Christ." By borrowing from Exodus the term "redemption," Paul places the work of Jesus Christ in parallel with Israel's deliverance from Egypt. But the new redemption is "the redemption through his blood," and it consists in the "forgiveness of sins." Referring to Christ's atoning death which He suffered at the hands of men by whom his blood was shed, Paul says in Ephesians 5:2, "He gave himself for our sake as an offering and sacrifice to God for a sweet odor." The Apostle does not compare Christ's selfgiving with sacrifice in general but rather with the sacrifice ordained by the divinely given law of Israel. Both have this in common, that they designate a work appointed by God for the remission of sins. In the Old Testament it consists in putting to death living animals owned by the sacrificer. Here it is the complete selfsurrender of the sinless Savior who was sent into the world as mediator for the remission of sins. In Hebrews this mediatorial office of Jesus is described as a priestly one or rather as that of the high priest. Again, the reference is not to priesthood in general but rather to the priesthood which had been appointed by the law proclaimed in Holy History. In Hebrews 10:1 ff. we find this contrast: the things ordained by God are accomplished through the activity of the high priest by the law which ordains the highpriestly sacrifice of the day of atonement; on the other hand, Christ offers Himself to God.

In both instances, it is an activity ordained by God in Holy History and it operates in that capacity. But the activities differ in the way expressed in Hebrews 9:13 f. The Old Testament sacrifice of atonement applied to the worship of the nation as a whole which was in that respect the congregation of God. Since membership in that community was but an external matter, it sanctified only as far as the purification of the flesh was concerned, whereas the sacrifice of Christ purges our conscience because it is the taking away of sin. He who brought purification made it effective. Just as in the Old Testament the high priestly sacrifice of atonement is offered for the national community as a whole, so the sacrifice of Christ is given for his church as a whole and for the individual inasmuch as he is its member. Thus when it is said in Hebrews 2:17, "for the propitiation of the sins of the people," the term "the people" does not designate the Jewish people nor exclusively Jewish Christianity but rather the New Testament community, inasmuch as it continues that of the Old Testament in an antitypical way.

It is said of Jesus, that having come to God, He is sitting at God's right hand. This expression is borrowed from Psalm 110:1, where God says to the king, "sit on my right hand," etc. The place where the king is to have His throne on Jehovah's side is Zion, since through David that locality has become the seat both of the king and of God of Israel. Hence when it is said that Christ is sitting on God's right hand the meaning of the phrase is identical in both instances. He who sits on the right hand of a ruler shares in his dignity and dominion, and thus he who sits on God's right hand shares in His authority as the ruler of the world. But the term is applied here to Him who through His death has passed on to God. The reign of Christ is therefore a supramundane one and will remain so until his Parousia. This idea of an interval is not found in the Old Testament. Christ therefore holds His sway not only over everything that is on earth but over every principality and power and He has become more powerful than the angels (Heb. 1:4). The latter term refers to the fact that all the activities of the Creator in this visible world are mediated through the ministration of the spirits. It is in this supramundane dignity that Christ is a "high priest after the order of Melchisedek." He is the high priest both as the antitype of Aaron, namely in sacrificing Himself, and of Melchisedek because He has passed on to God. Thus His relationship to mankind is the same as that of Melchisedek to Abraham.

Christ's future manifestation is called His coming "in his kingdom." This expression does not designate a royal power in general but rather He is called king as the antitype of David (Psalm 2). He will reveal Himself to this world as the one having power over it, because He is the divine appointed head of His congregation. Since in Isaiah 9:7 it is said of David's son that he should sit on David's throne forever, it is surprising that in I Corinthians 15:24 f. we read that the time will come when Christ will surrender His kingdom to the Father and subject Himself to God. This vision of the final end transcends the ideas of Psalm 110. The mediatorial activity of Jesus no less than the power which He exercises over all the non-divine forces including death will come to an end when its purpose has been fulfilled, namely, that God should be all in all; in other words when there will be a world which is entirely God's and in which there is nothing found which is alien to Him. It is obvious that these ideas cannot be found where the Messiah has not yet been recognized as the Son in the New Testament sense. However, the Old Testament too knows of a final end beyond which there will be no continuation of that history which takes place here on earth. Isaiah for instance speaks in 66:22 of a new heaven and a new earth. In other passages too the Old Testament prophecy foretells a final condition of things brought about by the ultimate revelation of God and the settlement of the conflict between Israel and the world of nations. But that state of things is described for example by Joel and Amos in purely earthly terms. There will be no history beyond the Son's "subjecting himself" to the Father, which is spoken of in I Corinthians 15:28.

In the above given instances, the New Testament witness of salvation was expressed in terms borrowed from the Old Testament. Accordingly the connection which exists between the saving facts and the saving truths recorded in the New Testament on the one hand, and the Old Testament on the other, finds its appropriate expression in the quotations from the Old Testament. The correctness of our interpretation of that connection is to be tested by them.

The connection with the Old Testament implied in such quotations is most easily apprehended when the New Testament events are introduced as fulfillment of Old Testament predictions. Nevertheless, even in those instances a bridge has to be built between the two facts. The demonstration of the adequacy of the quotation must not be facilitated by interpreting the prediction in the light of the event in which it is fulfilled. We have already mentioned such instances, as when in Matthew 1:21 f. the evangelist refers to Isaiah 7:14. In that instance the Old Testament quotation "behold a virgin will conceive and bear a son and they shall call his name Emmanuel," is preceded by the word spoken to Joseph, "she will bear a son and thou shalt call his name Jesus." From this arrangement it is obvious that it is not the name of Jesus which had been foretold but rather that His name actualizes what is contained in the Old Testament prophecy. Likewise instead of the expression "thou shalt call" as found in Isaiah, it is said in Matthew, "they shall call." In other words, when these things take place, people will be glad that God is no longer against us but with us (Emmanuel). Hence we conclude that the prophecy is not intended to be the exact model of the future event. In the Old Testament, the imagery describes the miracle of salvation as coming in the midst of a disaster which the people had brought upon themselves, and as taking its shape from those circumstances. This is confirmed by the way in which the Savior enters this world. In a similar manner Micah 5:2 is related to Jesus' birth in Bethlehem.

Likewise Matthew finds the fulfilment of Isaiah 53 in Jesus. In Isaiah the suffering of the servant of Jehovah and His appearance are explained as being caused by Israel himself. According to Matthew 8:17, the fulfilment of the prophecy lies in the fact that Jesus accepted the physical diseases of His nation as His own burden by allowing people to come to Him and by healing them. He proved Himself to be the Savior of His people by making it His own burden to remove its misery. His activity of healing showed Him as a helper in all evil and was a sign of His nature. Likewise the hardship of His ministry indicated His willingness to endure everything that was necessary to redeem them from all evil. It is particularly in His prophetic activity that He introduces Himself as the one portrayed in Isaiah. It is similar with the passage Zechariah 9:9 discussed above, which according to Matthew was fulfilled in Jesus' Messianic entry into Jerusalem.

Things are different when the quotations from the Old Testament refer to the antitypical relationship in which the New Testament events stand to the history of the Old Testament.

In Hebrews 10:4 f. for example the Christ who enters the world is introduced as saying what David said of himself in Psalm 40:6-8, namely, that He did not come to offer sacrifices which God did not desire, but rather that "in the scroll of the book it is written of me, I delight to do thy will," etc. Instead of appearing with animals to be sacrificed David appears with the will of God concerning himself in its written form, and he carries this scroll with him as a symbol of his willingness to act accordingly. He adds that that will is for him not a merely outward command, but fills his personal life. Since David is the king of the people, the content of the book with which he comes before God applies to him in a special manner, not only in the general way in which it obligated every other Israelite. It is his duty as king to see to it that the whole will of God which is contained in the book, both as promise and as demand, should be executed. Hence the words of that psalm as spoken by David give expression to the inner attitude which he takes towards his office. Its antitype is found in the attitude with which Christ entered into the world, namely, to do the will of God concerning Himself as found in the Scripture. Thus we understand why the author of the Epistle to the Hebrews introduces the passage from the Psalms in such a way. Spoken by Christ it has become an expression of the determination by which He has become man. He became man in order to execute God's saving will by offering Himself.

In Hebrews 2:12 f. the quotation from Psalm 22, "I shall proclaim thy name to my brethren, in the midst of the congregation I shall sing hymns to thee," is introduced as a saying of Christ and joined with the statement that Jesus is not ashamed to call the human beings His brethren. The reason for His doing so lies in the fact that "He who sanctified and those who are being sanctified are all of one" (Heb. 2:11). The common origin of Christ and of those who are sanctified through Him is expressed in that passage of Scripture. It is originally a word of David from the same period in which Psalm 22 originated, when he anticipated his ascent to the throne of his people for which he had been ordained. The words by which David expressed the fact that he had a common origin with those whose king he was to become is used to express a like awareness when ascribed to Christ.

The author of Hebrews adds two further quotations for the support of "out of one," namely, "I shall put my trust in him who has hidden his face from the house of Jacob," and "behold I and the children which God has given me." Both statements are spoken by Isaiah (8:17-18; and cf. II Sam. 22:3). In the former instance the prophet through whom the divine promise is given emphasizes that he, no less than those to whom he prophesies, must remain in believing expectation of Jehovah. It was the same with Jesus the true prophet. For in this passage He is referred to as the prophet of His congregation. All the things which He promises to those whom He addresses He must expect of God for Himself.

In the latter passage the children of Isaiah are His two sons called "A remnant shall return" and "Hastening to the spoil"* who share in the performance of His prophetic office.

The name of the former one points to the distant future of Israel and that of the latter one to its immediate future, both in connection with the meaning of the name Isaiah, that is, "Jehovah saves." In the case of Isaiah, his sons are united with him in the same office because they are of the

---

*i.e., Shearjashub, Isaiah 7:3, and Mahershalalhashbaz, 8:3.

same flesh and blood with him. Similarly those whom Jesus has made share in His ministry are with Him of the same flesh and blood. Thus these two statements characterizing the prophetic office and the one spoken by David are prophecies concerning the relationship in which the king and prophet of the New Testament stands with beneficiaries of His activity.

Having told how the child Jesus had to be brought to Egypt for safety because of the insidious plans of Herod, Matthew adds in 2:15 that this happened in order that the word might be fulfilled "out of Egypt have I called my son." The evangelist is aware of the fact that the passage Hosea 11:1 which he quotes speaks of Israel. There Jehovah calls Israel His son and reminds Him that He had called Him out of Egypt. In a situation where that people seemed to be permanently unable to perform its vocation Jehovah came to its rescue. Since this is an essential feature of Israel's history, it is also an essential feature in the history of Him who is in the fullest sense of the word the Son of God, and not merely in a relative way as was Israel who as a nation formed by God was the Son of God in contrast with the other nations which originated through the natural differentiation of mankind. Israel became a nation merely on account of Him who was to be born out of her and her history takes place for His sake. This purpose forms the basis of the typological relationship between the events in the life of Jesus and the things that happened to Israel. The Son of God, too, to whom Israel's prefigurative sonship pointed, had to be brought back to his mission from a situation in which He seemed to be lost for that purpose.

Things are the same when after the narrative of the murder of the infants in Bethlehem Matthew refers in chapter 2:17 to Jeremiah 31:15, "a voice was heard in Ramah." In that passage the prophet has a vision of Rachel rising from her tomb, and breaking out in mourning as she sees how the land of her children has been depopulated. It looks now as though God's people had been incapacitated for its mission.

In order to understand the way in which Matthew speaks about the fulfillment of this word, the following consideration is necessary. Those who had known of the child which had been born in Bethlehem and on which the hope of Israel depended inevitably could think that as a result of that massacre their hope had been crushed. Just as Israel seemed permanently to be lost for her vocation, when Nebuchadnezzar had depopulated the country and she had been dispersed among the nations, so Israel's hope seems now to be gone, and the mission of God's people again brought to naught. These two facts of Israel's history, namely, her sojourn in Egypt and her forced exile from the Holy Land, have their analogy in the history of Jesus, the son of David. They are both prophecies and they find their fulfillment in the history of Him whose appearance is in every respect the fulfillment of Israel's history.

In Matthew 13:34 f. it is said that Jesus spoke to the people in parables in order that the word spoken in Psalm 78:2 should be fulfilled, "I will open my mouth in parables." With these words Assaph introduced a psalm in which he gave a poetic and prophetic survey of Israel's history from her redemption out of Egypt down to the election of David. From this survey Israel is to learn a lesson for her own conduct. The poet uses the literary form of the "riddle" and "parable" in order to stimulate his audience to consider the lesson which God had given them in their history. The former term designates an artificial way of expression and the latter one an artistic one. What matters in the "riddle" is the purpose for which the object has been presented in that specific perspective. In the "parable" it is the deliberately chosen form of expression which matters. When Assaph says that in his psalm he offers instruction which in the historical facts is both hid and also given artistic expression, the evangelist points out that this is fulfilled in the fact that Jesus spoke to the people in parables. Since He is in every respect the fulfilment of Old Testament history He is so particularly as a prophet in everything which is characteristic of the prophet. One of the characteristic features of the prophetic office is the artful presentation of the message. When the new things which Jesus was given to teach were presented before the indolent populace, Jesus used His ability to express them in such a manner that people had to make a mental effort in order to discover the idea concealed in its literary garment. Jesus manifested Himself in this respect too as a prophet, that is, as a master of speech by proclaiming the word of God in a manner which was appropriate to its purpose.

Furthermore, since the manifestation of the power of Jehovah which had been promised in the Old Testament took place in the New Testament as God's manifestation in Jesus Christ, everything that in this respect is told of Jesus can be introduced as the fulfillment of a passage of Scripture that deals with Jehovah. The simplest form of this relationship is obviously found in those instances where reference is made to Old Testament predictions which found their fulfillment and realization in certain facts of the New Testament. Mark for instance opens his gospel (1:2) by referring to the word of the prophet Malachi (3:1), "Behold, I send my messenger before you," which he, however, combines with a saying of Isaiah. According to Mark this took place when John the Baptist made his appearance. In other words, there was in fact such a messenger who preceded the coming of the Gospel. But Mark changes the text of the Old Testament passage. There it is said that Jehovah would send a messenger before Himself who should prepare the way for Him. Mark alters this passage in such a way that God addresses another person saying, "I am sending my messenger before you." This Old Testament passage altered in the same manner is also found in a speech of the Lord recorded in Matthew 11 and Luke 7. The justification for this alteration lies in the fact that Jehovah's advent which was spoken of by Malachi has now taken place in the fact that God sent Jesus into this world. The manifestation of Jesus is that manifestation of Jehovah which was predicted by Malachi. However, Jesus' appearance in the flesh is but the beginning of God's advent into the world. We cannot have the complete fulfillment of that Old Testament prophecy unless we include the future manifestation of Jesus in His glory.

The case is similar in Acts 2 where at the occasion of the pouring out of the Holy Spirit, Peter quotes the promise given in Joel 2:28. While there it is Jehovah who promises, "I will pour out my spirit," etc. it is said in Acts 2:33 concerning Jesus: "Having received this promise of the Holy Spirit from his Father he poured out that which you now see and hear."

Things are about the same in Hebrew 1:6. There to the words, "But when he has again brought the first born into the world," the quotation is added, "All the angels of God shall worship him." The quotation goes back to Deuteronomy 32:43 and is introduced in the enlarged form of Psalm 97:7. However, what has been said concerning Jehovah with reference to the final end of the history of Israel and of the nations, is here referred to the future manifestation of Jesus. Like Jehovah at the end of history, so Jesus will be revealed as "the Lord of hosts" in His glorious reappearance.

There are also some instances in the New Testament where events which in the Old Testament are spoken of as having been brought about by Jehovah are ascribed to Jesus. This is the case for instance in Ephesians 4:8. There Paul describes God's spirit as He operates in the Church of Jesus Christ. Each member of the church has his vocation and his appointed place in the church according to the measure of the spirit given to him by Christ. Paul continues, "When he had ascended to the heights he took captivity captive and gave gifts to men." In Psalm 68 this passage refers to Jehovah. It is said there, "Thou hast ascended to the height, thou hast made prisoners, thou hast received gifts, in order to dwell among people, even among the rebellious ones" (v. 18). The author of the psalm rejoices in the triumph of the God of Israel who has made Zion His dwelling

place and thereby the seat of His dominion to which all the
world will be subject. As a victor He has so to speak made
men His captives and received gifts from the vanquished.
According to the author of the psalm this refers to the royal
glory which Jehovah has achieved in the midst of His people
to which He had previously stooped down moving before
them in the bleak country of the desert. Paul transforms this
statement into the praise of the triumph of Christ who
ascended from this world to God, rose above all the heavens
and became the king of a church which serves Him after
He had first condescended to mankind from His previous
height and glory.

Paul does not hesitate to alter the wording of the text.
Where it is said in the Psalm, "Thou hast received gifts" he
substitutes, "He has given gifts to men." The passage would
not fit the context of his reasoning except with this modification, for Paul points out the significance of the spiritual
equipment which the individual members of the church of
Christ have received. Yet there is no difference between
Christ's receiving gifts from those people who shall serve
His purpose or His giving to them gifts in order to equip
them for His service. Paul wants his readers to recognize the
relationship in which Christ's triumphal procession stands to
that of Jehovah in the Old Testament. Christ's ascent to
God is the antitype of the Old Testament fact in which
Jehovah made Zion the seat of His royal glory. Since Jehovah's advent as predicted by Malachi took place in Christ's
appearance in the flesh, the New Testament fact of Christ's
being exalted to God is the antitype of that Old Testament
history in which the God who had moved before Israel in the
wilderness had finally established His throne upon the royal
height of Zion.

From the way he quotes from Psalm 68 it can be seen that
the Apostle does not intend by means of the quoted passage
to prove the factuality of the things which he relates in Ephesians 4:1 f. Paul bases his reasoning upon the fact that the full
manifestation of Jehovah which is the aim of the whole

Old Testament has taken place in the appearance of Jesus. As far as Paul and his readers are concerned there can be no doubt concerning the reality of the New Testament fact. But in the New Testament fact his readers are to recognize what is stated in that psalm, namely, the historical triumph of Jehovah. On the basis of such reasoning the author of Hebrews can in 1:10 introduce a passage from Psalm 102:25 which is addressed to Jehovah, "Thou Jehovah hast established the earth in the beginning, etc.," as applying to the Son of God. The writer would not be able to do so if he were addressing himself to people to whom he had to demonstrate that Jesus is the Son of God or who had to be taught first what it means that Jesus is the Son of God. But by opening his treatise with the statement that God has now spoken through the Son and that it is through the Son that God has created this world, he indicates that both he and his readers believe in these facts. Yet he wants them to realize too, what follows from the fact that we have heard the word of God through the Son. Hence in agreement with the author the readers believe that Jesus proceeded from God and came into this world. Therefore what is true of Him from whom He proceeded is true of Himself also. The author merely transposes into a New Testament message a word chosen from the Old Testament which proves to be a convenient expression for the things he wants to state. The same things for which the author of Psalm 102 praised Jehovah his God are ascribed by the Christian to his Savior Jesus.

We conclude: the passage quoted from the Psalms was not interpreted as originally referring to the Messiah. Nor are all the statements which the Old Testament makes concerning Jehovah indiscriminately to be applied to the Christ of the New Testament. Rather, in Jehovah we have combined in one idea what in the New Testament is differentiated into the work of the Father and the Son. The method used in Hebrew 1:10 is the same as in I Corinthians 10:4, "the rock was Christ," or in I Peter 1:11 where the spirit operative in the Old Testament prophets is called "the Spirit of Christ."

The New Testament believers know that where Jehovah is, He is never without the Christ who mediates His revelation and that every spontaneous activity of Jehovah is an activity performed through the Son.

Furthermore, Christ is the Son of Man no less than the Son of God. Thus in Him the destination of mankind has been reached. When it is said, for instance, that to man has been given the rule over the world which surrounds him, this vital element is quoted in Hebrews 2:5 f. as having been fulfilled not only in mankind in general but above all in Christ Jesus who is the originator of the race. Hence the words of this psalm are applied directly to Jesus in I Corinthians 15:27.

A comparison of passages such as Mark 1:2, Ephesians 4:8 and Hebrews 1:10 shows that they have one feature in common. Things that in the Old Testament were predicated of Jehovah are applied in the New Testament to Christ. Nevertheless there are also differences between them. In the first passage a fact predicted in the Old Testament is presented as having been realized in the New Testament. In the second one the author of an Old Testament fact is recognized as being at work also in a New Testament fact. In the third instance, an Old Testament passage is simply transposed into the New Testament and placed into its context.

We have now to consider the fact that the quotations in the New Testament are sometimes given according to the text of the Septuagint which differs from the Hebrew original and that in other instances they disagree both with the Septuagint and the Masoretic text.

In Hebrews 10:5 for instance we find the Alexandrian rendering of Psalm 40:7, "Thou hast prepared a body for me," instead of the Hebrew, "Thou hast opened my ears" (i.e., to hear thy word). But the quotation as has been shown above does not stress the word "body." Rather it emphasizes the fact that David speaks concerning himself as one coming to do the will of God since God does not desire sacrifice. Furthermore, when in v. 10 Jesus' sacrifice of Himself is

called "the sacrifice of the body of Jesus Christ" the terminology is determined by the text of the Septuagint. In Hebrews 1:6 there is a quotation from Deuteronomy 32:43
which is found only in the Septuagint. Although it is evident
that the author knows the Hebrew text, he nevertheless
follows the Septuagint because it was used by his readers.
In this instance, however, he would not have done so except
for the fact that the same words were also found in Psalm 97.

Over against the scribes and high priests who challenged
Him because the children shouted, "Hosanna to the Son of
David," the Lord claims in Matthew 21:16 the authority of
Psalm 8:2, "because out of the mouths of babes and sucklings
I will prepare praise," quoting from the Septuagint. In the
original text the passage says, "from the mouths of babes
and sucklings hast thou ordained strength because of thine
enemies, that thou might still the enemy and the avenger."
In this passage the term translated "strength" refers to God's
power to keep in check His opponents. Accordingly the translation "out of the mouth" is inappropriate. Rather the word
translated "mouth," just as the term "hand," is used in the
place of a preposition. The psalmist says that from small
children and helpless babes God makes grow a force to
overcome His adversaries. In referring in this instance to the
word of the psalm Jesus wants to indicate that one should
not object to children's paying Him homage, since as the
passage shows, God does not deem children unfit for His
service. The evangelist found the inaccurate rendering of
the Septuagint convenient to adjust the general idea of the
psalm to the incident in question. However, in quoting from
the Psalm He wanted merely to emphasize the fact that
little children are used to glorify the divine name. Since God
has destined children to become the instruments through
which His strength will be manifested it is not surprising
that they are now manifesting His miracles when those who
should speak of them keep their peace. But quoting from the
Septuagint Matthew intimates to his readers that this is the
appropriate interpretation of that passage.

Thus far we have dealt with passages of the Old Testament which were quoted from the Septuagint where its text differs from that of the Hebrew Bible. We are now considering quotations which differ equally from the Septuagint and the Hebrew text. We start with Romans 12:19 and Hebrews 10:30 where the passage from Deuteronomy 32:35 is rendered by "vengeance is mine, I shall repay"; whereas the Septuagint text reads, "on the day of vengeance I shall repay." The way in which the quotation is given in the above passage is definitely closer to the original text than to that of the Septuagint.

Another quotation which differs both from the original text and the Septuagint is found in Matthew 2:6, "And thou Bethlehem, in the land of Judah, are not at all the least among the princes of Judah; for out of thee shall come a Governor, that shall rule my people Israel." As far as the correct rendering is concerned the text of the Septuagint is more in accord with the prophetic passage (Micah 5:2), "And thou Bethlehem, house of Ephrata, art the least among the thousands of Judah. Out of thee there shall come for me the leader who shall be the prince in Israel." The evangelist not only had a Hebrew text which meant "leaders" instead of "thousands," but he also established a different relationship between the two sentences by the conjunction "for," which was caused by the negation "not at all." The meaning of the quotation as given by him is this: When the princes of Judah will gather, Bethlehem will not be considered the smallest one, or the most insignificant portion of Judah, "for out of thee," etc. By doing so he adjusted the passage to the specific context in which it is found here, without essentially changing the meaning of the quotation.

The passage in Zechariah 9:9, "Rejoice exceedingly daughter of Zion, and be glad daughter of Jerusalem," and the subsequent words, "Behold thy king is coming to thee," is rendered in the Septuagint, "Rejoice greatly, daughter of Zion, proclaim, daughter of Jerusalem, behold the king cometh to you." Over against this we read in Matthew 21:5,

202 INTERPRETING THE BIBLE

"Say to the daughter of Zion, behold," and in John 12:15, "Fear not, daughter of Zion." John alters the passage in such a way that Zion has no reason to be afraid of a king who comes to her in such humility rather than as her judge.

In Matthew on the other hand the context shows that in order to be recognized Jesus Himself had made arrangements to present Himself to His people in the manner prophesied by Zechariah. For this reason the original injunction to rejoice is altered by the evangelist into the admonition "tell," etc.

It is obvious that the New Testament writers are not anxiously sticking to the letter of the Old Testament when quoting it. They will use the Greek version when its text is more convenient for the purpose for which they quote although it may differ from the original text. They also feel free to transform the original text or its Greek version in order to present an idea in that perspective which is most appropriate for their purpose. Nevertheless the original meaning of the Hebrew text is always preserved.

John 12:37-41 is a most instructive instance. There we read that although Jesus had performed so many signs among them the Jews nevertheless did not believe in Him in order that the word of the prophet Isaiah 53:1 should be fulfilled, "Lord, who has believed our report and to whom has the arm of the Lord been revealed." Things had to take place in accordance with that prophecy. Only when it was too late would Israel realize the significance of the servant of Jehovah. The evangelist continues that "it was for this reason that they were unable to believe." The subsequent conjunction "because" adduces a second reason for their inability, which however, is connected with the former one. According to another word of Isaiah (6:9), "He blinded their eyes and hardened their heart, lest they should see with their eyes and perceive with their heart, and should be converted, and I should heal them." In the original text we find a divine exhortation addressed to the prophet to harden the heart of the people and to make their ears hard of hearing, etc. The result of his prophesying will be blindness and hardening of heart on the part of the people. In the Septuagint the sentence has been changed in order to avoid the offence given by the imperatives "make blind . . . harden." There it reads, "The heart of this people was rendered fat, and their ears were hard of hearing, and they eyes became dim in order that they should not see," etc.

John quotes neither the Septuagint nor the original text but rather he introduces Jesus as doing what originally Isaiah had been commanded to do. He says, "He has blinded," etc. What refers originally to the prophet he makes a statement whose grammatical subject is Jesus Himself. In 12:41 John says, "Isaiah said these words because he saw his glory, and he spoke concerning him." Thus here as in v. 40 we find statements concerning Jesus because it was Jesus whose glory the prophet had seen and of Him he had spoken. The commandments which Isaiah records apply to Jesus, even as the fact that Isaiah had seen Jehovah meant that he had seen the glory of Jesus, that glory in which He is and had been before He entered into this world. In the person of Jesus we have a merger of the glory of Jehovah and the work of the prophet. Whether or not the people will listen to Him as the prophet, Jesus will nevertheless enter into His glory. His propetic work may be of no effect, which will fulfill Isaiah's prophecy; yet He is not just the prophet but also He who afterwards has entered into His glory. As the one exalted to God He will eventually be recognized by the people as their Savior, and He will say as it is said in Isaiah 53:1, "Who has believed our report," etc.

In the above passage we have an instance of how that which the Old Testament prophets said about their vocation is considered in the New Testament as a prophecy referring to Jesus. At the same time, however, it is also an instance of the way in which the Old Testament manifestation and apparition of Jehovah is considered a manifestation of that divine person, which as a man is called Jesus. For Jesus is both like Isaiah and like Jehovah. The one before whom

Isaiah stood beholding His glory has also become a prophet, another Isaiah. Like the latter one He was unable to illumine the populace, but rather blinded it. Nevertheless He could say in John 8:28, "When you have lifted up the Son of Man, then shall you know that I am he." Here, too, we find the same liberty with which the New Testament writers quoted from the Old Testament, but also that notwithstanding that freedom, the basic meaning of the Old Testament passage is preserved.

Thus far we have dealt with the significance which the contrast between the Old Testament and the New Testament has for the interpretation of the Bible because it is rooted in the very nature of Holy Scripture. We have also investigated the specific qualification which the Biblical interpretation receives from that fact. There is another contrast, however, which is found in both parts of the Bible and which is caused by the fact that the Scripture is not a text book teaching conceptual truths but rather a document of an historical process, and that it has originated within the history recorded therein. This fact implies that the Biblical witness of salvation partly records things past, partly refers to things present, partly foretells things future. It has already been shown that the traditional distinction of historical, prophetic, and poetic books in the Old Testament, and of historical, epistolary and prophetic portions in the New Testament, is not only inappropriate, but has also no significance for our work. In general hermeneutics, the rules of interpretation are given for the different kinds of speech found in Scripture. But it is our task to show how the general rules of interpretation are modified by the specific character of Holy Scripture. Thus our next task will be to investigate how the interpretation of Holy Scripture will be affected by the fact that its proclamation of salvation naturally deals with past, present, and future things.

CHAPTER FOUR

The Holy Scripture
as a Witness

A. THE REFLECTION OF THE PAST

The Biblical records of the past have this in common with the historiography of antiquity, that they are closer to epics than modern historiography is. In particular, when people are introduced as saying certain things this does not imply that they used exactly those words. In the Gospel of John for instance, Jesus and John the Baptist employ the same kind of language which we also find in I John. This explains why the speeches of Jesus in John's Gospel differ so much from those in other gospels. Similarly in Acts the language used by Peter and Paul on the one hand, that of the author on the other, are similar. We conclude that their speeches were freely reproduced by the author. It would therefore be methodologically wrong to judge the language of the Petrine epistles by the speeches of Peter in Acts and vice-versa. Similarly it is held that the way in which Paul in Acts 26: 12-18 tells Agrippa the story of his conversion is incompatible with the narrative of his conversion told to the populace in Acts 22:6-11. If that were the case we would conclude that this contradiction no less than the disagreement between his report and the narrative itself were due to the author of Acts.

205

The conversation between Agrippa and Festus which is reported in Acts 25:14-22 is not meant to be a literal report. Similarly Tertullus' accusation was certainly longer than that given in Acts 24:3 f. It was hardly confined to the few words recorded there. In the same way Luke does not intimate that the conversation between Zachariah and the angel or between Mary and the angel, or Mary's and Zachariah's praise of God were all uttered exactly in the way he records them. What had been oral tradition was molded by the historian in this manner, and his hand is clearly discernible. How much more this might be the case when speeches and conversations of the distant past have been recorded! Their present shape is due in part to oral tradition and in part to the redactor who put them down in writing.

While we delight for instance in the beautiful conversations recorded in Genesis 24, we do not hold therefore that Abraham, Eliezer and Rebecca uttered exactly those words. The literary form in which these things are reported in the Scriptures is meant to make them useful for us, because it was for that end that they were conceived under the influence of God's spirit. The fact for instance that the same speeches of Jesus are recorded in different words in Matthew on the one hand and in Luke on the other, requires in each case an interpretation which is in accordance with their context. In both instances they are an integral part of their gospel and they must not be amalgamated to a middle text standing in between the two. We must rely upon the form of expression in which they have become words of the Scripture rather than upon the form in which Jesus uttered them. Hence each of the two phrasings has its specific value in the context in which they are found, and their effect is conditioned by the peculiar character of each of the gospels.

It's the same way with the narratives. How greatly the story of the centurion of Capernaum differs in its details in Matthew 8:5 f. and in Luke 7:1 f.! In Matthew the centurion comes to Jesus with his request; in Luke he sends Jews who are his friends. There he asks Jesus to desist from coming to him; in Luke he sends his friends to keep Him back. Nevertheless, the things that matter are identical in both narratives, namely, the faith of the centurion and Jesus' marvelling about it.

Luke places great emphasis upon the details of the events reported. For instance in Matthew 9:18 f. Jairus says, "My daughter has died, lay thy hand upon her and she shall live"; but in Mark 5:23 and Luke 8:42 we are told that she was *about* to die, and that the report of her death did not arrive until later. But all three gospels emphasize the same point, namely, that Jairus was sure that Jesus had power over death. In this instance too Luke probably gives the more accurate record of the course of events. Whenever Matthew sees a number of events from the same perspective he joins them in such a way that they seem to have immediately succeeded each other; for instance the events recorded in chapter 8:1-15. A comparison with Mark and Luke will show, however, that in these instances the chronological succession is in appearance only. It is impossible to establish the chronological succession of all the events in Jesus' Galilean ministry. For the purpose for which Holy Scripture is given the complete picture of the external course of events is less important than the significance which the individual event has in its special place and the view of history implied in the arrangement of a number of events.

Particularly when events of a more distant past are recorded, the narratives have been preserved by an oral tradition which far from retaining an exact picture of the events, remembers only those features which were significant to those who passed on the tradition. It cannot be ascertained for instance in what manner the animals gathered in Noah's ark. Tradition only says that the animal world which surrounded him after the flood was that which had been preserved in the flood. Similarly when we read that flood was fifteen cubits above the highest mountains, this statement expresses the fact that the ark passed above the highest mountains. Yet for this purpose the Himalayas and Chimborazos are not to be considered. The narrative only wants to indicate that everywhere where people lived, the flood covered the earth above the peaks of their mountains.

Events of a far distant past were handed down by oral tradition according to the manner in which they were imagined in a much later and different time, and they borrowed the means of expression from their period. For instance, the events in the life of the first couple have been handed down for the sake of those and by those whose life was subject to entirely different conditions. It is beyond man's imagination to realize how that which became the body of the woman was taken from that of Adam. But the significant feature of the story lies in the fact that she was created from man, not beside man (I Cor. 11:8). Similarly we cannot imagine what transpired between the woman and the serpent. But what is of utmost importance is the fact that the stimulus to do what ought not to be done came to the human race, and in the first place to the woman, from outside of themselves. Nothing is said concerning the origin of Cain's wife who gave birth to his son. Yet it is evident that his sister became his wife. Similarly when it is said, "He built a city," this indicates the first definite settlement by means of which he became a resident of the strange country.

To this feature should be added what is usually called the mythical character of the narrative, namely, that events are directly ascribed to God, for instance, to His counsel as in Genesis 6:3 and 11:6 where God Himself appears as speaking. Yet such mythical features are derived exclusively from the facts themselves. When God is introduced in Genesis 6:3 as saying that He is giving to the human race another 120 years, this is but another way of stating at what time Noah received a revelation concerning the flood. Similarly when it is told in Genesis 8:21 that God said to Himself that no flood should cover the earth again, this statement gives expression to the same certitude which was symbolized to Noah in the rainbow, and which he interpreted in that sense. God's speaking to Himself is characteristic of the style of this type of narrative. In a similar way David gives expression to his conviction when he makes Jehovah say in Psalm 2, "I have set my king," etc.

We read that God spoke to Noah and to Abraham, yet it is not said in what manner it took place. What in Genesis 12:1 is stated as "God spoke" is referred to in Acts 7:2 by the words "the God of glory appeared." This in turn is reminiscent of the terminology in Genesis 17:1, "God appeared to Abram," whereas in Genesis 15:1 we read, "God spoke to Abram in a vision." No matter how the event took place, the narrative assures us that the revelation given to Noah and Abram did not proceed from human thought and will.

In other instances, things that have taken place are recorded as having been performed directly by God Himself. In Genesis 11:8 for instance it is said that after the building of the tower of Babel God scattered mankind over the whole earth. We learn from the narrative that the scattering resulted from the fact that they were unable to understand any longer each other's language. Likewise in Genesis 19:24 we read, "the Lord rained brimstone and fire from the Lord." When after the words, "from the Lord" it is said in opposition "from heaven," this terminology is meant to indicate that the God who called down judgment upon earth is identical with Him who sent it down from heaven. Similarly the passage in II Kings 19:35, in which we read that the angel of the Lord slew the army of Sennacherib is reminiscent of Acts 12:23 where it is said concerning Herod, "The angel of the Lord slew him." The fact that in the former passage it is a plague which annihilated the army of Sennacherib, and in the latter instance a disease that killed Herod, does not justify the application of the term "mythical" to these narratives if that term means unhistorical. Rather things which took place by means of secondary causes are reported as God's own work. The specific feature of Holy Scripture is precisely this that all history is interpreted and recorded therein as transpiring between God and mankind. Its purpose is not to provide exact knowledge of the external course of events but rather to point out the significance which certain events have for the salvation realized in Christ.

For it is this very salvation which is given expression in the Biblical narrative, yet it is described just as it had been realized at a given time in the historical process. However, such past actualization of salvation is always recorded from the viewpoint of the present salvation. Hence the things narrated are to be evaluated according to the significance they had for the salvation of those by whom they were recorded in retrospect.

At any given moment the experience of salvation allows one to envisage the past history of salvation from a number of different viewpoints. Thus we must always ascertain the viewpoint in Holy History from which the narrative has been told, in order to be able correctly to evaluate both the arrangement of the narrative as a whole and also the significance which its details have for the whole. By doing so we shall understand not only why these features of the narrative were selected but also why this manner of presentation was chosen.

What things are told in the first chapters of Genesis down to the beginning of Abram's history must not be understood as being the record of the legends concerning the origins of mankind which were known to the narrator. The Biblical history would be interpreted as secular rather than as Holy History if one saw only that and did not expect something different. For the author wanted to show his people what was meant by the fact that they were Jehovah's people. This intention is manifested in the total arrangement of the narrative, and its component parts have to be evaluated from this viewpoint. Given the fact that the major part of the Torah originated in the days of Moses, the experience of salvation from which the events of the past are viewed is that of his time. This explains why such features of Israel's history as the redemption from Egypt, her legislation, her march through the wilderness, but also the narrative of Israel's coming to Egypt, are reported in much greater detail than all the intervening events. It is obvious that from the viewpoint of secular history, more and different things should have been recorded concerning Israel's sojourn in Egypt.

Or let us examine an individual case, Exodus 4:21-23. At first sight it would appear that both here and in the preceding verses the order and the inner unity of the historical narrative had been neglected, and that details had been arranged in a purely arbitrary way. But when looked at in the right perspective, the things that in verses 21-23 and again in 24-26 are placed side by side have a very important inner connection both among themselves and with the whole line of narrative of this chapter. We read how God commanded Moses to tell Pharoah that he should allow Israel, his firstborn son, to leave the country; if not it would cost him his own first born son. This looks like a strange revelation, which Moses received by itself. But that is not the case. Rather God's revelation to Moses which is recorded in chapters 3-4 is repeated here again in relation to this special case and prior to the narrative in verses 24-26.

Let us now proceed to a later portion of that voluminous history whose initial part is formed by the Torah. In Judges 18 ff. begins a survey of the period of transition from the times of the judges to that of the kings. It starts with a narrative in which the origin of a special priesthood at Dan and the migration of the Danites is recorded, and this story has no connection with what precedes or what follows it. In chapter 19 the book continues with a similar narrative which describes the consequences of the atrocious crime which had been committed at Gibeah against the wife of a Levite. Let us carefully consider the manner in which the two stories are told. Those who do not accurately examine the arrangement of the two pieces will take subordinate things recorded therein as the real subject matter. Yet the latter story does in no way intend to explain how it happened that as a result of civil war the tribe of Benjamin had almost been extirpated; nor is chapter 18 intended to give a narrative of the migration of the Danites. Rather we hear of the migration of a section of the Danites because contrary to the law a special priesthood had come into being at Dan. Hence the narrator is interested in the one instance in a fact of the history of worship and in the other instance in a fact which is important for the history of morals. It is in these two respects that the period of the judges is to be characterized. Thus this characterization serves as an introduction to the record of the origin of kingship. It is shown thereby that by the establishment of the kingly office Israel acquired her special vocation, and we learn in what circumstances that development took place.

The history of the Genesis of the kingly office starts, however, as though a mere biography of Samuel were to be given. When the story tells that the people wanted a king and that the latter was annointed, this looks like an episode in Samuel's life. Yet this is precisely the impression which the narrator intended. It was through a prophet of Jehovah that the transition took place which was of such enormous importance for the realization of Israel's real vocation. The external circumstances in which the people lived at that time are described in a most sketchy way. Only incidentally is it shown that they too contributed to the people's desire to have a king. Quite incidentally one of the most important features characterizing the external conditions of that time is mentioned in I Samuel 13:19-21. For it is of little importance to know how it happened that the people wanted a king, but it is of utmost importance to understand how it came about that God appointed a king for His people. Even the reference in I Samuel 13 is merely occasioned by the fact that an heroic deed of Jonathan is recorded. The latter one in turn is not told for its own sake, but rather is found in the context of the story of a war which Saul waged against the Philistines. The latter one, too, has no special significance. It is depicted in such detail merely in order to make the readers realize that Saul was unfit to remain the anointed of Jehovah and to be the real initiator of the permanent royal office of Israel.

We have already pointed out above that the Books of Kings and the Books of the Chronicles tell the same history of the interval between the death of Solomon and the conquest of Jerusalem by Nebuchadnezzar, yet it is told in totally different ways. Everything reported in the Books of Kings is to be interpreted and evaluated as contributing to the provisional conclusion of the history of the nation whose origin and establishment has been recorded in the Torah. This national history has come to a provisional end in David and Solomon on the one hand and in the catastrophe of Judah on the other, and thus the history of the interval between Solomon and Nebuchadnezzar deals with the nation as a whole.

Things are different in the Books of Chronicles. The point of Holy History from which the past is seen in retrospect is the time of Israel's restored commonwealth, and the latter consists in the main of Jerusalem, that is, it is Judah restored. The purpose is now to point out what are the roots of the national life and the worship of this restored commonwealth. As far as the national life is concerned, its roots reach back to the sons of Jacob and to Abraham and it is even necessary to show whence Abraham himself came. The roots of the life of worship, however, which now is tied up with the sanctuary in Jerusalem reach back to David who had made Zion the center of Israel's national life and worship. This explains the fact that the consecutive narrative starts with the beginning of David's reign. It is true that the author ignores the northern kingdom posterior to the time of Solomon and that he records in great detail events which were of such momentous importance for the life of worship, as for instance the solemn celebration of the Passover under Hezekiah. But these features are by no means to be explained as an indication that the author of the narrative was a narrow-minded Levite. Rather the author sees the past from a legitimate viewpoint of Holy History, and this fact explains also the rhetorical character of his style.

A remarkable feature of the New Testament writings is

the fact that in Matthew and Luke the gospel starts with the conception and birth of Jesus, whereas in Mark and John with the prophetic activity of the Baptist. It would be historically wrong, however, to infer from this fact that the events which are omitted in the beginning of John's and Mark's historical writings were of lesser importance. Or to give another instance, John tells that immediately after his baptism Jesus began to manifest Himself in Jerusalem, whereas the other evangelists continue after the narrative of Jesus' baptism with His activity in Galilee. They point out, however, that this took place only after John the Baptist had been put in jail.

Again, concerning Jesus' teaching ministry in Galilee, John records only a single fact, namely his conversation with the Jews in the synagogue of Capernaum following the feeding of the 5,000, and its consequences. From the activity which for the other evangelists, particularly Matthew and Mark, provides the whole material for the story from the imprisonment of the Baptist to Jesus' march to the Passover John records only this single event. They in turn do not mention His several sojourns in Jerusalem, whereas John states that after the episode in Capernaum in chapter 6 Jesus stayed repeatedly in Jerusalem and He reports the things that took place at those occasions.

These features of the gospels have to be interpreted from the viewpoint from which the evangelists record past events. If we follow this principle we shall not be tempted to say, for instance, that the events which took place prior to the appearance of John the Baptist were of lesser significance to Mark and John than they were to Matthew and Luke. Nor shall we say that John followed a Judean tradition whereas the Synoptics' was a Galilean one. Rather since each of the evangelists interprets the events from his perspective of Holy History the specific details which we notice in each of them have to be seen in the light of the specific character of each of the gospels.

Matthew, for instance, looks back upon the history of the

Lord from the vantage point of a congregation of the Messiah which originated from Israel, yet lives its own life independent of the Jewish people. He indicates that the existence of such a separate community of the Messiah who Israel had expected was legitimate. For in those events of our Lord's life which led eventually to the formation of such a community of the saved the Scripture had been fulfilled. Thus it is essential to show how from its very inception the history of our Lord was the fulfillment of the Scriptures. Mark on the other hand looks back starting from the authoritative proclamation of salvation which is presently carried on in the whole world to its beginning. It started when the Baptist came forth with his witness.

Let us now consider another set of facts which we have already discussed, namely the course of Jesus' Messianic ministry as it is described in the Synoptic gospels. His specific activity is distinguished from that of the Baptist by the fact that not until the imprisonment of the Baptist did He become the prophet of His people. This work started in Galilee which He finally left in order to make Jerusalem the place of His prophetic ministry. On account of that perspective there is no need for telling what Jesus did prior to the imprisonment of the Baptist or what events took place in Jerusalem when He visited the city temporarily for the feasts. John on the other hand states clearly in 20:31 from what perspective he is reporting the history of the Lord. He wants to bring people to the belief that Jesus is the Christ the Son of God, and this purpose implies that they should know what faith is like and what it means to believe in Jesus. The fourth evangelist accomplishes this end by means of selected episodes in which Jesus deals with His people, showing that they did not believe in Him and that but few of them did finally embrace faith. Since for the Jewish people as a whole, the moment to accept the faith had come when John bore witness to Jesus, the event forms the beginning of John's gospel. Hence whenever Jesus during His public ministry and subsequent to the testimony of the Baptist bore witness to Himself in Jerusalem, He addressed Himself as it were, to the official gathering of the nation.

It was in Jerusalem that the people had to decide whether they were for belief or unbelief. For this reason John omits none of the instances in which Jesus bore witness to Himself in Jerusalem. The fact that John nevertheless also reports in chapter 6 the incident of Jesus' Galilean activity serves to show that in Galilee from which His disciples had come Jesus demanded the same kind of faith as in Jerusalem, and that such a demand was as offensive there as in Jerusalem. At the end of that chapter John uses the disciples who after that incident in Capernaum remained faithful to Jesus as an illustration of what it means to believe in Him.

The above statements are directed against an erroneous manner of harmonizing the gospels, namely, against a method which interprets the gospels as though in each of them the same things had to be told and everything had to be told in the same manner. This is but a different aspect of the erroneous view that things which are found in one evangelist but not in another were unknown to the latter one, or that the evangelists contradicted each other when one of them tells an event in a different way than another. Is it not obvious that the purpose for which Matthew writes carries with it an entirely different arrangement of the material than for instance in John, and even in Matthew different than in Mark? Since Mark looks back upon the gospel events from the viewpoint of the apostolic preaching that now is carried on in the whole world, it is appropriate that he should proceed from the witness of the Baptist immediately to that of Jesus and from the preaching ministry of Jesus to the training of the disciples who were to proclaim the gospel after Him. Matthew on the other hand, in accordance with his purpose, will dwell extensively on the teaching activity and the miraculous healings of Jesus as the two characteristic aspects of His prophetic ministry, in order that the reader should recognize that Jesus has fulfilled the scriptural predictions concerning the prophet. In this connection it naturally follows that Matthew will record the Sermon on the Mount. Yet he does not intend to give a literal report but rather he uses it as a characteristic specimen of Jesus' teaching. Consequently it can be presented by Luke in an entirely different form. Jesus' relationship to the Old Testament does not have the same significance for Luke as for Matthew who makes it the center of his gospel. Hence Luke will omit everything that deals with Jesus' opposition against the Biblical interpretation of the Pharisees. In turn Matthew inserts many things into the Sermon on the Mount because in his view they serve to characterize the teaching of Jesus, whereas Luke mentions incidentally the special occasion at which the Lord made these utterances.

Hence the facts reported in the Scripture are to be interpreted as forming part of an historical process in which salvation is realized. But we must also take into consideration the specific experience of salvation and the specific perspective from which that process is seen. Thus only is it possible to interpret it in accordance with the purpose for which the report is given and to understand both why it was reported and why it was reported in this specific way.

B. THE WITNESS OF EXPERIENCED THINGS

In these instances the interpreter has to identify himself with the moment of the experience of salvation to which the experience points. By the former requirement the passage will be differentiated over against those which originated at another period of Holy History and by the latter requirement over against other passages which belong to the same period of Holy History.

In Psalm 88:5 for instance, a leper seeing his imminent death before him says concerning the dead, "They lie in the grave, whom thou rememberest no more; and they are cut off from thy hand." We must consider that this statement was made at a time when the only prospect of the condition

after death was that the soul would share the fate of the
decaying body. How different are things in Philippians 1:21
where the Apostle says: "To me to die is gain"! For the condition of those who are "dead in Christ" (I Thess. 4:16)—the
Apostle is certain that he will be one of them—is "to be
with Christ," who has risen from the grave and is with God.

Nevertheless, this same Apostle will say in II Corinthians
5:4, "We do not wish to be unclothed, but rather to be
clothed with a new garment, that death should be swallowed
up by life." Although he is certain that once the tent of our
earthly body has been dismantled we will have another
edifice in heaven into which we shall be received and that
then we shall be with Christ. Death itself is nevertheless for
Him a hard destiny. Hence He would like to experience
during His early life a transformation into glory without
tasting the bitterness of death. In other words the statements concerning death, although made by the same Christian, differ nevertheless according to the perspective in
which death is seen.

In Psalm 66:13, 15, the psalmist says that he is to enter
the house of God with burnt offering, that he is to offer
"burnt offerings with the fat of rams" and to sacrifice "bul-
locks and he-goats," and that by so doing he would pay his
vows to God. Such evidences of gratitude were prescribed
in the law of Mt. Sinai. Nevertheless, in Psalm 50:9 Jehovah
says, "I will take no bullock out of thy house, nor he-goat out
of thy folds." Similarly the psalmist says in Psalm 51:15, "My
mouth will show forth thy praise." The reason he gives in
v. 16 f. is that God is not pleased with "burnt offerings and
whole burnt offerings," but rather that the real sacrifices
of God are a "broken spirit," etc. That Israelites of the same
period should differ so radically in the statements concerning animal sacrifices does not mean that they possess different degrees of knowledge concerning the function of
sacrifices but rather that in making their statements they
have different goals in mind. In the one instance the sacrifice
is an expression of gratitude, whereas in the other instance

it is emphasized that God is not interested in purely external worship but rather in the surrender of the heart.

However, when the Old Testament sacrificial worship had reached its climax in Christ's sacrifice of Himself, the author of Hebrews can say to his readers who worried about their being excluded from the sacrificial worship of their nation: "Let us continually offer through him the sacrifice of praise to God, that is the fruit of our lips, giving thanks to his name" (13:15). Notwithstanding this statement, however, Jesus exemplifies by sacrificial worship in Matthew 5:23 how one should purge oneself of a hostile attitude towards one's neighbor. Likewise according to Acts 21:26 Paul participated in the Temple in a sacrifice which people offered in consequence of a Nazarite vow. As long as the Jews who believed in Jesus remained within the community of their nation the temple at Jerusalem and its sacrifices remained their sanctuary too.

When at the end of Psalm 137 the psalmist in addressing Babylon expresses his indignation over the contempt in which the exiled Israelites were held, he exclaims, "Blessed is he who repays to thee what thou hast done to us." The poet promises to be grateful to him who will deal in such a manner with Israel's enemy and he wishes him well for doing so. This statement shows the same attitude which we find in Isaiah or Jeremiah who rejoiced in the fact that they were foretelling the destruction of Babylon. Their desire that God should vindicate his people against an hostile world is there expressed by saying that God's judgment should take place by means of war. Thus in Isaiah 13 for instance, the Medes are called upon to perform the judgment of Babylon. In the same way David will say concerning his adversaries in Psalm 69:24, "Pour out thine indignation upon them, and let thy wrathful anger take hold of them," because they block his way to the goal for which God had called him. This does not contradict the commandment in Leviticus 19:18, "Thou shalt not avenge, nor bear any grudge against the children of thy people, but thou shalt love thy neighbor as thyself."

For the same David will say in Psalm 139:21, "Do I not hate them, O Lord, that hate thee?"

Similarly in the New Testament there is no contradiction between Matthew 5:44 where it is said, "Love your enemies, and pray for those who persecute you," and such passages as for instance II Thessalonians 1:7 ff. There the Christians in Thessalonica are comforted in their persecution through a reference to the return of Jesus who "will repay vengeance to those who do not know God, and who do not obey the gospel," etc. Nor is it a carnal desire for revenge out of which the souls of the martyrs of Jesus cry, in Revelation 6:10, "How long dost thou not judge and avenge our blood on those who inhabit the earth?" The love of one's neighbor which cannot be disturbed by hostility is in no way incompatible with the desire that the time might end in which God allows the evildoers and the enemies of His Christ to sin unopposed. The passage Matthew 5:44 applies to the relation in which the Christian as an individual stands to individuals. Things are different when it is a matter of conflict between the world and the Church of God. To such a situation Psalm 139:19 refers. We notice, however, that both in that Psalm and particularly in Psalm 137 the form of expression is that of the Old Testament mind.

Jesus, as the Baptist before Him, makes His appearance by proclaiming that "the Kingdom of God is at hand." This statement is the same as that in Obadiah v. 15 and Isaiah 13:6, "The day of the Lord is near." It is repeated in Hebrews 10:25, "You see the day drawing near," and James 5:8, "The coming of the Lord is at hand." Nevertheless there is a difference between the statements in the Old Testament and the New Testament. In the fact that the distress previously foretold has eventually come to Israel, the Old Testament prophets see the moment approaching in which Jehovah will identify Himself again with His people, and will manifest Himself in the eyes of the whole world as the God of His people. In the New Testament, however, the realization of God's kingdom here on earth is near when Jesus makes His public appearance. One thing only is missing. He who came in the humility of the flesh must reveal Himself in His divine glory in order to bring about the final end which was inaugurated in His incarnation. In view of this fact Jesus can say in Luke 17:21, "The kingdom of God is in your midst" (not: "within you"). The kingdom is present in His person. It is established in their midst and realized in the church of His spirit (Col. 1:13).

Let me give a few more instances which will show how important it is always to take into consideration this special aspect of the experience of salvation. Considering that the Book of Proverbs presents a sane prudence which is rooted in the fear of Jehovah, we shall hardly hold, for instance, that in chapter 8:22-26 we have a description of the Logos, that is, of the second person of the Trinity. Such an idea would be completely alien to this context. Similarly, the author of Ecclesiastes is a man who ponders over the natural order of things as he sees them apart from Holy History. In view of this outlook no one should deny that in 3:21 f. the author speaks concerning death and the state after death as one who is ignorant of any hope pointing beyond death.

In general the New Testament letters describe an experience of salvation, from which they look both back to the past and forward towards the future. Hence it is necessary to discern in each instance the direction in which the experience of salvation points. The traditional method of construing the so-called "doctrinal ideas" of Paul, Peter and John and particularly of James and Matthew is therefore bad and has already been rejected above in a different context. For by doing so one is prone to consider a single book of the New Testament, for instance I Peter, as a document from which the whole doctrine of this Apostle could be derived. Scholars will therefore call him "the Apostle of hope" as distinguished from Paul and John. It would be more profitable, however, if one investigated why Peter was moved to turn his attention in both his letters so intensely towards the end. The reason is that he is writing to Gentile Christians, with whom the eschatological outlook was not as natural as it was with Israelites. The purpose of his writing, however, is to exhort his Gentile Christian readers to strengthen and prove their status as Christians. For this reason everything presented refers to two things, namely, the final revelation of Christ and the actualization of the blessedness or the judgment resulting from that fact. In this light he both encourages his readers to remain firmly established in their faith in Christ and also admonishes them to be mindful of the approaching judgment.

On account of his first letter John is usually called the Apostle of Love. Yet looking instead at the Gospel of John one might call him just as well the Apostle of Faith. For as he states himself in John 20:31, he wrote his whole gospel "in order that you should believe . . . and that believing you should have life." But since in the letter he wants to show what the Christian conduct is like, he has to discuss the love in which the knowledge of Christ manifests itself, and which shows us whether or not somebody has been born again.

Or take Paul, in order to see in how many different ways he discusses the experience of salvation according to the respective purpose of each letter. There is no other book of the New Testament, for instance, in which the "Church of Christ," is discussed so extensively as in Ephesians. Nevertheless the subject matter of that letter is the "being in Christ," which pervades the whole epistle. His Gentile Christian readers have to be reminded that their Christian fellowship is not a matter of individual whims and fancies. By considerations of this kind he is induced in chapter 1:22 to mention the church for the first time. He points out that the church has its origin in the fact that God raised Christ from the dead and exalted Him to Himself. The church therefore is the body of this exalted Christ, "the fulness of him who fills all things in all." Should this remarkable expression be considered as forming part of a special doctrinal idea? By no means. The term was suggested to the Apostle by the fact that concerning the relation between Christ and His church he had to speak in such a manner that any arbitrariness and contingency was excluded. It is similar with Ephesians 1:10, where it is said that by the counsel of God everything in heaven and on earth is held together in Christ. This term, too, does not introduce a peculiar doctrinal idea. Rather the Apostle describes the office of Christ in this most comprehensive way on account of the perspective from which everything in the letter is treated. If it can be shown that Christ has been appointed to an office that embraces the whole world, how then could the fact that there is a congregation of Jesus Christ be the result of their own decisions and their individual fancies, and how can it be left to one's arbitrary decision to deal with it as one pleases!

We have now realized how important it is in those instances where the Scripture speaks of the experience of salvation to ascertain the aspect of that experience separately in each passage and to make sure of the perspective from which the experience is described. Now we may at last discuss the witness of Holy Scripture inasmuch as it is a prediction of future salvation.

C. THE FORESHADOWING OF FUTURE EVENTS

We have already pointed out that whenever in the Old Testament witness of salvation future things are foretold it is essential to investigate the point in Holy History from which such prediction is given as well as the direction in which its fulfillment points. Their content is to be understood within this context and is not to be adjusted to events which have taken place in the meantime. Future things to which the Scripture bears witness are either events which take place within the present order of the universe or events by which this present world is changed into a new one, or finally, events that belong to a new world and will be realized in it. Since the language by which these predictions are expressed might be borrowed from present experience, the degree in which the expression is appropriate for adequate statements will vary.

a) Proper expression can be given to the prediction of things which will take place within the present order of things, but only to the extent to which the future conditions are of the same nature as the present ones. This applies to such predictions as for instance Numbers 24:17. There Balaam who had been hired by Balak to pronounce a curse over Israel sees Israel overpowering her neighbors, and speaks of a scepter which will rise from Israel and slay Moab and all the sons of the drunkard (i.e., of Lot). Similarly in Micah 4: 10 the prophet proclaims to the daughter of Zion: "Now shalt thou go forth out of the city, and thou shalt dwell in the field, and thou shalt go even to Babylon; there shalt thou be delivered; there the Lord shall redeem thee from the hand of thine enemies." Since these events belong in their entirety to the present world order, they can be described in a direct way.

Similarly when Jesus says in Luke 19:43, "Thine enemies shall cast a trench about thee, and compass thee round, and keep thee in on every side," and in 21:24, "And they shall fall by the edge of the sword, and shall be led away captive into all nations; and Jerusalem shall be trodden down of the Gentiles," the siege of Jerusalem is foretold in the most literal terms. However, when in the parallel passage, Matthew 24:15 f. it is said, "When you see the abomination of desolation standing in the holy place, as spoken by the prophet Daniel," Jesus predicts a repetition of that devastation of the holy place which was done by Antiochus Epiphanes. However, for that very reason one wonders how that tribulation is to be thought of because it is connected with the final end. The disciples were familiar with this idea on account of Daniel's prophecies. Since at that time the tribulation had passed and the end of the present world process had not taken place, the disciples had to infer from Daniel's prediction that it would be followed by a similar tribulation, but one which this time would bring about the end.

Similarly, Luke, by saying in v. 24, "until the times of the Gentiles are fulfilled" posits an interval between the judgment upon Jerusalem, and the event of which it is said in v. 25 and 27, "There shall be signs in the sun and the moon and the stars . . . and then they shall see the Son of Man," etc., whereas according to Matthew this event follows immediately the "great tribulation" (v. 21) whose beginning is indicated by the "abomination of desolation." Of the latter one it is said, "then those in Judea shall flee upon the mountains; he who is upon the top of the house shall not descend." As a comparison with Luke 17:31 will show, all these features are parabolic expressions for a hurried escape which must not be delayed by any physical or moral hesitation lest by this tribulation souls should be jeopardized. Since in this description events by which the present condition of the world is transformed into a new one are combined with an event to be expected within present history, the picture as a whole exceeds our imagination. For the "tribulation" which culminates in the final revelation of Jesus is not identical with the one foretold by Luke. Hence one wonders what idea of that tribulation should be formed.

When Isaiah says in 37:29, "I put my ring in thy nose and my bridle in thy lips and shall lead thee back upon the road upon which thou didst come," he intimates that Sennacherib the Assyrian must turn away in vain from Jerusalem and go home. Yet in chapter 10 where the prediction concerning Assyria is expressed in the same way, it is said in v. 12 of a conceit like that of Sennacherib, "it shall come to pass that when the Almighty will bring to an end all his work on the Mount of Zion and Jerusalem, that I will punish the fruit of pride of the king of Assyria" (Is. 10:12).

Then in v. 28 f. when the same man marches against Jerusalem, he is described in v. 33-34 as a forest which is being cut down. This prediction the prophet combines with the promise in 11:1, "There shall come forth a branch out of the root of Jesse." It might appear at first sight as though that march against Jerusalem had been fulfilled in Sennacherib's campaign. But that appearance vanishes when it is seen that that campaign terminates in the end of world power in general, though in this connection it is called "Assyria," because the prophecy is related to the contemporary state of things. Similarly, while the passage Isaiah 31:8, "Assyria shall fall by the sword of one who is not a man," looks like a prophecy concerning the judgment inflicted upon Sennacherib, the prediction has not been fulfilled therein since in Isaiah 32:1 it is followed by the promise of the true King of Israel. This promise transcends our concepts inasmuch as it implies a complete change of things. The same is true of the prophecy concerning Babylon in Isaiah 13 which in verse 9 ff. is coupled with the description of the "day of the Lord." When an army coming from afar has been raised, it is said in v. 6, "Rejoice because the day of the Lord is at hand." Then the prophet describes how sun and moon will lose their brightness and judgment will be executed over all the wicked ones on earth. Turning back to its beginning the prophecy finally says that the Medes will come and Babylon will experience all the horrors of a conquered city (v. 17 ff.).

The prophecy of the final judgment of the secular power is in every instance coupled with a promise that Zion will be saved and Israel will be restored. In Isaiah 11:11-16 for instance the latter change is described in features which are borrowed from events of the past and contemporary conditions. Since at the time of Isaiah Israel was divided into Ephraim and Judah we read, for instance, in v. 13 that "Ephraim will not envy Judah, and Judah will not vex Ephraim."

Similarly in view of the fact that those nations which once had been subjugated by David are now again oppressing Israel and occupying her territory, it is said in v. 14 that Israel as a reunited nation "shall fly upon the shoulders toward the west, and they shall spoil them of the east together. They shall lay their hand upon Edom and Moab, and the children of Ammon shall obey them." Likewise just as the sea and the river formed no obstacle when Israel migrated from Egypt to Canaan, so the natural obstacle will be removed which might be in the way of God's people on their return to the homeland. This idea is expressed by saying that Jehovah will dry up the Egyptian bay and that He will cut the river Euphrates into seven parts so that one may cross it dry shod.

In Revelation 8, 9 and 16, features which are borrowed from past or present experience are used to describe extraordinary occurrences in nature, which are signs of the judgment that will take place at Christ's final manifestation. John notices, for instance, a mixture of hail, fire and blood, that drops down like hail but burns everything. In another instance a star falls down like a torch and by spreading its heat over the rivers and the fountains of water it renders their water unfit for drinking. Again the Seer describes how human beings are tortured by something that seems to be an army of locusts; yet those locusts have the tails of scorpions. Thus the visitation begins with the green earth, the rolling ocean, the sweet waters, and the heavenly luminaries which give light to men. Then the plague turns towards mankind, first torturing them in a painful and unendurable way, and then killing them by the thousands. Again in chapter 16 the torments start as boils by which the people are vexed; the ocean and the rivers are transformed into a blood-like substance because the people have accepted the sign of the beast and have shed the blood of the saints like water. The terror continues as an unbearable scorching heat of the sun, followed by an eclipse. This is a foretaste of the eternal fire and the everlasting darkness. Similarly in chapter 11 the miraculous power of the two prophets manifests itself as fire which proceeds from their mouth and destroys their enemies. Furthermore they shut up the heavens so that no more rain falls, and they change water into blood. Details of this picture are borrowed from Old Testament stories featuring Moses and Elijah. Likewise in Revelation 9:20 we read that those people who were not killed by those plagues nevertheless "did not repent of the works of their hands, and did not desist from worshipping demons and the idols of gold and silver." This is the description of a final apostasy which will occur after the present one (cf. 1 John 5:21).

b) Since we are unable to form adequate representations of the events which precede the end of the present age though their description has borrowed features from the present experience and past history, how much more will that be the case with the images describing how this world will be transformed into a new one! We are thinking of the Old Testament descriptions of the "Day of Jehovah," and the "Coming of Jehovah," or the "Return" of Christ in the New Testament. Just as the "Coming of Jehovah" is analagous with Jehovah's descent in Mt. Sinai, so is the return of Christ with His ascension from Mt. of Olives. Hence we read, for instance in Acts 1:11, that "this Jesus who was taken up from you into heaven will come again in the same manner as you saw him going into heaven." Similarly in Isaiah 64:1 the prophet desirous that God's judgment over the enemies of His people should take place in a manifestation of His power, says, "Oh, that thou wouldest rend the heavens . . . that the mountains would quake at thy presence!"

According to Joel 3:12, the manifestation of Jehovah's power will take place at a definite locality. The prophet says concerning the nations, "They shall go up the valley of Jehosaphat" to be doomed there by the divine judgment. In Zechariah 14:3 this manifestation takes place when Jerusalem has been captured by assault, and Jehovah marches out "to fight against those nations, as when he fought in the day of battle." Finally, in Zechariah 14:5 it is said that Jehovah appears with his spirits ("all thy saints with thee"). This same feature occurs also in Joel 3:11 where those spirits are His servants who execute His judgment. More than in Isaiah 10, for instance, the moment in which the divine interference takes place is described in Zechariah as one of extreme oppression and hopelessness.

How do such descriptions agree with such a passage as Malachi 3:1? There "my messenger"—the messenger whom Jehovah sends "before him"—is identified with "the prophet Elijah" of whom it is said that he would be sent prior to the coming of the "great and terrible Day of Jehovah." Hence the coming of Jehovah is represented in v. 1 as the coming of the "Lord" and of the "Messenger of the covenant" who will sweep Israel clean so that she would be pleasing to her God (v. 3 ff.). Passages of this type are compatible with the former ones when one realizes that the coming of Jehovah has a two-fold purpose, namely, to purge His people and to redeem them from the hand of the enemies.

The apparent contradiction is resolved in the New Testament. There Christ's appearance "in the flesh" is distinguished from His final manifestation in glory (cf. I Tim. 3:16, "he appeared in the flesh" . . . "He was revealed in glory"). But what idea shall we form of the latter event? The vision in Revelation 19:11 ff. follows the descriptions given by Joel and Zechariah. The Lord will return in the same way as He once descended upon Mt. Sinai. He will come to the holy place with His heavenly hosts to destroy the army of the nations which is gathered there against the congregation of God. It is said in Revelation 1:7, that "He comes with the clouds" (cf. Luke 21:27). But also in Matthew 24:30 it is proclaimed that "all the families of the earth shall see the Son of Man coming upon the clouds of heaven." Furthermore in the same passage (Mat. 24:27) it is stated that Christ's return will be "as the lightening goes out from the east and shines to the west." In I Thessalonians 4:17 we read that "then we which are alive and remain shall be caught up together with them in the clouds, to meet the Lord in the Air." We find the same idea expressed in Matthew 24:31. There the Lord says that He sends His messengers "with a loud sound of the trumpet." This is a sign of His coming, "and they shall gather his elect from the four winds." All these passages make a two-fold statement con-

230 INTERPRETING THE BIBLE

cerning the coming of the Lord. It will take place in a definite locality, yet will be visible everywhere with equal clarity.

What is accomplished by His return? The coming of Jehovah as spoken of in the Old Testament is differentiated in the New Testament as a first and a second appearance of Christ. The latter is the final end, yet also the beginning of the end. This is in full agreement with the Old Testament. Two ideas are equally essential for the prophecies concerning the end. There is the final judgment in which the conflict between Jehovah and the world that was alienated from Him is finally settled. Yet we find there also the idea of a period in which at the end of the present age His glory will be revealed notwithstanding the fact that the world of the Gentiles will not recognize Him. These two ideas are so intertwined that the latter one can originate from the former one or can be overshadowed by it (cf. Is. 24, 25, 65).

In a similar way we read in II Thessalonians 2:8 that the Lord will "bring to naught the lawless one" through the "manifestation of his coming," as is also stated in Revelation 19. Yet we also read that He will "judge all those who do not believe the truth, but rather take pleasure in unrighteousness" (II Thess. 2:12), suggesting a final judgment. This passage is reminiscent of others, such as I Peter 4:5 where it is said that those who walk in their lusts will have to give account to Him "who is about to judge the quick and the dead," or also of John 5:28, where the evangelist refers to the hour "in which all those who are in the graves will hear his voice and shall come forth; they that have done good unto the resurrection of life, and they that have done evil unto the resurrection of judgment."

Conversely, however, the Lord promises in John 6:40 to him who believes in Him that He would raise him up from the dead "on the last day." This statement resembles I Thessalonians 4:16 where it is said that "the dead in the Lord will rise first," and also I Corinthians 15:23, where those who are Christ's are spoken of as rising at His return.

However, in the latter passage (v. 25) the final annihilation of death ("the last enemy death will be destroyed") is separated from that resurrection by the period of Christ's reign.

The things differentiated in those passages are merged in II Peter 3. There the "return of the Lord" effects the transformation of this world and brings about a new one (cf. Heb. 12:26). The return of Christ is either the beginning of the end or the absolute end, the former one when as in I Peter it is the return of the "Savior" of His own, and the latter one when it is the return of "the judge of the quick and the dead," which is referred to in another passage of the same letter. When the judgment of the generation which rejected the Lord is combined with the tribulation which precedes His return it can be said in Matthew 16:28 that the contemporaries of Jesus would not die until "they have seen the Son of Man coming in his kingdom." For that "coming" starts with the judgment of the Jewish people. Yet in a previous passage it is intimated that the Lord would come "in the glory of his Father with his angels and then he shall repay every one according to his work." That would be the absolute end. The eschatological prophecies are never meant simply to provide knowledge of the future course of events. Rather they serve an ethical purpose. Hence when Matthew 25:31-46 portrays the judgment of the Son of Man, the description is to give to Christ's own people the assurance that "He who receives you receives me" (Matt. 10:40). Nevertheless, it is impossible to form a clear idea of that judgment, for a distinction is made between the brethren of Jesus on the one hand and the righteous ones who have shown mercy to them on the other.

c) We had to give up the hope of forming a clear picture of the events which precede the actual termination of the present eon, and of the event itself, because the only way in which they can be described is by borrowing the means of expression from present events or the past. How much more will this be true of the description of the new conditions which are brought about when the final end has arrived! In Isaiah 65:17 and 66:22, for example, the new world is characterized as a new heaven and a new earth. This terminology is borrowed from this present world which according to the Scripture consists of heaven and earth (Gen. 1:1). The same language is used in Revelation 21:1 and II Peter 3:13. Yet the lattter passage is immediately preceded by one in which it is said that the present world will be destroyed by fire. The only thing we learn from this passage is that in contrast with the flood, the earth will be destroyed in the same way as an object is destroyed by fire. The new world is further characterized in contrast with the present one as a world in which "righteousness shall dwell," i.e., nothing but what is righteous will be found in it. Hence both sin and evil are excluded from it. In another passage (Heb. 12:27) it is described as "the things that shall not be shaken."

The glorification of Zion is described by Isaiah in chapter 60, as an event taking place in this world which in every other respect will continue. This can be seen from v. 11, where it is said that her gates will remain open all the time, "that people should bring to thee the wealth of the Gentiles." Her glory is pictured in terms and colors furnished by experience. In v. 17 for instance it is said that in the place of brass there will be gold, and silver in the place of iron, brass in the place of wood, and iron in the place of stone. In this connection gold and silver symbolize the most valuable and brass and iron the most durable ones. Farther in vss. 19 and 20 it is said that Zion would no longer be illuminated by the sun and the moon but rather by the glory of Jehovah, and that the sun would no longer set down nor the moon wane. This means that without alteration the holy place will be brightened by the manifestation of God's presence which shines more brilliantly than anything else. Finally, in Isaiah 11:6 f. where the prophet describes the reign of the true Solomon, it is said that the wolf would lie with the lamb and the leopard with the kid. A little child will lead small calves and young lions and fatted cattle together, and the cow and the bear will walk together to the pasture. In this picture the prophet utilizes images and colors furnished by the earth in order to depict a state of peace which will be enjoyed conjointly by both man and all the other creatures.

Since Jesus was exalted to a supramundane existence with God, the life of fellowship which His own have in Him though in a hidden way is not to be found within this created world but rather beyond it. For this reason Paul speaks in Galatians 4:26 of "the upper Jerusalem" and similarly the author of Hebrews of the "heavenly Jerusalem" (Heb. 12: 22). Yet in Hebrews 13:14 she is called a "coming city" since in the future she is to be manifested together with Christ within this world. Similarly in Revelation 3:12 we read of a "new Jerusalem which descended from heaven." These designations are borrowed from the Old Testament city of God. This explains the language in Revelation 21 and 22. John is to be shown the new heaven and the new earth and in that new world the "bride of the lamb."

In those chapters the new Jerusalem is described in a manner reminiscent of Isaiah's description of Zion glorified, namely, as a city with gates, walls, and streets. In this portrayal of the new Jerusalem certain features are found which seem to suggest that she is situated in a world which in every other respect has remained unchanged. In chapter 21:24 for instance it is said that the kings of the earth "shall bring their glory and honor to her," and in 22:2 we read of the tree whose leaves serve to heal the evils of that portion of the world which is outside of her: "the leaves of the trees are for the healing of the nations." This impression is due to the fact that the new Jerusalem which in Christ's final revelation descends from heaven will remain intact throughout the transformation of the universe which will take place when the "one thousand years" of the reign of Christ and His glorified Church (Rev. 20:1 f.) are over.

All these features are indicative of the fact that the glory of the Church of God is one into which it will be transfigured at the moment when Christ returns to bring her home, and not only when God creates the new world. These concrete features of the picture would be automatically dropped if the latter, rather than depicting the final stage of this world, referred to the eternal bliss which begins with the creation of a new world. The picture refers to the period in which the transfigured congregation is engaged in teaching and assisting the non-Christian world. In the new world, on the other hand, the Church which originated in Abraham and was brought to its completion in Christ has become the integral mankind of God, in which all those are incorporated who in the final separation of the good and evil ones were deemed worthy by God of the life everlasting.

The condition of the life of eternal bliss is described in three different ways:

1) Firstly it is contrasted with that of the present time. Hence everything is excluded from it by which the spiritual conditions of the believers are adversely affected in this earthly world, for instance Revelation 21:4, "there shall be no more death nor weeping, nor any more pain"; or Revelation 7:16, "They shall hunger no more, neither thirst anymore; the sun shall not strike them, nor any scorching heat."

2) It is described in analogy with the present condition, for instance as a bodily life, yet in a "spiritual body" (I Cor. 15:44); or in a body "fashioned like unto his glorious body" (Phil. 3:21). In a similar fashion the Lord says in Luke 22:30 with reference to the Passover, that "you shall eat and drink at my table in my kingdom." This is said in particular to the Apostles, who are promised: "you shall sit upon thrones and judge the twelve tribes of Israel." These privileges no less than the common reign of the believers with Christ and their sitting upon His throne (Rev. 3:21) characterize the interval between Christ's second appearance and the final end.

3) It is described in analogy with past events. In Revelation 2:7 for instance, the phrase "to eat of the tree of life" is reminiscent of Genesis 2, and in Revelation 2:17 the expression "to eat from the hidden manna" recalls the manna which was deposited in the Holy of Holies of the tabernacle and thus hidden with God. Fellowship with the Christ who has been exalted into the true Holy of Holies with God will have the same significance for His own people as the manna had for Israel when she migrated in the wilderness. Similarly, just as the Tree of Life in Paradise was fit to endow with everlastingness the life which was given in Creation, so the believers will receive that gift by which the life obtained in their redemption will be made to last forever.

The condition of the unsaved is in an analogous manner described by a term borrowed from experience, namely as a lake of fire of burning sulphur (Rev. 19:20), or in analogy of present conditions, as "the second death" (Rev. 20:14). The fire consumes and the fumes of the sulphur suffocate. The two effects must be thought of in combination, in order to form a concrete representation of the second death as a state of existence which in every respect is separate from God. The image of a lake is used to indicate that they will be immersed into an element by which they will be continually consumed and suffocated.

It is obvious that none of these descriptions is given for the purpose of satisfying man's curiosity. The task of the interpreter is to separate the content from the form in which it is given. In other words, the literary form has to be treated merely as a means of giving expression to things which transcend our imagination.

The true interpretation of these materials has been missed by two otherwise antagonistic groups. One is that kind of belief which desires to know the things that cannot be known. The other is the kind of unbelief which uses the literary form as a pretext to thrust suspicion upon the things meant thereby. The Book of Revelation, in particular, more than any other book, has been misinterpreted and misused in these two ways, quite apart from the fact that the rules of general hermeneutics too have often been disregarded in its interpretation.

* * *

To sum up. Our first task consisted in describing the specific character of Biblical exegesis by defining it in terms of the relationship in which the theologian stands to Scripture as a whole.

A further qualification of the task of interpretation was derived from two facts: first, that the historical fact of salvation in Christ had an historical preparation; and secondly, that the Biblical proclamation of salvation originated step by step in the course of Holy History. As a result of these facts, the process of salvation itself and the Biblical witness concerning it had to be differentiated. These are the only features which are relevant for the interpretation of Holy Scripture. There are no further distinguishing features in the Bible which would make it necessary further to modify the general rules of hermeneutics as they apply to Holy Scripture. Consequently, we deem that the objective of these lectures has been reached.